NACHEMIA

NACHEMIA

GERMAN AND JEW IN THE HOLOCAUST

NACHEMIA WURMAN

with MARGARET RUSSELL

NEW HORIZON PRESS
Far Hills, New Jersey

Library of Congress Catalog Card Number
88-92789

Wurman, Nachemia
Russell, Margaret

ISBN 0-88282-046X
New Horizon Press

ACKNOWLEDGMENTS

I would like to express my special thanks to Ted and Ethel Shuster for their assistance, and to Margaret Russell for co-authoring the manuscript.

Heartfelt thanks to my dear sisters Chania and Chaika for their devotion and love throughout.

My deep appreciation goes to my daughters Hanna and Sara, and my son Avi. Without their constant encouragement, this book would not have been written.

And finally it goes without saying that without the patience and support of my dear wife Gloria it would have been impossible for me to see the completion of this book.

I dedicate this book to the memory of my parents, Gershon Henoch and Sarah Wurman, my brother Moshe, my brother Eliezer, his wife Zivja and their child Ester.

In memory of my wife's parents, Moishe and Hana Weinberg, and her brothers Chaim Mordechai, Leizer and Hershel, and sister Etta.

All of whom perished in the Holocaust.

ONE

August 1944

The forests were in full bloom and birds sang as they always had sung in the fields; daisies and cornflowers blossomed profusely alongside the rows of barley and wheat. Copses of trees formed rough demarcations between the fields. The crops grew toward harvest even though the farms had been abandoned.

The deserted villages were marked by burned-out and fire-scarred buildings.

I could not travel on the main roads. The German army travelled on them and checked all civilians carefully. I couldn't travel on the main paths. They were mined. I had seen the mines sticking out of the ground.

I couldn't find food anywhere. Not in the abandoned farms. Not in the deserted villages.

I had to reach Sandomierz.

The Soviets had made a bridgehead there. I had to reach them. I would have to cross the front lines.

I headed east from Opatov. It was about twenty miles to Sandomierz. I walked continuously, stopping only occasionally to rest. I could tell approximately how far I was from the front lines by the sound of artillery that broke through from time to time.

No one was about. The only sounds, outside of the gunfire, were from the birds, the rustling of the leaves, and the drone of low-flying aircraft. Russian aircraft. Whenever I heard one approach—and it was frequently—I dove for cover.

As I neared the front my progress became more difficult and dangerous. The entire area was full of German
soldiers. The firing from both sides was without let-up. At
night the Soviets fired rockets which ignited the countryside
as if it were midday. I wasn't able to move from my hiding
place for hours on end.

I emerged twice from under cover only to see soldiers
milling about. I dove back into the nearest thick growth.
Something told me that I wasn't going to be able to smuggle
myself across the front lines.

I had no choice. I had to try my luck in another place.

I emerged from my hiding place as darkness fell and
headed, I thought, southeast. I would approach the Russian
front from another direction.

The forest tracks and the smaller tracks through the
fields were almost completely covered by darkness. Occasionally I had to stop to wait for the Soviet rockets to light up the
sky so I could regain my bearings.

By the time daylight broke I was exhausted. And rav-
enous. Then I saw the "village": ten to fifteen scattered
homes, each with a barn, each about a hundred yards from
the other. They were made of wood with thatched roofs. Most
of the walls of the houses were standing; some had been
burned down. There were no roads through the village—only
walking paths through the fields.

A few dogs ran freely among the houses. I couldn't see
people anywhere—a situation I had come to expect by now.
Then I heard horses snorting and stamping, and suddenly
soldiers appeared among the houses, stretching and yawning,
talking idly among themselves.

I peered closely. They were German soldiers. I froze in
my tracks.

It was too late to hide or run. Lying down in the field
and crawling toward the forest was out of the question.

I stood there for what seemed like forever. It was
probably a matter of seconds. Then I walked toward them as
if it were the most natural thing in the world for me to do so.

As I got closer to the village I noticed a portable wood-burning stove with a chimney standing on a platform between a barn and a well. Behind it was a wagon of food and utensils. A large pot sat in the middle of the stove with two smaller pots on either side. It was a military field kitchen, and the soldiers were all heading for it.

A middleaged soldier was ladling out coffee to the others. He was, I judged, about six feet tall, graying hair. He wore a red bandana around his neck. I studied his face as I got closer: his expression was neither pleasant nor harsh, but simple—neutral.

After he finished serving the others I went over to him.

"Please give me a little coffee," I asked him in German.

He handed me a thick slice of bread, covered with black currant jam, and a mug of coffee.

"Thank you. You're very kind," I said. He shrugged.

I went off a little way and sat down. I wolfed down the bread and coffee. It tasted wonderful.

When the soldiers dispersed he began to clean up. I went over to him again.

"Can I help you?"

He didn't object. I began working at once. I scrubbed out the pots. I cut wood for the kitchen fire on which lunch would be cooked. I worked diligently. And tried to be unobtrusive.

The old German seemed to like me. He bent towards me. "What is your name?"

"Marion Schmidt," I answered, without really knowing why I picked that name.

"My name is Michel."

We grinned at each other. Up close I saw that there was a sort of twinkle in his blue eyes. His face and arms were tan and weathered.

When the soldiers gathered for lunch, they didn't seem to notice me—at least they paid no attention to me. Again I helped Michel clean up. Again he gave me food. Was there good feeling between us? I thought so. Perhaps my fluency in German helped. Perhaps he needed my help. I certainly needed his goodwill.

Trying not to be noticed, I slowly scrutinized the area. I had to find a place to slip away if anyone suspected me.

During the hours free between lunch and dinner I made my way toward the shade of a low tree and lay down with my back against the trunk, watching the soldiers. Who among them would find out what I was? Who would look suspiciously at me—if I stayed around long enough? Would my shabby clothes clue them in?

They, too, seemed relatively idle during those hours. There seemed to be genuine camaraderie among them. I shouldn't have been surprised: friendship among men in arms, especially in a combat situation, is natural. But these were Hitler's beasts, I reminded myself. These were not human beings.

Michel woke me gently. "Time to prepare for dinner." I was astounded. I must have dozed off. He smiled at my startled expression. "It's no surprise you slept. You've worked hard," he said reassuringly.

"What village is this?" I asked him as we walked toward the kitchen area.

"Oh—Nova, I think," he shrugged.

In the midst of dinner preparations a young sergeant made his way over to the kitchen. Tall, slim, dark-haired—he was attractive. He glanced at me, then took another, longer look. He called Michel aside. They talked, gesturing toward me. Shaking, I busied myself with the tea.

After the sergeant left Michel ambled over to me. "That's my commander," he said. Looking closely at me, he asked, "What are you doing here?"

I felt my blood run cold.

"I told him you were helping me," he continued. "He ordered me to ask you if you are ready to help in the kitchen every day."

I lost no time in responding. "*Ja*. I'm willing."

Michel smiled and patted me on the shoulder. Quickly, we began to prepare dinner.

"What is the sergeant's job," I asked, leaning over a pot as I sliced the beans.

"He's responsible for the supply and for the kitchen. We feed the battalions."

Working without stopping, I brought water from the well; I cleaned the thickened soup from the pots; I brought wood; I started to make coffee for dinner. By the time I had finished straightening out the kitchen it was dark.

"I'm going to inform the boss that you're ready to stay with us," Michel said. "Come on. We'll both tell him."

He put his hand on my shoulder and we started for the nearest house. I had no desire whatever to see the sergeant again. But I had no choice.

The house where Michel and the sergeant were quartered seemed in better condition than most. The wood had aged to a gray-brown; the straw of the roof was pale yellow— it had probably been re-thatched not too long before the village was abandoned. The windows on the first story were small. The second floor was accessible by a narrow outside staircase. Michel went up first.

I could walk away, I thought as I followed him up the steps. They probably wouldn't bother to shoot me. I took a deep breath.

Then we were inside the sergeant's quarters.

The second floor consisted of one big room which ran the length and width of the house, except for what appeared to be a small hay storage area at the far end. The room, broken only by support posts placed at regular intervals, was dim: only a small, irregularly shaped window at the other end afforded light. The ceiling slanted in the line of the roof. I made out two piles of straw, about three feet wide and six feet long, covered by blankets toward the hay storage room. Storage cases were stacked neatly where the ceiling met the wide-planked floor. Towards the window a table and a few chairs stood. A candle on the table attempted to augment the fading daylight. Michel walked over to one of the straw piles and began to search in a rucksack.

The sergeant sat at the table writing. He stopped, leaned back on the chair, and said in a quiet but commanding voice, "What is your name?"

"Marion Schmidt," I responded as confidently as I could.

"Marion is a French name," he said, narrowing his eyes. "Are you German—Volksdeutsch?"

"Yes," I replied. "I am Volksdeutsch. "My father was German; my mother was Polish."

He seemed to accept that answer. He smiled slightly. "Do you want to help us in the military kitchen?"

"*Jawohl!*" I replied without hesitation.

His smile broadened. "Okay. Come here first thing tomorrow morning. We've made a deal. See you tomorrow." He turned back to his papers.

Michel had apparently found what he was looking for in the rucksack. Silently, I left the room.

As I reached the bottom of the steps I realized I did not know where to go or where I could spend the night. I wandered around the "kitchen" area, watching the deepening shadows in the woods beyond the village. What did I feel? Relief: I had, for however long, a base, a means of being fed. Fear: what if they found out? Yes, I must stay alert for suspicion; I must remember the background I was fabricating for Michel and the sergeant, but the fear mustn't show. Thoughts gnawed at me. I shook them off.

Right now I needed a place to sleep.

I went back up the stairs. The sergeant looked up as I stepped through the door.

"It's past six," I said. "We—civilians—cannot be out after six. The curfew."

He studied my face. *What does he see there?* I wondered.

"What am I going to do?" I asked.

"If you want you can sleep here," he said. He called to Michel. "Michel, show Marion a place to sleep."

Michel led me to the hay storage room. It, too, had an irregularly shaped opening which could be closed with a shutter. Bales of hay were piled floor to ceiling. He walked back into the large room and returned with an olive-drab blanket and a knife.

"It gets chilly at night," he said. He cut the rope binding a bale of hay with the knife, hesitated then cut the rope binding a second bale.

"There you go," he said.

"Thank you, Michel. You are very kind."

"Ach," he shrugged. "What did I do?"

I looked into his eyes. They were not as blue as my father's. But they seemed as gentle.

He shrugged again. "Get a good sleep. We get up at dawn."

I spread the straw into a three-foot-by-six-foot pile. It seemed wonderfully soft and comfortable. I was asleep almost from the moment I lay down on it.

I dreamt of Kurov.

We called it Korev.

The town was rows of soft grays and soft whites, broken by the green of the ample trees which lined Lubelska, the main street. By decree the two-story attached brick houses were painted a cream color, and the wooden one-story houses were painted light gray.

I dreamed of the maples swelling into buds, then leaves, the shoots of grass that pushed up between the stones that paved Lubelska, bravely attempting to withstand the constant crushing of horses' hooves and human shoes. I saw the goats, dogs, pigs, and cats that roamed freely through the town, all seeming to congregate in the market square on Thursdays, when peasants from neighboring villages came into Kurov to sell vegetables, eggs, butter, cheese, chickens and all, hanging around the food stalls hoping for something to drop—or be thrown—to the ground.

Kurov was about eighty miles southeast of Warsaw, and twenty miles west of Lublin, capital of the Lubelska province. It took its name from the small river, Kurovka, that circled the perimeter of the town.

Kurov had been founded in the sixteenth century. The

Jews began arriving in the seventeenth. That was when the synagogue was built.

The church was built one hundred years earlier. It stands there today.

Two flour mills and a lumber mill were the main "industries." They provided some employment for people of the town. Mainly, however, the residents of Kurov were craftsmen, and proud of it: they were tailors, seamstresses, shoemakers and manufacturers of leather goods. Many sewed sheepskin coats, which were sorely needed during the winter. And many, many, like my family, were shopkeepers. A few people in Kurov were comfortable; most subsisted.

The land surrounding Kurov was fertile, and farms abounded and provided good harvests. One farm consisted of about a hundred acres: it belonged to a family by the name of Jeruzalski. Today, General Wojczech Jeruzalski, of that family, is Prime Minister of Poland.

Everyone knew everyone in Kurov—except for some of the gentiles who refused to associate with Jews.

Our house was on the main street. It was one of the nicest houses in Kurov. Warm, comfortable, and welcoming. Our bookstore, where we also sold stationery, fancy goods, even cosmetics, faced onto Lubelska, where most of the shops were located. The dining room, off the large, wonderful-smelling kitchen, could be converted into a guest room at a moment's notice—and usually was; my father brought a guest for Shabbat every Friday evening.

And often relatives were also present at those feasts: there were about thirty of us in Kurov.

Those evenings, everyone—my father, my mother, my brothers and sisters, our guests—sang the old hymns around the table: *Henne Matov Umanium, Beshoov Hasen Shivat Zion, Kol Mekadesh Shvyi, Ysmach Bemalchutcha.* The candle flames danced in my mother's large brown eyes. My father and my older brother, Eliezer, engaged in loving competition as to who could sing the most lustily. My mother and sisters urged me to eat more. Did I want to remain so thin all my life, she would say. And Zivja joined us more and more frequently.

Eliezer had met Zivja Rozen in *Betar*, the Revisionist youth movement. He was the leader of the Kurov branch. Zivja was from Urzendov, where my father's father lived, and stayed with relatives in Kurov. She had become almost as active in *Betar* as Eliezer. Eliezer was about 5 ft. 11 in.; Zivja came up to his shoulder. Like our mother, she had large, brown eyes and dark hair—as did Eliezer also. Brilliant and activist, when she turned her eyes to Eliezer it was as though she were looking at God Himself. Soon we took it for granted that Zivja would be joining us for dinner.

Moshe and I would kick each under the table when Zivja looked at Eliezer. Eliezer seemed to grow visibly at those times.

Our mother was fond of Zivja from the first and the affection between them grew rapidly. "Mrs. Wurman," Zivja said, bowing her head slightly. On the day it became "Mother Wurman," Mother was totally wreathed in smiles.

Mother's face was made for smiles. Her eyes would sparkle, her rosy cheeks would get pinker.

I could hardly remember Mother being still for long. Short and slender, she constantly rushed about—helping in the store, preparing meals, supervising Chania and Chaike in the housework, checking on our homework. Daddy towered above her, and whenever she looked up into his eyes her face took on a glow that assured me that everything was right in the world.

I could see my father again as he had been at those *Shabbat* feasts—his tall, sturdy frame, his warm, gentle blue eyes, his short, immaculately groomed beard.

Guests in our house were automatically considered one of the family. After the meal we all gathered around the large wood-burning stove in the center of the living room and exchanged news and stories. Our guests, whom my father often met through the *Hachnusos Orchim* (the "Welcoming Guests" organization which provided Jewish visitors to Kurov shelter over *Shabbat*), usually brought news from outlying districts and even from different parts of Poland.

More and more, the news was that the anti-Semitism was becoming stronger.

We knew. It had filtered down to Kurov.

Nearly half the six thousand inhabitants of Kurov were Jews. And there was a vital Jewish life there—as there was in many towns and cities in Poland. Children went to Hebrew and Yiddish school—Kurov's Hebrew school was about two hundred yards from our house. There were active political and religious groups, with their youth organizations which went from left to right—from Communism to *Agudas Yisroel*.

My family was very much a part of this life. My father was a founder of the *Mizrachi*, the Zionist movement, in Kurov; he was a member of the board of the Hebrew School, chairman of the Fund of Redemption of the Land of Israel, chairman of the merchants' union of Kurov. And the only Jew on the city council. There were people in our house practically every evening; Mother would smile warmly and quietly serve them tea and cake. But Daddy always had time to talk to us, tease us, play with us.

It seemed that all Jewish families in Kurov were close-knit. There was constant visiting back and forth between us. Eliezer and Moshe Naimark, my mother's nephew, were best friends. At sixteen Moshe was very tall and, like Eliezer, had dark hair and eyes. He helped his father, my uncle, in their leather and shoe shop. Always, when the families were in each other's homes, one would find Moshe and Eliezer in one corner of the room, deep in conversation.

Yacov Feinschmidt, my mother's cousin, was always ready to laugh or smile. He never failed to bring candy or other treats for us when he visited our house. He never failed to have a joke or funny story ready for us. We all loved him.

Sometimes Eliezer would play the violin for the guests. He could make the instrument talk. His eyes—large, brown, soulful, like Mother's—would be in another world as he played. And I guess I got on his nerves from time to time.

"Spoiled brat" was the phrase he'd utter as he smacked my bottom.

When he and Zivja got married it was the most joyous wedding in Kurov. In stature, Eliezer and my father, it seemed to me, were next to God.

Of my two sisters, Chania and Chayale—Chaike, as we called her—Chayale was my favorite. Chania, who was older, considered herself my mother's deputy—and I guess she was. In fact, both she and Chaike were virtual duplicates of my mother, except for their blue eyes. Chania held herself straight and proud—thinking, I suppose, to intimidate Moshe and me when Mother wasn't around. She had high cheek-bones and an arched nose. She was beautiful.

Chaike was younger and plumper. She laughed easily. Chania probably wished that Chaike were less easy-going: it was difficult to control two younger brothers if one was always bubbling over with laughter. Chaike's eyes twinkled constantly. I loved them both. But Chaike was special; she helped me with my homework.

Every Jew cared about every other Jew in Kurov.

The *shtetl* had its social welfare groups, such as the *Linas hatzedek*, which helped the poor with medicine and doctors and which had brought a Jewish doctor into Kurov. If the *Linas hatzedek* determined that a patient could not afford the doctor's fee, the doctor treated free of charge. The cooperative bank gave free loans for the needy and for small businesses; local merchants—and Jewish welfare associations in the United States—contributed to the cooperative bank. Care was supplied to the sick, the elderly, widows, and handicapped. There was always anonymous giving. And there was even a group which aided poor girls in finding husbands.

There were class distinctions among the Jews of Kurov, and I suppose our family was toward the top of this scale. Our home was the gathering place of the important Jewish men in the town, and of the Poles who despised the growing anti-Semitism and stood behind the hurt Jews.

I could see them, my father's friends and peers, very clearly.

Schmuel Chanisman was the same height as my father, and had almost the same blue eyes. He owned the shoe supply business and was, like Daddy, one of the most respected merchants in the town. He never failed to greet Eliezer, Moshe, and me with real affection. I often wondered if that was because he also had three sons.

Levi Weinbuch was built like a soccer player: blond, muscular, huge shoulders. I guess his physique helped in his cutting meat in his butcher shop. Not as thoughtful nor as intellectual as some of the others, he was nonetheless straightforward.

Hershel Zukerman, my friend Yosek's father, was tall, thin, and introverted. I frequently reflected that his face seemed to hold the woes of the world.

Antek Kordovsky, a "pure" Pole, was very sympathetic to the plight of the Jews. He, like Mr. Weinbuch, was tall, blond, and well built. Mrs. Kordovsky was a regular customer in our store and she and mother had become quite friendly. Often she'd bring a cake or cookies to the store and hand it to one of us with the smiling admonition, "Not till after dinner."

Mr. Kordovsky and Daddy were very good friends; he had been instrumental in getting Daddy on the city council.

Yacov Feinschmidt was family. But Wolf Ginsburg was my favorite—and perhaps Daddy's. Short, rotund, with mostly gray hair, he was constantly adjusting his glasses. A wholesaler, he travelled to Warsaw at least once a week to purchase merchandise for the other store owners in Kurov. He always managed to spend a few minutes with Moshe and me, regaling us with tales of his trips to the city, or funny stories. Intelligence and warmth beamed from his eyes.

These gatherings lasted well into the night. Huge, steaming kettles of tea were consumed; mountains of cakes were eaten, topped off by more tea. And as the meetings went on, the voices became louder and, I sensed, more despairing.

I was supposed to have been asleep. But I made a habit of making my way as quietly as I could, to a space between the china cabinet and the wall that divided the dining room from the kitchen where, though hidden, I could hear every word. As I sensed a gathering coming to an end I would make my way back to my bed—just as quietly, if more rapidly.

One night I got caught. Mother came into the kitchen to refill the teapot and I jumped back into the space between the cabinet and the wall just in time—I thought.

Mother went about refilling the teapot quietly and efficiently. Suddenly her melodious voice floated across to me.

"I saw you, Nachemia. I know you're there. Why aren't you in bed?"

I didn't know whether to move or stay where I was. I stayed where I was. Then she was in front of me, the teapot in one hand, the other hand outstretched to me.

"Come on, son," she smiled.

I crawled out of my hiding place.

She put her free arm around my shoulder and helped me to my feet. She always smelled so good! A field of wildflowers. She kissed me on the forehead.

"Go on, now, back to bed. This talk will just upset you, Nachemia. Go back to bed."

She patted my shoulder and gently shoved me towards the bedrooms.

I looked into her eyes. I should have gotten a scolding, at least. But only love and concern shone there. She smiled. "Go on," she said.

I returned to bed.

Why were Jews so resented? What had we done? I asked myself continuously. Hadn't we helped Poland's economy? From what I could hear, huddled in my corner, there were no answers.

In the late 1930's, Poland was an underdeveloped country compared to the rest of Western Europe. Agricultural production took care of the population's needs, with enough left over to export pork, sugar, and produce. But the typical town and village in Poland was backwards. The fields were cultivated as they had been for centuries—primitively.

Poland had a narrow industrial base, but the textile industry was an important part of the economy. It was propelled by Jews. The city of Lodz was compared to the English city of Manchester. Still, Poland had chronic unemployment; the economy was not able to absorb the millions of availlable workers. The three million Polish Jews suffered most from this—they were the last to be given jobs. The regime saw to the needs of the "pure" Polish population first. Jewish engineers, technicians, and other skilled workers had no access to government enterprises or to factories that belonged to Poles. They were barred from commerce and agriculture by means of various laws. And the government bureaucracy was hermetically sealed against them. Jewish students faced quotas. Jews had to sit on separate benches in the rear on public transportation and in public buildings. They were attacked and beaten.

Polish Jews were in an economic and social ghetto long before Hitler's ascendancy. Tens of thousands of families lived a precarious existence with no prospect for better times. Many thousands lived in poverty.

Voices rose. We must fight this discrimination with all our strength and might. But how? Other voices chimed in, with edges of despair: there's nothing we can do. They are much more powerful than we are. Always, my father's voice— and my mother's—were the soothing voices, the voices of reason. My father will solve whatever it is, I thought then. Everyone looked to him.

Huddled in the corner of a warm, comfortable house, nurtured by my family, my heritage, and my community, I couldn't understand the danger. Weren't we also Poles? Weren't we part of Poland?

But nothing was solved. There was the young priest who used to come to the market square on Thursdays, when it was busiest, leading a group of teenagers who stood by the shops and stalls of Jewish merchants and called to everyone in the square to boycott Jewish merchants and goods. They handed out anti-Semitic leaflets. They actively stopped Poles from dealing with Jews.

Slogans were painted on the walls of buildings: "Jews

to Palestine!" "Jews Are Blood Suckers of Polish People!" "Do Not Buy from Jews!" I walked by them on the way to school.

We were not allowed to wear our yarmulkes in school, and we had to sit in the back of the rooms. At recess we were the butt of jokes—and pranks. I didn't understand it, but I came to expect it.

One night there was a secret consultation between Jews and Poles in our house, and I was in my usual hiding place, listening. They were trying to find ways of getting rid of Kurov's mayor, Boleslva Panetski, who was notoriously anti-Semitic. They decided to put up Stanislav Sheleziak, who was a friend of both Poles and Jews, as a candidate.

He was elected by a large majority.

I was in the fifth grade. My teacher was Panetski's wife.

The day after the election she marched over to my desk.

"Put those books down!" she shouted. Her eyes were blazing.

I put the books down on my desk. My stomach began to churn. What was she going to do?

She grabbed a notebook and tore it into pieces. She grabbed another and ripped it apart. "Dirty," she hissed, "like all the Jews . . ."

I tried to save the notebooks. It was impossible. They were in shreds. She threw the remains against the nearest wall. "Take your filthy notebooks and get out of here!" she screamed. "Go home!"

I don't remember getting home from school. I was crying very hard by the time I stumbled into my family's shop. My father was there. He put his arms around me.

I gulped out what had happened.

"We will see about this," he said. "I will go personally to the school and see."

That night my father related his meeting with the school inspector.

"I told him what Mrs. Panetski had done to your books, Nachemia. He tried to dismiss it as nothing. 'Mrs. Panetski didn't mean it,' he told me.

"I reiterated that she had torn *two* notebooks, one after

the other, that it was not merely a gesture of impulse. I reiterated what she had said to you. Still, the inspector attempted to defend the woman.

"Finally, I became emphatic. 'Mr. Kulovski,' I stated—and he became very aware that I meant business, then. 'I am going to personally lodge a complaint to the district inspector against this treatment of my son. I think you are aware that as a member of the city council it will carry some weight.' "

Mother, Chania, Chaike, Moshe, and I all smiled broadly at this.

"So," Daddy continued, "Kulovski backed down—a bit. He proposed a compromise. Nachemia, you will be transferred to another class. And Mrs. Panetski is to apologize to you."

I returned to school the next day to a different teacher. I saw Mrs. Panetski in the hallway. She looked the other way.

Things did not get better.

Jewish students were hauled into fights involuntarily during recess. The gentiles threw stones at us. By pooling our meager allowances we began to hire strong boys to defend us on the way to and from school. It was worth it.

Not long afterwards a rumor made the rounds in Kurov: Jews were spies for the Germans. Any unknown Jew that came to Kurov was arrested immediately and accused of spying. The Jewish community leaders invariably deposited money to bail him out.

The situation worsened daily. The scent of war was in the air.

Two

August 1944

The first thing I saw when Michel woke me was his red bandana tied around his neck.

"It's not light yet . . ." I mumbled.

"*Ja*, well, I told you. Come, we have to start breakfast."

I pulled my boots on.

Sleepy as I was, I could hardly see as I shambled alongside Michel towards the kitchen area. Everything looked gray and foggy. Perhaps it was.

Except for the patrol there wasn't a soul about. "What part of the army is this?" I asked.

"We're the headquarters company of the Seventy-Second Fusiliers," he answered noncommittally.

"Oh."

"By the way, where did you get those boots and trousers?" he asked.

I tensed immediately. "Oh—I don't know. My clothes had gotten into such bad shape; some Poles gave me these to wear. They happened to fit."

Breakfast consisted of coffee, which was mostly chicory, and slices of bread with margarine and jam.

The troops wolfed it down.

We no sooner finished cleaning up from breakfast than we began preparations for lunch. That day it consisted of meat patties, which we fried in huge skillets, and potato salad. After I chopped the wood Michel asked me to peel the potatoes and put them in a huge pot of water.

"Michel, what are the patties made of?"

"What do you mean?"

"What kind of meat?"

"Why?"

"Why don't you want to tell me?"

He sighed—then grinned. "It's horsemeat."

"Horsemeat." I wished I hadn't asked. He caught my expression.

"It's good meat," he declared.

"Yes," I said. I guess I didn't sound convinced.

"Listen," he insisted, "it *is* good meat. In my shop in Dresden many customers asked especially for horsemeat. Not too much fat in it. They came back for more."

"What shop, Michel?"

"Oh, my shop. My butcher shop. I'm a butcher—I *was* a butcher before the army got me. It was a good business. Kind of cold in the refrigerator, though."

I brought the conversation back to the job at hand before he could ask me about myself. "How would you like these potatoes cut up?"

"Oh—like this." He cut one in thick slices to show me. I busied myself with the knife.

Lunch varied only slightly from day to day, I learned. It was either meat patties, goulash soup, or meat balls with potatoes in some form, and vegetables—usually cabbage.

We didn't cook for dinner. We sliced up loaves of military-issue bread—which somehow was never fresh—and laid out dozens of slices of canned meat or fish and salami. It usually disappeared quickly once the troops reached the long tables.

"The boss is pleased with your work," Michel said to me after a couple of weeks.

I had noticed that the sergeant appeared increasingly friendly. He asked me how I was. He grinned. Once he clapped me on the shoulder. Often his left eyebrow would quirk up when he was amused by something.

That was fine. Perhaps I could begin to feel secure, if I

did my job and kept my mouth closed. They'd never know. He couldn't engage me in lengthy conversation while we were preparing meals—we were just too busy. And Michel and I were awake and in the kitchen area long before he—or anyone else—was awake. Evenings I either got into "my" room while he and Michel were still outside, talking with the others, or, if either of them was in the large room as I made my way toward the storage area, I would wish him a good night and keep going.

Heinz was a *wohler Kerl* (good fellow), Michel assured me. And it seemed that he was. The other sergeants and officers—and troops—seemed to genuinely like him. He himself always seemed to have a pleasantry or joke to exchange with someone. I had noticed one sergeant—Emil—with whom Heinz seemed to have a game going: who could tell the best joke. The supply of jokes seemed bottomless between those two. It seemed that whenever Heinz and Emil were together in a group the group never stopped laughing.

September 1944

I headed toward "my" room. The sergeant called out to me. "Marion! Come join us! A little rum!"

I turned. They were both sitting at the table, a wine bottle and two glasses between them.

Michel grinned and nodded at me. "You'd make a *good* soldier, Marion; you do your job, you're hardworking, you keep your mouth closed. But you keep to yourself too much. Come on, join us. Relax."

While Michel urged me to the table Heinz had somehow produced another wine glass. I moved towards the table. I smiled. I could be fond of both of them, I thought, under other circumstances.

The sergeant pointed at the bottle. "There are definite advantages to being in charge of the food supply," he laughed.

He filled my glass as I sat down on one of the chairs. "So Marion, how do you like army service?"

I tensed. What did he mean? I watched him closely. Why did he ask this question? His eyes seemed friendly—but was he looking for clues in what I might say?

"Fine, sir."

He smiled at me. "Marion. I'm Heinz. If you want to be formal in front of the troops—well—you don't even have to be that. But here, in this room or when it's only the two of us—or the three of us—it's Heinz. Why—" his smile broadened. "You're not much younger than me, are you?"

"I'm eighteen, s—" I caught myself.

"What? What's my name?" The left eyebrow quirked up.

". . . Heinz."

"That's better."

Michel chuckled goodnaturedly.

Now he's going to ask me about my background, I thought. *Best to keep the conversation on him.*

I leaned forward, took a sip of rum. It *was* good. "How did you get into the food area of the army, Heinz?"

"Believe it or not, I studied cooking and nutrition at the university in Hamburg, where I'm from. I got a degree in it. Then the war began. I was drafted. We all were—except for this old man here—" he gestured playfully toward Michel— "he's a lifer!"

"Careful! I could be your father," Michel pretended to grumble. "Yours, too," he winked at me.

"So. Shall we call you 'Papa'?" Heinz grinned.

Michel grunted and poured more rum into his glass.

The light was fading rapidly in the room.

"That was three years ago," Heinz continued. "I went to Odessa, fought in the Crimea. See—" he turned the jacket of his uniform which hung from a peg in the slanted ceiling behind him. It bore the insignia: a map of the Crimea with the word *Krim* through it. I had noticed it before.

By the end of the bottle of rum I was more than ready for bed. Michel had fallen asleep in his chair.

"Marion, give me a hand with him," Heinz chuckled.

"Between us we can get him over to his bed. If he wakes up he can walk himself."

We each took Michel under a shoulder. As we began to lift him he woke up with a loud snort.

"Aha, you're awake!" Heinz laughed. "So—you can get to your bed by yourself."

Michel mumbled something and ambled over to his straw pallet.

"Marion, bring your bed out here. No need to be off by yourself," Heinz clapped me on the shoulder.

I went into the storage room and got my straw pallet and blankets. No sense in seeming unfriendly.

As I drifted off to sleep I caught sight of the insignia on Heinz's uniform which he had earned in the Crimean War. The Crimea. I remembered vividly when war broke out in Kurov.

September 1939

I woke up earlier than usual on September first. We were to start a new year at school that day.

Chania, Chaike, Moshe and I all spoke at once at breakfast. I was happy. I had learned at the end of June, as school let out for the summer, that my two closest friends, Abraham Kenig and Yosek Zukerman, would again be in the same class with me.

"Abraham, Yosek and I are in the same class again," I crowed.

"That's so the three of you can cheat on tests," Moshe said derisively.

"Like you and Yosel Chanisman?" I shot back.

"Get out of here!" Moshe sneered.

"Well, at least we won't have Mrs. Panetski again," I said.

"Watch out! Maybe she got herself transferred back to your class!" Chaike teased.

"Hey, do you think we'll have to hire guys to protect us again on the way home from school?"

Chania shook her head. "Why does this happen to us?" she asked no one in particular.

Daddy had switched on the radio in the middle of our increasingly silly speculations—probably preferring to listen to it rather than us. Suddenly they shushed us.

"The Army of the Third Reich has attacked Poland on all its borders," the voice boomed over the air.

The six of us sat glued to our seats.

General Rydz Shmigly, Poland's Chief of Staff, came on the air. "The Poles will defend their country to the last drop of our blood! We will throw off the German attackers!"

Mother, Daddy, Chania, Chaike, Moshe and I locked eyes with one another in total silence.

"Eliezer," I said suddenly. Eliezer and Zivja had moved to Urzendov, where our grandfather, Abraham Wurman, lived. Was he listening to the news? Would they be all right?

I jumped up from the table and turned the dial on the radio, searching for a foreign radio station. I found one.

". . . You have no choice but total surrender! We will surround Poland! We will take Poland! Our destiny has decreed this . . ."

"The beast!" Mother muttered.

She got up from the table and went to the stove for more coffee. I watched her. Her hands were shaking.

I wanted to run over to her, throw my arms around her, tell her everything was going to be all right.

But I didn't. Because it wasn't.

Yes, the voice was unmistakable: the distinct, husky, hysterical tone of Adolf Hitler filled our kitchen like a noxious gas.

"We will destroy all your cities. We will burn all your farms. You have no choice. It is the destiny of the Third Reich—"

"Oh God, turn it off!" Chania almost sobbed.

We did not go to school that day, nor the next. Of course, there were panicked meetings in our house every night.

"What will we do if they destroy Kurov," Mr. Chanisman asked over and over.

"Leave. Do you want to become part of the rubble?" Mr. Zukerman asked. Mr. Zukerman was a practical man— almost as practical as my father.

"I'm not leaving," Levi Weinbuch stated flatly. "Kurov has been my family's home for generations."

"What if there's no more Kurov?" Antek Kordovsky put in. Kordovsky was highly sympathetic to the Jewish cause and had helped my father get on the city council.

"Why would they bother with a small town like Kurov? We are insignificant compared to Warsaw and Lublin," my father observed.

"To break Poland's spirit," Hershel Zukerman said. "Yes, they'll probably get Warsaw. And Lublin. But they won't stop there until we go to them with our arms raised over our heads."

There was a very loud silence.

"And listen," Yacov Feinschmidt mourned, "we all know that when the Germans attack the Poles, the Poles are going to attack us worse."

There was another long silence, broken only by sighs.

"Henoch, when is the city council meeting?" Mr. Weinbuch asked. "Shouldn't they have an emergency meeting?"

"Yes. I will let you know." Daddy's voice sounded strangely flat. Despairing, I thought.

The city council convened. They established a Civil Guard on which every member of the council had to serve. My father was nominated as its leader.

We spent a week moving the merchandise in our shop to our cellar, which was constructed of brick and had a steel door. We wanted to save it from the fire that would result from bombings. Then, with our customers wanting to stock up on supplies, we spent the next few days running between the shop and the cellar retrieving the merchandise to sell.

Mother sewed small bags of cloth, into which she put money. One evening after dinner, she gave them to each of us. She had tears in her eyes as she spoke:

"My children, there is a war going on. We don't know what will happen tomorrow. If, God forbid, we have to separate or if we lose each other, you must have money at least to buy food."

Shortly afterwards she prepared rucksacks and filled them with underwear, pants, shirts, skirts for Chania and Chaike, and socks.

At the end of the week a rumor that the Germans were going to bomb Kurov spread through the town. Panic broke out yet again. Most Jews locked up their homes, took what valuables they could, and made their way out. The streets were jammed. Some families drove carts or wagons; most travelled by foot.

In school, which had finally resumed by the end of the week, I could not keep my mind on what was being taught. Neither could Yosek or Abraham, I learned.

"What did she say about the textile industry in Poland?" Yosek asked on the way home.

He pulled on his ear. We had been in the same class since we'd started school. Yosek's thin face, with its bushy eyebrows and humorous twist to the mouth, was as recognizable to me as my own. Often I felt closer to him than to Moshe.

Abraham was kicking pebbles along the roadway, distracted. His head, with its mop of auburn hair, was bent into his chest; he was frowning.

"I dunno," Abraham said. "She acted funny herself— on the verge of crying, almost."

"Listen, do you think they'll close the school?"

"I dunno."

On Friday morning my father went to the city council to find out what he could about the rumor. He returned to the house dispirited.

"No one seems to know the source of the rumor," he sighed, "but everyone is sure that they're going to bomb us."

"Henoch," Mother soothed, "we are prepared for anything. Flight, if necessary. You and I prepared the rucksacks. As long as we're together."

"Perhaps they'll just drop a couple of minor bombs and then leave," Daddy said. I wondered if that's what he really thought.

Less than two hours later, at noon, we heard the sound of airplanes in the distance. Within minutes bombs began to fall. We were petrified.

"I want to see what's happening." I made for the door.

"Nachemia! You come back here!" I had never heard Mother shout so loudly.

I don't know what impelled me to run outside, but I was out before she could stop me.

It was a scene from hell. Buildings burned on all sides. Flames leaped five to ten feet into the air with a loud hissing sound. Flames engulfing the police station were twenty feet high. Trees burned, their branches splitting off and crashing into the street. I began to walk down Lubelska.

Then I saw the bodies. Wounded and dead men and women lay in the street and on the sidewalk. Blood ran from their mouths. The eyes of the dead were open, staring. Some of the wounded groaned; some screamed. Some tried to stretch out their hands toward me as I walked up the street.

I couldn't stand it. I turned and ran back to the house. Mother and Daddy were handing out the rucksacks so we could leave. Tears rolled down their cheeks.

"Nachemia, never disobey your mother again," my father turned a stern face toward me.

"I won't, I promise!"

Why did the Germans bomb Kurov? It had no military camps or ammunition dumps, no strategic importance for the Polish army, nor did it matter that it was located on the road between Lublin and Warsaw.

The Germans seemed to want to create panic among the civil population of Poland; perhaps, to break our spirits. Hitler had meant what he said.

Our rucksacks were in place. Tears were streaming down our cheeks. My father had his arm around my mother's shoulders. Chania and Chaike stood close together. "We'll be back, children. It is not the end of the world," my father said.

A windmill stood on a hill just outside Kurov. We headed for it on the Kloda road, about half an hour's walk from the center of town. We saw friends and family among those who trudged on Kloda Road. The greetings among us were mostly silent, except for an occasional *"Shalom."*

At the top of the hill we stopped to catch our breaths and to consider where we were going.

"Listen, before we go too far, I think I should go back to the house to check on it," Daddy said.

"Henoch, no. What if a bomb falls on you while you're back in town?"

"I think they've done their worse, Sarah. Look, there are also things we forgot to bring—"

"Such as?"

"Well, blankets. Who knows where we're going to spend the night?"

"I'm afraid—"

"Sarah, I'll be fine. I would not leave you and the children if I thought I would not come back."

Her eyes clouded. "All right, Henoch."

We sat down on the grass to wait for him. Chania and Chaike huddled together; Moshe and I sat close. Mother sat between the two boys and the two girls. She was murmuring: I decided it was a prayer for my father's safety.

"Look, Mother, we can pick out our house," Chaike suddenly said.

We all looked to where she pointed. "All right," she said, "now there's the *cheder;* now look to the right . . ."

"Well, it's still intact," Mother finally said.

"Just as Daddy said," Moshe chimed in.

Daddy returned about two hours later. I had never seen him so bitter. He carried woolen blankets and some cooking pots—and loaves of bread and a big salami.

He sat down heavily beside us.

"Henoch, what is it . . .?" Mother asked.

"I don't know, Sarah," he sighed. "It's just that—well,

when I turned the key in the lock of the door as I was leaving, it broke . . . I feel it's an omen."

We gathered around him. Suddenly Chaike screamed: "No! Oh, NO!" Her eyes were fixed on Kurov.

We looked. Again, we picked out our house. It was engulfed in flames.

Wordlessly, we reached for each other. We wept uncontrollably.

"It is *Shabbat*," Chania said quietly. It was. It was five in the afternoon.

We turned away silently. Daddy walked first and we followed him.

September 1944

Our battalion received orders to pack up and move to the village of Volka Voynowska.

After we cleaned up from breakfast I stood and watched the soldiers load their belongings onto the wagons. Blankets, rucksacks. The kitchen equipment. Heinz gave orders for the loading of the kitchen equipment and food supplies. Michel walked around and around the wagon to see that it was done properly.

What was I going to do now? Who was I to them? I counted for nothing. Well, maybe now I would locate the Soviets, I thought. Maybe this was the opportunity.

I glanced at the trees at the edges of the fields. Already some of the leaves at the tops had begun to turn burnt orange and yellow. Soon winter would be here again. I *had* to find the Soviet army. They would shelter me.

I didn't hear Heinz come up behind me.

"Marion, you will come with us, yes? We need your help."

I smiled almost in spite of myself. "*Jawohl*, Heinz."

I looked into his eyes. There was utter friendliness in them. My heart pounded: why do we have to be sworn enemies?

We marched—trudged, rather—through deserted

countryside all day. We passed many abandoned villages such as the one we had left. The officers rode on horses. Michel and I travelled on the supply wagon which was horsedrawn. Heinz frequently teased Michel.

"What's wrong, oldtimer? Too far for you?"

Michel shook his head and snorted. Heinz laughed. There was real affection between them.

I noticed that Heinz was well liked by practically all the other sergeants and officers. He had an easy, friendly way. But he brooked no nonsense.

Chickens, pigs, and goats ran freely about the streets of Volka Voynowska. I thought of the market square of Kurov. Here, the seventy-five or so houses were made mostly of wood and had thatched roofs, although there were a few wooden roofs here and there. Most of the houses had been painted white, and some even had windowboxes where flowers made a small splash of color Children ran through the streets with the animals, barefoot.

"Well, the other quartermaster should have places prepared for us," Michel commented. "Hope so. I'm tired."

"What quartermaster?"

"The battalion that's meeting us here. Well, we'll see."

We soon learned that a storehouse had been set aside for the food supply and kitchen—and that we would sleep on its floor. Heinz was not pleased.

"Marion, you speak Polish. You be our *Dolmetscher*. Find us a better place than this. Why should we sleep on the floor?"

Think fast, I told myself as Michel and I walked through the town. We came to the schoolhouse. *Aha!* I thought. It was locked. I stopped a fat, old peasant waddling alongside the building.

"Who has the keys to the school building?" I asked him.

He took off his cap. "Mostly likely the schoolmaster," he replied.

"Can you show us where he lives?"

"I'll take you there."

"See," Michel mumbled in German as we made our way to the schoolmaster's house, "we've got them well trained here. The army has been occupying this place for five years; they do as they're asked—or told."

I nodded.

The schoolmaster's house was a rather large one—one of those with windowboxes filled with flowers. It seemed to have lots of windows on the first floor. I knocked at the door.

When he opened it and saw Michel, he straightened up. "Yes?"

"We need the school building for the kitchen and food supply for our battalion," I told him in Polish.

He frowned, his thin face creased into dozens of horizontal lines. "That cannot be," he said. "The children are supposed to begin the new school year next week and the quartermaster has promised me that on no account will he commandeer the school house."

"Well, do you know of another place where we could set up our kitchen and store our supplies? A place near a well?"

He looked at us for a moment.

"If you want, you can set up here in my place," he finally said. "There is a well in the yard and also a storage shed." He looked at me closely. "I have a spare room on the second floor of my house. Nothing fancy. How many are there in your unit? There are mattresses on the floor."

"You are very kind," I said. "Thank you. There are three of us."

The schoolmaster smiled. "It will be tight—but, yes, there is room."

Michel and I hurried back to Heinz. Mattresses! We would be sleeping in luxury!

"Good for you, Marion." Heinz said when I told him.

"*Ja!* Mattresses!" Michel exulted. We all laughed.

On the way over to the schoolmaster's house Heinz explained the setup. "See, we're more or less joining another battalion. We, as headquarters, supply the food to them—it'll be about one hundred and twenty meals a day. Don't worry—

you can always commandeer help from the village. I think you have to speak to the *soltys*—he's the village elder. We also have a field hospital here, a munitions stockpile, and clothing supply."

We were busy, even with the help we were able to recruit from the village. Every peasant had to be shown what to do every mealtime. They seemed to rotate: one would show up for a few days, then disappear. I'd have to then recruit someone else.

The men of the battalion began to recognize me and call me by my name. Of course, I was instantly recognizable in my shabby clothes and uncut hair. I smiled at them. I returned their *Gut morgens*. I was constantly watchful for the too-long glance, the suspicious stare.

The schoolmaster's spare bedroom *was* snug with the three of us in it. Michel had managed to fit cases of Moselle and canned meat and cheese into the space under the eaves. so the nightly camaraderie continued, fuclled mostly by Moselle, but once in a while by cognac. Heinz assured us that it was excellent cognac.

Once Heinz took a photograph from his shirt pocket. It was of a lovely looking young woman—blonde and blue eyes. There seemed to be no artifice about her.

"Your mother, Heinz?" Michel grinned.

"*Ja,* my mother, you old woodchuck! Marion, that is my fiancée, Elsa."

"She's beautiful, Heinz." I meant it.

"Jawohl, she is. But—I'm biased about that."

"She suits you, Heinz." I meant it. When was I going to admit how much I truly liked this man?

He looked at me for what seemed a long time, a questioning expression on his face. I expected him to ask me to explain what I'd said. But he remained silent.

Michel broke the silence. "So, Marion. What about *your* fiancée? Girlfriend?"

"Uh—she may well be dead," I said slowly. I regretted it immediately.

"Have you no family now, Marion?" Heinz asked.

"I don't think so," I answered. "The Bolsheviks murdered my father and they deported my mother—I don't know where they sent her. I've heard nothing about them."

"What town was this, Marion?"

"Sandomierz," I answered uneasily. Did he notice my nervousness?

"Ah yes, Sandomierz." he took another sip of his cognac. What was he thinking?

"No brothers or sisters?" Michel piped up.

"No."

"Ach—that's sad." Michel poured himself more cognac.

"So, Marion," Heinz said gently, "you are alone now."

I nodded. What was this leading up to?

"Lots of people are alone now—severed from their families—because of that maniac."

I looked at Heinz in utter astonishment.

"Come on, Marion," he prodded softly. "You don't think Michel and I are in this stupid war because we want to be, do you? Michel separated from his wife and children, I from my parents and sister and Elsa. Because we believe in Adolf Hitler? Why—the man's insane!"

I didn't utter a sound. He continued.

"Take over all of Europe! At what cost?"

Michel nodded.

I was dumbfounded. Was this a trap? Were they waiting for my response in order to find me out?

Later, in the darkness, I thought—at what cost indeed? At least Heinz and Michel still had families and knew where to rejoin them when and if this war ended. I hadn't the faintest idea whether I still had a family or not.

September 1939

My father knew a Polish peasant, Dombrowski, in Kloda, the tiny village not far from Kurov. We dragged ourselves to his house and knocked on the door.

Dombrowski opened it immediately.

"Mr. Wurman, what is going on?"

"The Germans are bombing Kurov, Dombrowski," Daddy told him sadly. "They've destroyed our house."

"Oh, dear God."

"Could we spend some time in your barn—until we decide what to do?"

"Of course!" Dombrowski's weather-tanned face broke into a smile. "Can I get you anything?"

"No, thank you. Just now we'd like to rest."

The barn was large; the straw was fresh. We lay down and tried to sleep. I was restless. Moshe was awake, and I detected Chania and Chaike weeping softly. I had to know what was going on outside. I left the barn and walked toward the main road. Hundreds of men, children, and women, pushing baby carriages and wheelbarrows filled with their belongings, trudged by. The luckier ones walked next to carts hitched to horses. A terrible confusion permeated the air; the din of shouting was almost impenetrable.

An old black carriage hitched to two horses moved with the crowd; it was the rabbi from Modzic with his attendants. His thin, ascetic face with its sparse beard seemed to have aged by ten years. They stopped the carriage near the well to let the horses drink. It was instantly surrounded by women and children who cried and sobbed.

"Rabbi, I have no candles for *Shabbat*," one woman blurted out.

"Today you do not have to light candles," the rabbi answered. "Look around you; you will see that your candles are already burning."

Another cried, "Rabbi, what am I to do; I can't stay here. I must get to my children in Miechov. I might, heaven forbid, lose them—"

"The duty of saving life overides the *Shabbat* laws. You can go," he replied.

He guided the horses back to the main road.

I was tired and shaking by the time I returned to the barn. We were all hungry but no one wanted to eat.

During the evening more people came to the barn—

some of whom we knew. We offered them straw on which to sleep.

Somehow my cousin Moshe Naimark found his way there late at night. He woke us and told us that by now the entire town was in flames except for a few houses in the new market section. Apparently our cousin Yacov Feinschmidt's house was still intact, and a number of Jews had taken shelter there.

None of us could get back to sleep. My head spun with the thoughts racing through it, but I dared not say anything— I was the youngest. Then my father sighed:

"God, Master of the world, more than twenty years of hard labor are now burning in the fire, and, may his name be obliterated, Hitler will be coming."

At sunrise we left the barn and hid in the bushes along the edge of the field. Shortly afterward, German planes began to bomb the area—as we had expected. They fired at those moving on the roads and in the fields with automatic weapons. By afternoon hundreds lay dead along the roads and paths. We remained in the bushes, hardly daring to breathe, all day long. And we escaped the bullets.

When it got dark we returned to the barn. Daddy went out to look for food, and returned with some bread, cheese, and fruit. We ate it thankfully.

On the following day Daddy decided to go back to Kurov yet again to check the situation with his own eyes. Again my mother protested.

"They are shooting bullets from planes!" she exclaimed.

"Sarah, Sarah, I will be careful, I promise you. I will not leave you."

Again we hid under the bushes and trees and found shelter from the German bullets. We returned to the barn as darkness fell.

Later that night Daddy returned carrying a loaf of bread, homemade cheese, and some vegetables. We jumped at it.

He was weary. "The town is almost completely destroyed," he sighed. "The Jewish section has suffered the greatest losses, of course: the big synagogue, the *cheder*, and all the other of our institutions are gone—except for a pile of ashes. The church is still standing, and the city hall, the post office, the school. Also a few houses in the non-Jewish section."

We looked at one another without speaking.

"Yacov's house somehow escaped the bombs; they were sheltering Jews who've not left Kurov," he continued. "But," he shook his head sadly, bewildered, "they bombed again today. They got Yacov's house this time."

We held our breaths.

"Yes," he nodded, "Aunt Hena is dead, and Hershel Naimark, your cousin, also.

The tears began in us again.

"I also met with the Mayor, Shelezniak, and a few Christian friends from the city council, like Kordovsky, and the chief of police. The bombings and the targets seemed very suspicious. We figured someone was giving the Germans information on just where to strike in the town. We thought it was probably Ulrich, the mill owner just outside town. You remember," he nodded at Mother, "the man is a rabid anti-Semite.

"Anyway, we decided to search Urlich's place. A few police officers got together with us. We went to the mill. There was a secret radio station there. We turned the radio on: there was a German speaking. The police officer—I forget his name—who speaks German told us that the voice was that of a pilot commenting on the bombing."

"So—" Mother prompted.

"The military police arrested Ulrich and his son."

After about a week in the barn we were given a gift: Eliezer walked in.

We laughed, we cried. We took turns hugging him. "Okay, Eliezer," Daddy finally said. "Tell us how you got here. You look tired; you've no shoes on."

"Well," Eliezer said, one arm around Mother, one

around Chaike, "Zivja and I of course heard the news about Kurov. I set out immediately on my bike. You know, it's about fifty miles; I figured I could make it in a day and part of a night. No such luck. About twenty or twenty-five miles on the road, I was attacked."

We gasped as one person. "By whom?"

"Just hooligans. Polish. Not Germans, not any army. There were about four of them. They took my bike—and my shoes. I didn't have a chance."

"So how did you get here—to the barn?" Daddy asked.

"On foot. It hurt for the first ten miles or so. Then—" he shrugged. "Oh, you mean how did I know to come *here*. Well, Daddy, I remembered that you were pretty friendly with Dombrowski and—I just used instinct. Yeh, I examined every face on the road. But somehow I knew you'd be here. And you are."

We hugged and embraced again.

"Eliezer," Daddy said. "There's something we must tell you."

Eliezer stiffened. "What is it?"

"Our house—"

"No! Don't—" I covered my eyes.

Daddy nodded sadly. "Yes, Eliezer. It's gone. Burned. Rubble."

Eliezer sat down suddenly on the straw and, openly, unashamedly, wept. "Bastards!" he muttered. "I'll get them. I will."

Again, we wept for our home.

Finally, Mother said, "But we are together."

"Yes," Daddy joined her, "and we must decide what to do."

"I think we should separate temporarily," my mother stiffened her back.

"Why?" I asked, my voice breaking.

"So we stay alive," my father said resolutely.

"But we're together," Chaike interrupted.

"Yes, Chaike, but it is probably more expedient—we

can move better—in a smaller group. Don't worry. It's only temporary."

Do you really believe that, Daddy? I wondered sadly.

Suddenly the barn door burst open and Shumel Chanisman and his son Yosel ran in.

"Henoch, Henoch!" Mr. Chanisman was out of breath. "The Germans have entered Kurov. They are there now, walking around our streets!"

"Dear God—" Mother said.

"Listen, listen!" Chanisman pressed on. "They released Ulrich and his son. They've made Ulrich town commissar."

"What!" Daddy reeled at hearing this.

"Yes, yes!" Chanisman bobbed up and down nervously. "And listen, you know what Ulrich is saying? That his first job is to locate Henoch Wurman and his family and hang them in the market square."

Chania and Chaike both burst into fresh tears.

"Henoch, you've got to get away," Chanisman continued.

"Of course," Daddy said, folding his hands across his chest. "We were just discussing that."

"Now! Now!" Chanisman placed his hands on my father's shoulders and shook them.

"You're right, Shumel," my father said. "I want you to tell everyone you meet that we've headed for Russia. And that we've gotten a week's start."

"Russia," Mr. Chanisman said, still on the verge of hysteria. Then he nodded. "Yes, Henoch, I will tell them. Everyone?"

"Everyone," Daddy repeated firmly. Then his face lightened; his old hospitality intervened. "But we shall talk of all that later. Stay and have dinner. It's not fancy, but we would enjoy your breaking bread with us."

Mother, Chania, and Chaike laid bread, cheese, and milk on the board we had elevated between two milking stands and used as a table. When they had arranged things to their satisfaction, they beckoned to us.

The conversation continued, interrupted only by the blessing of the food.

"Let Chaike and Nachemia return to Urzendov with me," Eliezer said over our meal of bread and cheese. "There is room in Grandfather Wurman's house. It is large—for Urzendov. Zivja and I have moved in there."

"All right," my father pondered this. "Then Mother, Chania, Moshe and I will head for Lublin. There are 45,000 Jews there. They can't kill them all, can they?"

It took us about seven hours to get to Urzendov. Often we hitched rides on carts; most often we walked. We had found a pair of shoes for Eliezer: someone had donated them. Chaike wept for most of the journey. "But Chaike, we are going to Grandfather Wurman's house."

"I don't want to leave Mother!"

"It's only for a short while, Chaike."

Urzendov was about one-sixth the size of Kurov. Basically, it consisted of a large market square around which all the homes in the town clustered. Here also houses were painted off-white and gray. Ducks and goats were roaming the streets freely as we approached.

Two years before, the Polish government had built a large munitions factor—Budzyn—which the Germans had taken over, as they had Urzendov itself. A German commissar now ran the town and heavy financial "tributes" were imposed on the Jews. Jews were taken to Budzyn to clean the roads, to load and unload supplies, to clean the horses.

My grandfather's house, made of brick, had a large backyard but was smaller than our house in Kurov: it consisted of two bedrooms, a large kitchen, and a hardware store in front. Eliezer managed the hardware store, and he, Zivja, and their baby daughter Ester lived in one of the bedrooms. With Chaike and me, there were six of us sharing the rooms. Then, a month later, the rest of our family, unable to stay any longer in Lublin, arrived in Urzendov. That made ten of us sharing the three rooms.

We looked all over Urzendov for larger quarters. There

were none. Grateful as we were for the shelter, we were also despondent. And there were the decrees that the commissar posted every day:

> All Jews had to give capital contributions—individually and then community contributions—to the Germans.
>
> All Jews had to give their radios and bicycles to the Germans.
>
> All Jewish store owners had to submit a list of the merchandise in their stores to the Germans. Written permission must be obtained from the commissar before purchasing any new merchandise.
>
> All Jews must have a permit to travel between towns.

We could not stay in Urzendov, we knew. But we didn't know how we would leave.

Then my father's brother, Matityahu, who lived in Ostroveic, got a message through to us. He had speculated that we might have arrived in Urzendov and had sent a messenger to my grandfather's house: we were all invited to live in his house.

Another family consulation ended with the decision that I, the youngest, would go first and the rest would come later on.

So I left Urzendov.

THREE

January 1940

The first thing I noticed in Ostroviec were the armbands. Each was about four inches wide and bore a blue Star of David. Men, women and children wore them: the bands identified them as Jews. The bands seemed to appear everywhere: Jews made up about half the population of Ostroviec.

Next I noticed the Judenrat. They also wore armbands—only those had the word "Judenrat" inscribed on them. The Judenrat were Jews who had been drafted by the Germans to enforce the restrictions and decrees imposed on Jews. The Judenrat moved freely in areas where other Jews were forbidden access. They collected tributes. They distributed the food rationing in the ghetto. They supplied the Germans with workers for forced labor. And when the expulsion to the death camps began, the Judenrat were the ones who supplied the numbers required for the "transportations."

Most Polish cities with a sizeable population had Judenrats.

Jews also made up the "ghetto police." They were supposed to keep order in the ghetto. They enjoyed perhaps more privileges than the Judenrat.

My uncle, Matityahu Wurman, explained these distinctions to me on the first day I arrived in Ostroviec.

Uncle Matityahu owned the fur factory in Ostroviec and was one of the wealthiest industrialists in town. His house was among the finest, and he, like my father, was respected by Jew and gentile alike.

He still had to live in the ghetto and wear the armband. I noticed it when he threw his arms around my shoulders in welcome.

I looked at him: he wasn't nearly as tall as Daddy, and was rotund. He had black hair and a black, well-groomed beard. And he radiated energy. I was drawn to him on sight.

"So. We will make a furrier out of you, Nachemia! A skill you will never fail to put to good use. Come, now. Let me show you where you will sleep and explain our restrictions."

I had observed one already. There was no radio in the house. Jews were forbidden to listen to the radio, Uncle Matityahu said, and had handed all radio sets over to the Germans months ago—on penalty of death.

"They want us cut off from the world," he explained, "so that we cannot know the progress of the war. Whether the Bolsheviks rout the Germans from Poland, whether the English defeat them on another front. They're trying to keep the Poles cut off from the news also, but they're easier on them—of course. They have concealed radios—and the Germans know it—and can listen to broadcasts from London and Moscow. They can move about freely. They're not confined behind barbed wire."

He put his strong arm around my shoulder and walked me into the kitchen. "Here, Nachemia, I hope you like this."

The bed was in an alcove off the large kitchen. The kitchen had a feeling of warmth and light—and, somehow, affection. The bed was soft and inviting.

"Uncle Matityahu," I said. "Would it be all right if I took a short nap?"

Smiling, he nodded.

Ostroviec was settled by a Polish prince by the name of Yanusz Ostrouski. During the sixteenth century he built a white stone church on top of a hill on the perimeter of the town. It is still standing.

The first Jews arrived in Ostroviec early in the seventeenth century, and soon built its synagogue.

The town is bordered by two rivers, the narrow Kamien

and the wider Lias. Unlike Kurov, Ostroviec had heavy industry. The town was surrounded by tall chimneys which comprised a smoke-belching jagged horizon. Tens of thousands of Ostroviec's citizens worked in its cement, sugar, vinegar, soap, brandy, brick, and iron plants.

And there were the flour mills, the lumbermills, a tannery, and a brewery. The industries had developed over the past century.

Of the forty thousand residents, approximately thirteen thousand were Jews, and Ostroviec's Jews derived their living primarily from three sources: crafts—tailors, cobblers, and furriers; merchandising—selling textiles, clothing, and hardware; and money—sent from relatives who had emigrated to Canada or the United States.

The Germans had divided Ostroviec into two regions: Christian (Aryan) and Jewish—the ghetto. The ghetto included the market square and the narrow lanes leading to and from it and surrounding it. Jews from every area of the city were moved into the ghetto. It had literally doubled the number of people in the area. Two or three families crowded into one room. The sanitary conditions became subhuman. Then the Germans moved about three thousand refugees from Austria and from the western regions of Poland into the ghetto.

Certain wells were designated for the use of the ghetto. I don't remember ever passing a well where there wasn't a long line of people. Food was rationed through coupons—which the Judenrat distributed.

The fur factory was close to the Christian area at the perimeter of the city. My uncle had a special permit from the Germans to leave the ghetto to go to and from the factory, and he saw to it that I was issued one as well. He had no difficulty: his factory had begun to manufacture fur coats for the Gestapo.

In fact, most of the officers, as well as the town's commissar, came to the factory to order fur coats for themselves and for their wives. They visited the workshops frequently and chose the best skins available. They never paid a cent. Motchald, the town commissar, put in frequent appearances at the factory, because by law a license card had to be issued for every coat we made, and he was in charge of these. He had a long scar on his face, (made by a knife, I was told), and he always wore a murderous expression. He devised every form of persecution of the Jews in Ostroviec.

Uncle Matityahu himself taught me how to cut and sew skins into coats, collars, and hats. For the first couple of months I was clumsy, so I considered the work tedious. By the time I began to get the hang of it, Daddy and Chania arrived from Urzendov.

We made it a joyous occasion. Uncle Matityahu uncorked at least two bottles of wine.

"Henoch," he said a number of times, "we have nothing to worry about. We are safe—*you* are safe—here in Ostroviec. Practically every one of the Gestapo does business with the factory. They get for themselves or their wives. Or their girlfriends. And we get along well. We'll be all right."

Daddy looked doubtful.

"Then we'll get Sarah and Moshe and Chaike here. Soon," he continued.

"Please, God," Daddy intoned.

At about that time the barbed wire went up. It enclosed the ghetto. Gates were installed at regular intervals, and each was manned by police: Polish and German on the outside, Jewish police on the inside. No one could leave without a special permit.

The first time I passed by a gate and saw a Jew shot down by a guard, I stood and gaped. What had the man done, I asked myself? Then I noticed one of the guards staring hard at me. I rounded the nearest corner. That evening I related the incident to the family.

Uncle Matityahu sighed. "His permit probably didn't conform to the day's rules."

"The day's rules?" I asked not understanding.

He frowned. "Yes. No one but the guards know what they are—I think they change them from day to day—and the penalty is death."

"God—"

"Yes, Nachemia." My uncle pressed his fingers to his temple. "One wonders: Is He watching?"

In July a typhoid epidemic broke out in the ghetto. The Germans closed the area down completely. Jews were allowed to leave their houses for only two hours a day—to receive their portions of food and water.

The big synagogue was turned into a hospital, because there was no other place to treat the victims. Signs were posted all over the ghetto directing that the sick be brought to the hospital. If a typhus case were found in a private house, all residents of the house, as well as the sick, were shot. Not surprisingly, the improvised hospital was not properly equipped, and people died there daily. Doctors were among the victims. It became common knowledge that the sick went to the hospital to await death.

When I broke out with typhoid fever, my father, my uncle, and Chania told everyone that I had a bad flu with a high fever.

I lay in bed, half alive, for two weeks. The town medical assistant, Avraham Beinerman, did everything he could to save my life. And he risked his own by keeping my condition secret.

Chania never left my side. She was tireless. She fed me, cooled my head with cold compresses, administered the medicine Avraham had prescribed.

"Chania," I managed to croak, "I'm glad it's you. If I can't have Mother, I'm glad it's you."

"Why, Nachemia!" Her features softened. "I thought it was Chaike you loved best." There was a twinkle in her eyes. "It was Chaike who helped you with your homework. Chaike who laughed at the pranks you and Moshe pulled."

"Go on, Chania. Tease me."

The crisis passed. I slowly began to regain strength. My father declared it a miracle. I think the miracle was Chania.

Once on my feet, I resumed my life as a Jew in a ghetto. I was fourteen.

It was Friday. Weiler, a Gestapo officer whom we knew better than most, appeared at the factory and said that Uncle Matityahu was to come with him. We thought nothing of it. Uncle Matityahu was frequently called to Gestapo headquarters to take the measurements of the officers who ordered furs.

We began to worry when he did not return by sundown.

The following day Gershon asked Weiler of my uncle's whereabouts. "Mr. Wurman left the Gestapo after taking care of some things," he said. He did not meet our eyes.

Two days later a Polish policemen we knew told us that he had seen Uncle Matityahu, together with some other Jews, being taken to prison.

Two months passed.

One day we received a package with no postmark. My uncle's clothes were in it. We searched them frantically and found a small note in his jacket pocket in his handwriting; he was, it said, in the concentration camp in Auschwitz.

"I guess they got all the fur coats they needed out of him," my father said. I had never heard such bitterness in his voice.

A couple of weeks later we got an official telegram from the German authorities: "Matityahu Wurman died of a heart attack."

The telegram also informed us that if we wanted the ashes of his body we would have to pay the authorities a certain sum of money. It was a huge sum.

Ironically, the "fur operation" took place not too long afterwards. All Jews in the ghetto were given eight days to hand in their fur coats, their fur collars, fur hats, fur gloves. On the ninth day the Gestapo, along with the Jewish police, searched every house in the ghetto. They arrested and executed every Jew who was still in possession of some furred garment or material.

There followed the "money operation." The "gold operation." The "jewelry operation." The "silver operation."

The work at the fur factory continued under the management of Uncle Matityahu's two sons, Moshe and Gerson.

April 1942

I woke at about 3:00 a.m. Screams and gunfire had penetrated my sleep. I made my way to where my father slept. He was awake.

"Nachemia, whatever you do, don't go outside."

"What's going on?"

"Stay here," he answered.

A dim lamp threw shadows all over the room. Perhaps I had not really taken notice before, but it struck me right then how gaunt my father was, how deep the shadows were under his eyes. His bearing was as proud, his grooming as immaculate as ever, but—he had aged. Overnight. Of course, he and my mother were separated for the first time since their marriage. But I sensed it was deeper than that. And it was consuming him from the inside out.

"Maybe we should go down to the cellar until morning," he was saying.

At that moment Moshe and Chania came into the room. "Yes," he said. "Take pillows; take blankets. We may not get much sleep, but it's a measure of safety."

He was right. We didn't get much sleep. Even in the cellar we could hear the gunfire and the screams.

Later that morning, as I made my way through the ghetto towards the factory I saw the bodies. I recognized a number of them. Some wore unforgettably anguished expressions. They were slumped in front of their houses; their blood was still fresh on the walls behind them. There were gaping, bleeding holes in their chests or in the foreheads—sometimes in both. Their eyes were open, staring, horrified.

I stopped when I recognized someone I'd known. After the third or fourth time a Judenrat accosted me.

"What are you staring at? Move on!"

By nightfall I learned what had happened. The Gestapo, armed with carefully prepared lists and firearms, had entered the designated homes and arrested more than one hundred men and women—including doctors, lawyers, engineers, merchants—the most respected people in the community. Those they didn't shoot in front of their houses were sent to Auschwitz.

No one was allowed to remove the corpses in front of the houses until the following day.

The Germans termed it *aktsia*.

It was meant as a warning to the Jews not to evade the work program they had set up for us.

There were two factories on the perimeter of Ostroviec which were integral to the German war industry: the Herman Goering Industries, which manufactured iron and steel utensils and railway carriages, and the Yeger factory which manufactured bricks and had been confiscated from its Polish owner. There was a German-appointed manager. They wanted to set up the labor force in both factories to round-the-clock production.

A week or so prior to the *aktsia* they had established an "employment bureau" at which all Jews had to register. The bureau issued cards designating the place of work. Not that they meant anything. Jews were kidnapped routinely for particularly hard or dirty work—or for labor camps.

So the Jews prepared hiding places in their houses.

While this was going on, word reached the ghetto that the Lublin ghetto had been liquidated and the Jews there sent to Sobibor or Belziec. The Germans refuted this with statements that the Lublin Jews had been sent to the Ukraine to work on farms.

Most of the Jews in the Ostroviec ghetto believed it. I was astounded at their credulity.

"Nachemia, of course, they want to believe it," my father sighed. "Who wants to think about what really lies in store for one's neighbors, friends, relatives—for himself?"

"And you, Daddy—do you want to deny that this could happen to Mother and Chaike and—"

My father raised his hand. "Stop, Nachemia! No I don't. And neither do you. Let us at least have a grasp on reality."

The next rumor from the Gestapo was that those working at the iron or brick factories would not be sent to the camps. There began a mad rush for the working cards stamped with Yeger or Eisen Fabrik. Huge amounts of money crossed Gestapo palms; all connections with Judenrat and Jewish police were employed, to secure a place in one of these factories.

The Germans, the Judenrat, and the Jewish police cleaned up.

Daddy, Moshe, Gershon, Chania, and I wondered what, if any, influence our having supplied the Gestapo, the Hitlerist officials, and the gendarmerie with fur coats collars, and hats would have on our securing cards for Goering or Yeger.

"After all," I reasoned, "they treated us like human beings when they came into the workrooms. They obviously respected Uncle Matityahu's judgment in furs."

"Yes," my father shook his head sternly. "And they sent him to Auschwitz."

No one had a reply for that.

When I received a working card for the iron factory, and Daddy and Chania received cards for the brick factory, it was as though we'd been given a new lease on life—such as it was.

There was a square near the edge of the ghetto, bordered by weather-worn old buildings on three sides and open space on the fourth.

Posters nailed to the doors of the ghetto houses ordered us to report there—"the assembly point"—at 6:00 a.m. every morning.

From there we marched, escorted by Ukrainian guards, to the two factories.

The first time a guard beat one of the older men with the butt of his rifle for "breaking the pace of the march," I winced and closed my eyes. When I opened them I saw the guard looking at me menacingly. From then on I kept my eyes straight ahead, my face expressionless, and never broke the pace.

I was assigned the setting of the railway lines. I carried—dragged, rather—the iron and steel beams for the tracks, set them in place, and went back for another load. The first few times I could not believe how heavy they were. We worked from about 8:00 a.m. till five in the afternoon. Sometime during the middle of the day we were given about a pint of watery soup in which a few pieces of cabbage or radish floated.

And Niebedkofsky, the Polish overseer, did not allow us as much as a minute's respite. I came to despise his corpulent blond smugness, his red-veined face. But there was a solution. I don't know who it was, or when he figured it out, but someone discovered that a bottle of vodka did wonders for Niebedkofsky's temperament. Things went a little easier.

About three weeks after the *aktsia,* as we trudged toward the ghetto, we noticed that the market square was surrounded by Gestapo and gendarmerie. As we drew closer we saw the gallows. Ten men were hanging from them. No one stopped us from approaching the structure, and we were able to identify the victims: they were not Jews, but Poles—among the most respected and honorable in Ostroviec. They were left there on the gallows for twenty-four hours. We saw them on the way to the factories the following morning, and again on the way back to the ghetto the next afternoon. In fact, the Gestapo forced the Polish workers from both factories to pass by the square. It was another "Lesson."

The Gestapo published the "reason" for the executions a few days later. Apparently, the Poles had blown up a bridge that German trains passed over on their way to the Russian front. The Poles had to be punished.

At the same time the Gestapo informed the Poles in Ostroviec that the Jews had handed over the ten Polish men to the authorities, presumably because those men were Jew-haters and belonged to the Polish national underground movement *Armia Krayova,* which was fighting against the Germans and against the Jews. Woe to the Jew who happened to fall into their hands as he escaped to the forests, they said. They even pointed to two Jews who had allegedly handed over the ten men. Then the Germans eliminated those two Jews.

Daddy, Chania, and I were able to keep contact with the rest of our family in Urzendov with the help of Polish messengers. It involved large sums of money, because the messengers literally risked their lives in delivering letters to and from Jews. At first it was relatively easy, if costly, to keep these contacts by merchants and Polish smugglers. But the situation changed drastically in 1942. Connections between towns ceased almost completely; contact between the ghettos was, of course, even worse.

While in Urzendov, we'd struck up an acquaintance with Kovalevski, a welder who had married a woman from Ostroviec and moved there. He worked in the iron factory, and we continued the friendship. From time to time he visited his parents in Urzendov, and carried letters to Mother, Chaike, Eliezer and Zivja—as well as messages to us from them.

That was how we learned that the Germans had liquidated the ghetto in Urzendov and expelled all the Jews to the death camps. Eliezer, Moshe, Chaike and my mother escaped to the forests. Zivja and their little daughter, Ester, found a hiding place with a Christian family in the village.

Several months later we learned that Zivja and her daughter were executed. A Pole had informed the Gestapo of their hiding place. The gendarmerie took them out of the house where they were staying, led them to the Jewish cemetery of Urzendov. They ordered Zivja to hold the child in her arms. She'd begged them to shoot her and spare the infant, Kovalevski told us. They shot the baby first, then Zivja.

That was when Eliezer determined to actively avenge himself on the Germans—and the Polish informer. He had already made some contacts with the partisan units; now he asked to be accepted into their ranks. The answer was that they didn't accept Jews. It seemed that the Jewish partisans had two enemies: the Germans and the Poles. And it seemed that the Polish partisans were even more anti-Semitic and nationalistic than the Germans.

It should have been no surprise. Eliezer my mother, Chaike, and Moshe had found no help among the Polish population in the area when they'd escaped the liquidation of the ghetto. They'd asked the farmers who lived close by the forests for food and had been refused—mostly with threats that they would be handed over to the Germans. There was one exception.

It seems that they'd met up with a Polish family of farmers whom they'd known slightly. By the time they'd reached this family's house they had been two days without food, they were dirty, and their clothes were torn. The farmer's wife took them in, gave them hot soup, bread, and her sympathy. The farmer announced that he was going out to feed the cattle.

When my family left the house the gendarmerie were waiting for them. The farmer had gone straight to the authorities. They were taken to the concentration camp Budzin, close to Urzendov.

Fayeks, the commander of Budzin, had a reputation as a bloodthirsty beast. He was known to murder Jews caught in the area on the spot. This time, a miracle occurred. The Germans needed a good electrician in the camp, and both my brothers were skilled in that. Friends of our family who had already been incarcerated in Budzin, informed Fayeks about Eliezer and Moshe. Eliezer became the chief electrician of the camp, Moshe his assistant. All four of my family were spared.

That was the last news we got through Kovalevski about Mother, Eliezer, Moshe, and Chaike.

October 1942

Day after day, the news was the same: Jews from the small towns in the area were being sent to Treblinka.

Morale in the Ostroviec ghetto was ghastly. There was

not one inhabitant who didn't expect the Nazi angel of death daily. We felt that liquidation was a matter of weeks—if not days.

Some escaped. Women dyed their hair blonde and red, obtained false identification documents, and said they were Poles. Some were caught; some survived. Men with "good looks"—i.e., non-Jewish features—grew moustaches, like the Poles. Some managed to escape, hoping to somehow join a partisan unit or find shelter with Christian acquaintances. Those who were wealthy or had valuables "bought" shelter from a Pole and hid their families there. Often these shelters were burned and the Jews hidden there died. Often the Poles robbed the Jews and then handed them over to the Gestapo.

But the majority of the sixteen thousand Jews in the Ostroviec ghetto had nowhere to go. So they waited, tormented and fearful, for the fatal day. And they knew it was approaching rapidly.

One Saturday in October my father and I went to the horse stable adjacent to the fur factory. We had built a double wall, in there, a hiding place. The Polish factory guard had seen us do it. That evening Kredel, the head of the German employment bureau, came to our house in the ghetto and requested the fur coat he had ordered for his wife.

"Mr. Kredel, the coat is not quite ready," my cousin Moshe said. "Another three days, and it will be finished. You will be pleased."

"No, Wurman. I must have it now. Tonight."

"Mr. Kredel, your wife will not want to wear it as it is now. I tell you—we will work all day tomorrow on the coat and we'll deliver it to your house tomorrow night. Your wife will be very pleased with it."

"Didn't you hear what I said? I *want* the coat—*must* have it—*now!*"

"As you say, Mr. Kredel," cousin Moshe sighed. His eyes, when he glanced at me, were full of despair. "We will have to go to the factory to get it, if you don't mind the walk."

"Not at all. Let's go."

I knew. Cousin Moshe knew. My father knew. Tomorrow was the last day of the ghetto.

In the factory workroom, as I handed Kredel the coat, I asked him whether my iron factory working card would save me from Auschwitz or Treblinkna.

He nodded sadly. "This is a good card, Nachemia. There is no need for you to worry."

"Thank you, Mr. Kredel. What about the cards for the brick factory—Yeger?"

He turned away and stroked the coat. "The coat looks nice, Nachemia. You've done a good job. Good night."

It was close to midnight by the time we got back to the house. Apprehension was like an iron weight over us all.

A decision was reached: Daddy and Chania would go and hide in the double wall in the stable. I would remain in the house with my aunt Rachel and my cousins Chana, Chaya, Moshe, and Gershon. Each of us prepared a rucksack with a few articles of clothing and underwear. We got into our beds fully dressed and waited.

I was tired. My eyes closed automatically. I was on a boat in the middle of a stormy sea. The waves were higher than any I'd ever seen; they overflowed the cabins. Somehow, I could see the passengers, as they drowned, plummeting down to the depths of the ocean. The boat sank, also.

A loud knock at the door woke me. Then I heard the angry shouts:

"Jews out! Jews out!"

It was the Gestapo. They were accompanied by Lithuanian, Polish, and Ukrainian police.

They went from house to house. Everyone, with no exceptions, was to report to the marketplace within fifteen minutes.

I grabbed my rucksack and ran out to the yard. Gunfire sounded from every direction. The savage shouts were everywhere:

"Jews out! Jews out!"

They held whips in their hands. They used them on

everyone who got in their way—women, children, old people, anyone who moved slowly.

It was about four in the morning. Cold and dampness penetrated my bones. I didn't know exactly where to run. The main door of the house led right onto the market square; I left through the back gate and began to run down the street that bordered the yard.

An old man was walking slowly to the market square. An S.S. man in black uniform approached him and began to lash him with his whip. "Bloody Jew bastard!" he yelled.

The old man fell down. The S.S. man savagely kicked him. When the old Jew stopped moving, his attacker shot him in the head three or four times.

Many Jews did not reach the market square.

The shouting, the yelling, the crying tore the sky. Mothers became separated from their children, and the children ran wildly about, looking for their parents. The S.S. men shot at them.

Sick people who couldn't leave their beds were shot where they lay; their bodies were later thrown onto the streets.

As I ran, my whole being cried in anguish: *God, Master of the World, where did this horrible cruelty come from? So merciless and bestial—how did it get into beings created in Your image?*

I found myself on the far side of the ghetto. I was exhausted. Suddenly I noticed a wooden lean-to sagging against one of the buildings. I cautiously approached it.

I prodded the hatch gently with my foot, testing if someone was inside. The hatch door opened all the way; there seemed to be no occupants. I crawled in. It was damp and musty inside. But it was a hiding place. I shut the hatch and fell asleep instantly.

As soon as light began to show between the cracks I peeped out of the lean-to. No one was around. Still, as I inched my way out of the lean-to I was alert for the Gestapo; they were clever at figuring out where people might hide. I made my way toward the square in front of the church.

A Jewish policeman stood at the edge of the square in front of the church. I went over to him and showed him my Fabrik card.

"Get right over to the employment bureau," he said. "The workers are assembling there. And listen—don't go near the market square. Don't go near it. Go across the city hall building. And hold that card in your hand. No one will stop you."

I ran all the way to the employment bureau holding the red card in my hand.

At the bureau, I went through a gate which led to the square where the factory workers gathered. It was guarded by Gestapo—and there was the known murderer, Schield. He'd been sent from the district headquarters in Radom. His name was an anathema to the Jews, the Poles—even his subordinates. He stood on the other side of the gate.

He was dressed in civilian clothes. He held a short stick in his hand.

"How old are you?" he asked.

"Seventeen!" I lied self-confidently.

I guess he wasn't satisfied with my answer. I guess he wanted to check my physical strength. He hit me across the shoulders with the stick as hard as he could. For some reason, I had bent down a bit and his hardest blow struck the rucksack—but I still thought my back would break in two.

Then he kicked me. Afterward he pushed me to the place where other Jewish workers were gathered. I soon learned that we were not allowed to move or even open our mouths. We stayed there the entire day. We were not given food or drink.

Late in the afternoon a unit of the Ukrainian guards showed up, together with Hauptman Zviezina, commissar of the iron factory, in the lead. We were ordered to stand in two rows. He checked us over himself. Those whom he did not like were sent to the market square, where the bloodshed was still going on.

When the "nondesirables" had been weeded out, the Ukrainian guards surrounded us, and we were led to the

Fabrik. There were four hundred and twenty of us. We were divided into groups of twenty to twenty-five males, and led to a row of small cabins. But they ran out of cabins; a few of us spent the night outside on the cold, wet October earth.

Fabrik consisted of a walled-in compound of about ten acres, containing many buildings. Railroad tracks ran right into the compound through huge gates; this facilitated the delivery of raw materials into the factory, and finished goods out to wherever the Third Reich required them.

As I looked around, I resolved to learn the layout and workings of the factory as intimately as possible. I also resolved to find Kovalevski, who had carried letters between Urzendov and Ostroviec for my family.

The Polish workers arrived at the factory in the morning, and we learned what had happened to the Jews of the ghetto. The second *aktsia* had eliminated thousands of Jews. The stones in the market square were drenched in blood, they said. Hundreds of bodies still lay in the square and in the nearby streets, while "mass graves" were being prepared for them.

Those who had survived the *aktsia* were led to the railway station, put on cattle cars, and taken to the death camps.

By now there were about seven hundred working at the iron factory: more Jews had been sent there even before we arrived, and after the *aktsia* even more arrived there from the liquidated ghetto.

On October 28 we were ordered to assemble in front of the factory at two o'clock in the afternoon, with our personal belongings. No one knew what was going to happen. Most of us were convinced that it was the end.

The Ukrainian guards were there, as usual. They ordered us to stand in two rows. Then they made us run towards the open field where the Gestapo men and their Ukrainian minions waited. We were convinced we were to be shot.

I remember the sky: it was a clear, deep blue, as only October skies can be.

In the field we were ordered to stand with our hands

above our heads. Soon a car arrived. Gestapo emerged, among them the renowned executioners from the Nazi security service, Peter and Bruno. I almost had to laugh: Peter was tall and thin, Bruno was short and squat. They looked amusing together. I believe every Jew in that field resigned himself to death then.

Then Hauptman Zviezina got out of the car. A long table was set up; empty boxes were placed upon it. Zviezina spoke to us in German.

"You Jews are most fortunate Jews!" he declared. "You are working at the iron factory. Nothing is going to happen to you—if you hand over your money, your valuables, your jewelry, and your clothes."

A buzzing began among us. We still stood with our hands above our heads. Zviezina held up his hand.

"We will conduct a personal search of every one of you. If something valuable is found, that person will be shot."

He then pointed to three youngsters and called them out of line. He signalled the nearest Ukrainian guard. The guard raised his rifle and shot them to death.

"Do I make myself clear?" he asked.

Each of us passed by the long table. Each put his money, his valuables, and then his clothes into the bins. I shivered with the chill and clutched at my coat. A Ukrainian guard yelled at me: "Take the coat off! Drop it in the bin!"

I took off my jacket also. That left me wearing my shirt. They took that, too.

In our underwear, we were again made to stand in two rows, and were marched out of the area. Again, we were all sure we were to be shot.

They marched us back to Ostroviec. As we passed through the town we saw that the shops and houses were empty—their doors hung open. Everything had been taken. Death and silence were everywhere.

I shook as though I had a fever. My teeth chattered; my cheeks were wet with tears. The march through the market square seemed endless. I could hardly drag my feet. Every step was torture.

When we reached the ghetto area we saw what they had done.

They had shrunk the ghetto to one small street—Ilzietzka—about hundred yards long. Fifteen, small, old, broken-down houses lined one side of it; the Jewish cemetery ran along the other side. All was surrounded by an eight-foot wooden fence. One well served the entire area. This was where we were to live.

After all, they had reduced the population considerably.

Polish police guarded the fence. Jewish police kept order in the ghetto—the "small ghetto"—itself.

We were divided into working groups: each group got a small house which had already been "purified" of its former residents,. Ordinarily, one of these houses could hold ten people; we were huddled eighty to a house. In fact, thirty members of the *Reumungs Kommando* had already settled in the small ghetto. Their job was to collect the dead for burial; they were also to load the furniture, household goods, and clothing taken from the Jews and transport them to the warehouses. There was also a contingent of the Judenrat and a unit of the Jewish police.

Saddest of all were the dispossessed: men, women and children who, having survived the liquidation of the ghetto, had no working permits. They crept into the small ghetto in a variety of ways, desperately wary not only of the Germans but also of the Judenrat and the Jewish police.

They bribed the Polish police and the Jewish police with what money they had for a place to sleep and for a minimal ration of food. And since searches of houses were conducted regularly, they could not even stay temporarily with relatives or friends. They lived on the streets, waiting for the German or Jewish police to find them and end their suffering.

I saw them every day on my way to and from the iron factory. I got into the habit of hiding a piece of bread from my "lunch" in a pocket so I could give it to one of the children. *Things could be worse for you, Nachemia,* I told myself.

It wasn't long before starvation became virtually a way

of life in the small ghetto. Poles and Ukrainians could be bribed to smuggle food into the small ghetto, but the bribes were exorbitant.

The younger Jews literally risked their lives to sneak back to their former houses where valuables were hidden. Certain Polish or Jewish police accepted part of what they had to allow them out of and back into the small ghetto, but many young Jews paid with their lives: they were caught in the town proper, or in trying to crawl under the fence.

The Gestapo made sure to drive the lesson home. Every day as we left and re-entered the small ghetto, bodies of teenaged boys who had risked all were strewn along the fence. They left them there purposely, the blood from the bullet holes dried on their faces and bodies. Yet others continued to try.

For the most part, I didn't care about food. I did all right. It was Daddy and Chania about whom I worried. I had no idea what had happened to them. Had their hiding in the false wall of the stable been successful? Had they gotten to shelter? If they were still hiding in the stable wall, how were they able to obtain food and water?

I had forgotten about Julek Manovski. A gentle, God-fearing man, he lived near the fur factory and raised fish for sale in small pools on his property. It seemed only natural that he and my father would strike up acquaintance; they were alike in many ways. My father had intimated that Manovski had some sort of connections to the underground, but never elaborated. It was dangerous to even think about it. I liked Manovski: medium-tall, muscular, he had a fair complexion with dark hair and moustache and found humor in any situation—an excellent survival tool. One day on the forced march from the iron factory Manovski appeared as if by magic at my side, walked next to me until the guard chased him—but not before he was able to slip me a letter from my father.

Alone in my small corner of the house I shared with dozens of other men, I read it; I think my father must have reached new depths of despair:

. . . We cannot stay in the shelter any longer. We are starving. Worse, Martin, the guard who saw us constructing the double wall has come here a number of times to tell us that he is going to turn us over to the police if we don't vacate the hiding place . . .

They had to be saved. I got an idea. I asked my cousin, Gerson, to contact Manovski and ask him to bring my father and sister to the borders of the old ghetto; Gershon would meet them there and bring them to the house where I was staying. They would be illegals but at least Martin would not hand them over to the Gestapo.

Manovski agreed. The plans were confirmed. But—my father had decided by then to attempt to make it to the ghetto on his own. His idea was that Martin would see him leave and assume that Chania had also left and presumably not bother going to the stable any longer. So when Manovski showed up at the meeting place he met only Chania and escorted her to the boundary of the old ghetto where Gershon waited.

Both Chania and my father made it to the small ghetto—to the house where I resided. Our joy knew no bounds.

Then I learned what had transpired during the three weeks we had been separated.

"The trip to the fur factory went safely," Daddy related. "But when we got to the entrance, Martin refused to let us in. I pleaded, I begged, I promised him the world—in addition to all our valuables. Chania and I were both in tears. Finally, he relented. He knew about the false wall in the stable. He allowed us in.

"We were there two days when the Gestapo showed up. They combed the factory for Jews. We were sure we were doomed. What would Martin do?

"Well, Martin kept quiet about us. But his wife! That miserable woman! She got hysterical—began shouting that Jews were hiding there. The Gestapo—praise the Lord— didn't understand Polish and didn't know what she was saying. I heard them ask Martin why she was yelling; and he answered in broken German that she had been mentally ill for a long time. They believed this, apparently; they left.

"That was fine. Then, a few days later, Martin came to the stable and demanded more money from me. I had no money on me there; but I told him that I'd hidden large sums in the house in the old ghetto, and that when things cooled off I would take him there and give him a good part of that money. That held him for a few days.

"But, a week or so later, he was back, with more demands for money. I placated him again, but the situation was deteriorating. That's when I wrote you through Manovski. And that's when I decided to try to make it here by myself; I'd hoped to throw Martin off. Whatever, Nachemia, we're here, and we're together again."

FOUR

October 1944

Heinz called the corporal responsible for the clothing supply into his quarters.

"Marion, give Willi these three packs of cigarettes and double portions at lunch."

"Yes, sir."

Willi, blond, blue-eyed, rather short and with pock-marked skin, did not strike me as the brightest soldier in the battalion. His face first registered surprise, then broke into a grin which stretched from one large ear to the other.

"Willi," Heinz addressed him, "I want you to outfit our newest recruit. Now."

I gazed at Heinz in utter surprise.

Willi led the way to the headquarters clothing supply; I followed almost in a trance.

There, having determined my size, he handed me underwear, boots, and a complete German army uniform, including a leather belt with a metal buckle that flew the German eagle with the swastika in its claws and the motto *Gott mit uns* emblazoned on it.

"So," Willi urged. "Take off those rags and get dressed!"

I removed my shabby clothes and dropped them to the floor. A piece at a time, I donned the clothes the corporal held out to me. Still in half a trance, I turned toward the mirror.

I couldn't believe my eyes.

Was this me, Nachemia Wurman, Jewish boy from Kurov, in the uniform of Hitler?

It was a dream. Like the one in which I'd watched people plunging to the depths of the ocean.

It wasn't a dream. It was the insane reality of this era of horror and brutality. It was, more important, another step in my survival.

Still, I stared at the reflection.

"Marion, you want these clothes or shall I burn them?" Willi's voice brought me back to where I stood.

"Oh," I replied as nonchalantly as I could, "yes, Burn them. Okay, Willi. I'm going back to the kitchen now."

"Don't forget what Sergeant Klockman said—double portions for me at lunch."

"I won't forget."

Back at our quarters, Heinz approved. "But now let's get you to the barber. He'll make a man out of you."

It was the standard military cut. More hair wound up on the floor of the barber's quarters than on my head. I was completely indistinguishable from the soldiers around me—except that I did not yet shave.

Again I returned to Heinz. Again he smiled his approval. "Good for you, Marion! You look great!"

I grinned as best I could.

Heinz had forms before him on the table. He began to fill them out. I saw the words, "Marion Schmidt" across the top. He filled in my birthdate; the fictitious names of my parents. He also wrote down that I was a Volksdeutsch who had volunteered to serve in the German army—a "FIVI" volunteer.

In my uniform, I was obliged to salute officers, sergeants, and corporals by lifting my right hand and shouting "Heil, Hitler!" And, of course, I received all the rights of a German soldier.

My head spun rapidly. *A Jew in German uniform! A Jew shouting "Heil Hitler!" Have I gone mad? Am I insane?*

Had I endured the concentration camp, my father's death—had I hidden for interminable days in the tunnels for this?

January 1943

There were about three thousand of us jammed into the "small" ghetto in Ostroviec. About thirty young Jews, ranging in age from about seventeen to twenty-five, had managed to organize an underground network. I knew most of those who were part of it, but I was too young to be in it. Somehow, they bought weapons through liaisons with sympathetic Poles in the factories and other working places. They had also opened communications with the *Armia Krayova*. They didn't know the A.K. was anti-Semitic.

The ghetto network hatched an escape plan which involved their dividing into three groups. The first group, of eight, escaped to the nearby forest and into a bunker. The other two groups were to follow shortly.

But the A.K. bombarded the bunker with hand grenades. Only one—Schlomo Zweigman—escaped to warn the rest of the ghetto network.

The A.K. had, of course, also informed the Germans of the underground network. One day the Gestapo ordered the Judenrat to deliver Noah Zukermann, one of the group's leaders, to them. They threatened to eliminate the entire Judenrat and Jewish police were Zukermann not turned over.

"Nachemia," my father gripped my shoulders tightly as he spoke. "Tell me the truth—as you always have—are you part of this underground?"

"No, Daddy. I swear I am not."

"All right, son." He looked intently at me. "They'll get all of them soon. I know it."

"Not me, Daddy."

He patted my shoulders, then. His eyes filled. As far as he knew, Chania and I were the only family he had left. "Daddy, Mother's still alive, don't you think? Wouldn't we have heard?"

"Sure we would have, son." Now he was fabricating. But only to soothe me. And himself? "I am sure that she and Chaike and Moshe are alive. And will stay alive." He turned away and stared into the distance.

They found Zukermann hiding in a cellar in one of the homes and dragged him over to Gestapo headquarters. They shot him in front of the Jewish cemetery—but not before they severely beat him with whips and rifle butts. They left his body lying there for two days. No one dared to move it.

Daddy and Chania, having working cards for Yeger, the brick factory, were "legal" residents of the ghetto. They were assigned living quarters with other Yeger workers. We saw each other at the assembly point in the early morning and on the marches to and from our factories, but, of course, we could only signal to each other silently. As often as we could, we visited in the evenings. We were all alive and, in a strong sense, together.

The "illegals" were sent to Treblinka and to Blizin, a labor camp. One week the Gestapo rounded up one hundred and fifty of these hapless souls. And they found new ways to round them up.

Every morning, when we assembled at the designated point, the gendarmerie entered and searched the houses. Those whom they found hiding were shot on the spot.

The mass graves at the Jewish cemetery became wider and deeper.

And the Ukrainian guards who escorted us to and from the factories and the ghetto devised a new form of harassment; as we marched we were forced to sing a hymn—any hymn, it didn't matter which one. Of course, those who didn't march in rhythm with the singing were beaten with rifles.

The Ukrainians were all over the factories, as well. And while we had found a way to mollify the liquor-loving Niebedkofsky, any Ukrainian guard who observed a Jew taking a breather from work invariably ran up to him and beat him mercilessly.

We didn't take breathers.

We were given about thirty or forty minutes for lunch, though.

It had taken a few days to discover where the welding department was located—and to meet with Kovalevski.

Often we shared lunch—to my benefit. A small dining hall had been built for the Polish workers, where they could obtain food, coffee, tea, and milk. Kovalevski usually had food, which he must have obtained there, for me.

"You are so kind, Mr. Kovalevski," I would tell him over and over.

"It's nothing, Nachemia. Eat," he would say soothingly.

The train that brought the materials into the factory ran through this area between the buildings. Piles of wood, iron, and coal lay right next to the tracks.

I noted almost unconsciously that it was a good place to hide.

Late in January I was transferred from the loading/unloading section of the factory to the building section—which was easier work. I hadn't been there two days when all of us in this section were marched to an open field where boundaries, which appeared to be the outlines of buildings, were marked in chalk or lime. Huge piles of lumber were stacked everywhere.

More than one hundred men from the brick factory arrived just behind us in the field. We were ordered to stand in two rows while a Gestapo gave us our orders in German.

We were to build six structures, fifteen feet high by about one hundred and twenty feet long, and six more only slightly smaller than that. We would begin immediately. Our duties in Fabrik would be suspended until we finished.

In all, the work was not nearly as backbreaking as laying iron railroad lines, although for the first few days I found the splinters I got from the rough-cut lumber unbearable. After that, I must have gotten used to it.

The speculation as to what we were building was rampant. Yaacov Tarlovsky, a tailor about five years older than me, and I worked closely together.

"What do you think this is, Nachemia?"

"There are no windows in the walls—just up close to the roof. It must be stables."

"Stables? This big?"

"Who knows what they're going to bring here."

We weren't professional builders. And we could tell that the structures, whatever they were, would be drafty in winter and would not let in much light or fresh air during the rest of the year.

"Nachemia, do you think we're building a death camp?"

"If we are, I've seen no place for mass execution—you know, gas lines, furnaces."

It had occurred to me. But I didn't let on to Yaacov. I don't know why.

"Listen, Yaacov. Do the splinters bother you?"

"Nah. When you've stuck as many needles and pins into your hands as I have—nah."

It took about two weeks to complete all the squarish structures. We were sent back to the factories to resume our work there.

Not five days later, having assembled at the usual place in the ghetto in the morning, we were ordered to run in the direction of the railroad station.

There wasn't a doubt in anyone's mind. The end had come: we were going to be put on the trains and taken to the death camps. I looked frantically for Daddy and Chania; when I located them, I saw that they were also looking around for me. Tears began to stream down our faces. Tears streamed down the faces of everyone.

"*Sing, you bloody Jews!*" The guards brandished their rifles.

Someone began the chant. His voice was choked with sobbing. Soon we all took it up:

"*Sh'ma, Yisroel, Adonai eloheinu*" ("Hear ye, Israel, the Lord thy God is One").

The Ukrainians laughed.

Then I noticed we were running past the station. Gradually, everyone realized it.

The chant continued.

When we reached the group of structures we had built we saw that there was a wire fence around the area, with a tall tower at each corner. And a gate. There was a sign over the gate:

"Arbeits-lager." (labor camp)

Those of us who had built the structures realized then what we had been building: the huts that seemed to have been designed to stable horses were for prisoners. And that's what we were.

The Jewish police were waiting for us just inside the gate. They divided us into groups of about two hundred. I saw fleetingly that my father and I had been shoved into the same group. Chania, of course, was shepherded into a group of women.

The orders began: "You will each run—not walk—to that pile of straw over there; take an armful of straw for your beds. That is your mattress. Then run—don't walk—into the huts assigned you."

We began to run to the huge pile of straw. Those of us who didn't move fast enough were beaten with broad sticks across our backs.

Plank beds, arranged in three levels, lined two walls of the hut. Three heaters, burning woodscraps and sawdust, stood in the aisle down the center. There was a mad rush for the plank beds on the upper level. I wasn't as tall as most others and had trouble climbing up. A short, fat man in police uniform rushed over to me.

"Why aren't you on the plank bed?" he screamed in Polish, and hit me with his stick.

I was confused. I was climbing as fast as I could. *Calm*, I told myself. I saw that my father had reached an upper-level bunk not far from me and was lying on it, watching.

"Why are you hitting me?" I replied quietly.

He glared at me, then suddenly punched me between the eyes. Blood spurted onto my shirt and trousers. Somehow I scrambled up onto the plank bed and began to wipe the blood off my face. I couldn't control the tears any longer.

My father, I knew, had seen everything. I knew, also, that he didn't dare utter a word. Tears ran down his face, as well. My heart ached for him.

The short, fat guard turned to go. A tall, black-haired

fellow about my age looked at me. There was utter compassion in that look.

Soon a short man who loked like a balloon stuffed into a German uniform entered the hut accompanied by men whom we would later learn were the "Jewish management" of the camp and the head of the Jewish police. As he stepped inside, one of the policemen yelled *"Achtung!"*

We all jumped from our beds and stood at attention in front of them. The balloon was Golditz, the commander of the Ukrainian guards. He would have been amusing had he not been so menacing. He carried both a pistol and a whip. He sauntered up and down the center aisle, staring hard at us randomly.

"All right! Everyone outside!"

As we filed out, the tall, black-haired youth managed to surreptitiously pat my shoulder. "Bastards!" he whispered to me.

We automatically formed into two rows. Outside, the Jewish police directed us to a squarish area, and prodded us into some sort of formation. Daddy managed to squeeze my shoulder as we got ourselves into the order they wanted. We found ourselves in the middle of a "square."

"You are now on the parade ground," the balloon barked. "You will get into this formation here every morning before leaving for your labors in the factories, and every evening when you return from the factories. After that, there will be free time for socializing." He sneered on the last word.

"Will they serve tea and cakes?" someone towards the rear murmured. Golditz's head shot in the direction of the murmur. None of us moved.

"Now I will familiarize you with the buildings of Lager." He chuckled maliciously. "After all, quite a few of you built them."

He pointed to the structure nearest the gate. "This is the *'Workschutz'*. It houses the headquarters of the Ukrainians who are your guards. You will pass it on your way in and out of the camp every morning and evening.

"Over here," he indicated a rather larger one-story building, "reside the members of the camp management. They are your fellow Jews: Ephraim Shafir and Avraham Zaifman. They will distribute food and clothing; they will assign you to different jobs—according to our instructions. Remember, however, that Shafir and Zaifman are under the direct command of Commanders Blumenfeld and Puczic, and it is from them that the orders originate."

As if on cue, Ber Blumenfeld and Moshe Puczic appeared out of the hut. I wondered fleetingly if the Germans deliberately paired tall slender men with short rotund ones: Blumenfeld was about forty, tall, attractive, with dark hair and eyes, and clean shaven. Puczic was also about forty—short, fat, blond curly hair and a long nose. We would come to refer to him as "Napoleon."

"Over there," Golditz barked, "is the prison. I need not tell you that we will not hesitate to incarcerate anyone who doesn't obey orders and obey them rapidly. This small structure houses a bath and a disinfection oven."

A palpable shudder went through every one of us.

"You are required to take a shower once a week; at the same time your clothing will be disinfected.

"There is the kitchen and, next to it, the dispensary. Doctors Peker and Ulman will see to it that you are kept in good health," he smiled. "Also, the food and clothing supply is behind the kitchen. We will issue you new uniforms when your own are beyond wearing.

"Now! Into two lines! Go to your jobs!"

We marched out the gate. Two lines of us headed in the direction of the iron factory; two lines in the direction of the brick factory. Daddy and I were able to make eye contact as our respective formations passed one another. I noticed that most of the women headed for the brick factory. Chania turned her head slightly in my direction; she must have seen where I was in line.

We had a sign over our hut when we returned that evening: it read "Yeger."

To my utter astonishment, Daddy was already in our hut, sweeping the floor. He explained during "free time":

"I guess they felt sorry for my age. I'm in charge of cleaning and maintaining our hut. Also, I must make sure that there's enough woodscraps for the heaters."

"What's that sign in front of the hut?"

"Oh, 'Yeger.' That means that those of us in here work at the bricks factory—Yeger."

"But I—"

"I know, Nachemia. Probably an oversight. Let us pray they don't check or fuss so we can at least have this together. Chania is in the women's huts. I don't know quite which one yet."

We were ordered to line up for dinner. On line, I again found myself near the black-haired youth who'd comforted me that morning. "I'm Abek Fridenthal," he said.

"Nachemia Wurman."

"How does your head feel?"

"Sore. But I'll live."

"We all must. We have to."

Dinner virtually duplicated the watery soup and slice of bread we received at the factory. We were allowed to "socialize" during dinner, also. Abek and his father, Aaron, sat with Chania, Daddy and me.

Abek and his father were cut out of the same mold. Each had the same slender, intelligent, sensitive face, framed by black hair.

Mr. Fridenthal was about four or five years younger than Daddy. He had been a lawyer/accountant for a flour mill in Ostroviec before the employment cards had been issued. He had been teaching Abek the business. Now he was working at Yeger.

He and Daddy invariably got into political discussions which ran the length of the time we were allowed to "socialize." Chania, Abek, and I usually discussed what had gone on at the factories that day.

"Most of the women work at the bricks factory," Chania

explained. "But some work at the sugar refinery. That is wonderful, because they can smuggle the sugar beets, from which they manufacture the sugar, into camp. We won't starve."

We didn't—at least for a while. It was also possible for those who worked in Yeger to smuggle bread, butter, and, on occasion, vegetables, back into Lager. Yeger wasn't as closely guarded as Fabrik, and, as Chania described, bartering for food was practically a sub-operation of the factory.

Abek and his father also figured they could smuggle food into the camp.

"We will not die of malnutrition, don't worry," Mr. Fridenthal said.

"We will escape here," Aaron said. "They cannot keep us."

"The guards will kill you instantly."

"There will be a way."

Sneaking food into the camp was very dangerous, of course—and sometimes involved the death penalty. So the smugglers invoked the cooperation of the Jewish police—for a price, of course. They knew exactly when searches would take place and when food could be smuggled in without danger.

It was not altruism. The Jewish police became partners to the food smugglers—and it was in their best interests to prevent epidemics that would break out as a result of starvation. After all, were we to die, their jobs would be eliminated—and they might be, also.

Chania was one of the smugglers. She helped Daddy and me to stay alive.

We each received a round disk on which were a blue Star of David and a number. It had to be worn at all times. So we were numbers: names, family names, individuality had been eliminated. My number was 245.

I somehow wound up back in the loading/unloading section of Fabrik. I unloaded coal, coke, iron, iron junk, and other heavy material from the carts. There wasn't one day when I did not return to the camp tired and broken—looking forward only to meeting with Daddy and Chania again.

That's how I became friendly with Hershel Zilberberg. He worked alongside me and, I'd noticed, also lived in Yeger hut—unnoticed, like me, by the authorities, I guess. He was short and slim with dark, wavy hair. But he seemed physically strong. I guessed him to be about eight years older than me. We had one thing in common—and perhaps in common with everyone else in camp: we planned on escape. The questions were: How? When?

"We could hide in the carts after we've unloaded them; when they've gotten them out near the forest we could make a dash for it."

"Are you crazy, Hershel? Don't you think they check the carts leaving the factory? They'd shoot us on the spot!"

"Yes. Probably true."

"We certainly can't run at night. The bright lights they've got all over the camp are like daylight."

"Yes. They'd keep me awake, but I'm so damned tired after this business here . . ."

"Who isn't?"

"Nachemia, we've got to get away. I can't stand it anymore. The 'parades' in that damned square! One inconsequential misstep—someone doesn't take off his hat; someone doesn't stand up straight; someone doesn't keep the row even—and he's murdered! Right there. Five, six, seven at a time. God above, that square is *drenched* in Jewish blood. We *can't* stay here! *I* can't stay here!"

"I know, Hershel. But we've got to get out in a way that our blood is not spilled, either. And if I escape . . ."

"I know, Nachemia. Your father and sister. They will kill them immediately if you escape."

At first the Germans assigned four workers to unload twenty-five tons of material in eight hours. Then they decreased us to three, then to two. The amount of material remained the same. When two could not unload it in eight hours, they were forced to stay for another eight to finish.

It happened to me once. By the end of the sixteen hours I was totally broken. I fainted by the cart.

The Polish inspector noticed that I was lying virtually unconscious. I heard him shout at the Jewish foreman:

"What's the matter with you? You trying to kill him? How old is he? Twelve? Thirteen?"

The foreman stammered in fright as he replied: "Sir— the orders were that the material had to be unloaded. And if the two didn't finish in the eight hours we were to make them work the next eight hours. Those were the orders, sir."

"*Ja,*" the inspector replied. "But it doesn't mean you kill children. I don't want to see this boy doing this anymore!"

"Yes, sir."

I lay there unmoving. I couldn't believe my ears at his showing compassion?

The following day I was transferred to another part of the factory. There, I was ordered to dig deep holes; these were for the foundations of new buildings in the factory compound. I also had to carry wheelbarrows loaded with concrete, bricks, and iron.

The foreman, a tall, hefty Yugoslav with a Hitler-like moustache spoke German with a heavy Yugoslav accent. "*Haida, haida,*" he shouted, all the while brandishing a heavy stick. One day as I pushed a concrete-filled wheelbarrow across the area I got dizzy and lost my balance. I fell next to the wheelbarrow, and waited for the stick to come down on my back.

The Yugoslav must have been frightened that I had expired. He called the Jewish supervisor and they both picked me up and propped me into a sitting position. To my utter astonishment, the Yugoslav berated the Jew:

"Why do you send the weaker people to the hard jobs and the strong ones to the easy jobs? You can't have this boy pushing concrete around! Stupid bastard!" I listened, my eyes closed, once again astonished. Were there human beings among them?

They assigned me to assist in repairing the smelter ovens. That was easy. I helped out a bricklayer: all I had to do was "serve up" the bricks, water, and sand. The ovens were constantly in need of repair. Periodically, some of them were shut down for days, even weeks, for repair. After a couple of weeks I got to know which oven would shut down—and when.

I still managed to see Yaacov Tarlovsky from time to time at the factory. He began to join Daddy, Chania, Abek and Mr. Fridenthal regularly at free time at camp. The Fridenthals were a good source of information—how Abek found things out I will never know.

He filled us in on Ephraim Shafir and Avraham Zaifman, our "managers."

"Shafir and Zaifman are by no means loyal to the Germans—although they 'serve' them. They think they are serving the Jews by representing us. They're not entirely without their own interests though. You know, Shafir's wife and Zaifman's wife and father are also here in camp. They figure they'll receive better treatment. Have you seen the quarters they occupy? They're like a palace!"

"Ha!" I retorted.

"Well, listen—both Shafir and Zaifman have special rooms for their families, with regular beds, tables, chairs, closets and stuff," Abek continued.

"How did you find out?"

"I saw through the window."

"How come you didn't get caught?"

"I'm here, aren't I? Anyway, it's working for those two. Yes, they're sympathetic to us—to an extent—but they're looking out for their own interests." Mr. Fridenthal snorted.

Daddy shook his head.

Somehow, Golditz had disappeared. His replacement, Rade, made him seem benevolent. Tall and fat, he somehow resembled Hitler in the way he wore his hair and moustache—and he was proud of that. He devised an especially pernicious form of harassment: he'd enter the huts in the middle of the night and order everyone out onto the "parade ground." It was still terribly cold in March. More often than not we didn't have time to put on shoes or clothes. Once outside, he'd order us to run around the square—a dozen times, a few dozen times. Or we would merely stand at attention for a few hours. Someone would shiver—and would be beaten for it. Some of the older men dropped to the ground and were dragged off. Every time that happened I would utter a swift, silent prayer: "Please, dear God, not Daddy."

The intensity of Rade's harassment depended, we learned, on how much liquor he had consumed.

He increased the severity of the checkup at the gate, and it soon became just about impossible to smuggle in food. Those towards the back of the line would hear a shot—or shots—at the gate and would either consume the food they'd hidden in their clothing immediately, or throw it into the field.

We began to suffer from hunger.

June 1943

One hundred and fifty Jews from the city of Pjotrkov arrived at the camp. Not long afterwards, five hundred and forty were brought in from another concentration camp— "Plashov." All arrived barefooted and in rags. The rags were painted with colored stripes so that they would be recognized immediately if they tried to escape. Quite a few wore wooden shoes brought from Holland. The shoes made it difficult for them to walk—let alone escape.

The sanitary conditions at the camp deteriorated proportionately. Overcrowding and lack of soap and water were the least of it. There wasn't one person not frightened that epidemics would break out.

"They would probably throw us into mass graves even before we were dead," Hershel mourned.

The only protection against it were the disinfection ovens. But our clothes would return from the ovens with a terrible smell—and tore as if they were paper. One had to be virtually naked before being issued a new "uniform."

Moreover, the soap we were given at the entrance to the baths was strange. It was the color of human skin. Carved in it were the Latin initials: "RIF"—pure Jewish fat. Were we bathing with something manufactured from the dead bodies of our fathers, our mothers, our brothers, our sisters? Were *we* one day going to be turned into soap? Many of us refused to use this soap. We would scrub ourselves with the rags issued us as washcloths, pretending that the "soap" was contained in the cloth. It seemed to work.

The Gestapo visited the camp more and more often. On each visit they imposed a new decree.

One time they took Ber Blumenfeld with them. We never saw him again. A couple of weeks later, Ephraim Shafir went with them. We heard he was shot.

One morning the Jewish police yelled into every hut: "No one leaves the hut!" For the most part, we stayed on our plank beds. Many went back to sleep, glad for the respite. Those of us on the top levels were able to see out the small windows. After a few hours, a large group of Gestapo arrived, led by Peter and Bruno. Yeger hut buzzed when we relayed this information: an *aktsia* was in the works.

Then Hauptmann Zviezina from Fabrik arrived.

"Outside! Arrange yourselves in formation on the parade ground!"

We rushed out to the square. Zviezina stood before us, his hands clasped behind his back. "The labor camp of Ostroviec is the best in all of Poland," he proclaimed. "We have good conditions and enough food."

No one as much as raised an eyebrow.

"In spite of this," he continued, scowling, "there is a black market going on here. And you all know that this is absolutely forbidden. There is only one way to stop this. Right now, you will each hand over all you have to the officers here," he indicated the Gestapo men ranged around behind him. "Tables are being set up for this."

He concluded with the usual words: "Those who do not obey orders will die."

As we stood at attention the Gestapo entered each hut.

They searched our belongings and our plank beds. Out of the corners of my eyes I searched out my father's face. Had he hidden anything at all in his bunk? Had we anything left to hide?

A Gestapo officer emerged from Fabrik hut holding a roll of bills in his hand. "Who is the Jew who sleeps on plank bed number three in Fabrik hut?" he barked.

Two young men stepped out of the row. Each said that they slept on that plank bed.

"*Which* of you sleeps on plank bed three?" the Gestapo man shouted, visibly angry. "Who owns this money?"

Both answered at once, in shaking voices, "We don't own this money—or any other valuables."

Zviezina interrupted. "One of you will have to die for this crime."

The young man on the left, who seemed to be the older of the two said, with amazing calm, "Then you will have to shoot both of us, because we are brothers."

Zviezina, momentarily taken aback, ordered them to kneel down. He signalled to the nearest Ukrainian guard.

Both brothers were shot at close range through their heads.

Those of us watching scraped together some small comfort; they died quickly.

October 1943

It was a cold, clear morning—a beautiful fall day. The kind of day when, only four years ago, I'd be so energized by the snap in the air that I'd get to school earlier than usual, even though I'd taken time to kick up piles of leaves on my way.

About seven Gestapo officers arrived at the camp. They went right to the headquarters of the Jewish police to confer with Moshe Puczic, who had succeeded Ber Blumenfeld.

Suddenly Jewish police invaded every hut armed with a list. They called out the names. One of the names was

Henoch Wurman. About sixty men and women were herded onto the "parade ground."

"All right! What are you looking at? Get into formation for breakfast!"

I was in shock. Hungry as I was, I didn't eat. Timidly, I asked one of the Jewish police—whom I thought to be more sympathetic than most—where the prisoners were going.

"The prisoners are being taken to the camp near Radom Firley."

"My father, too?"

"You can find that out at headquarters."

I was shaking.

The policeman put his arm around my shoulders.

"Listen, Nachemia. From what I can find out, the Gestapo requested only forty people—those who could not work or are sick. You know they gave your father the maintenance of the hut because of his age. So they arrested sixty. They say the twenty "surplus" arrest can be redeemed by money. Look—go to headquarters and see."

I ran to headquarters as fast as I could.

I recognized the man who sat at the headquarters desk: Leibush Zeifman was a Jewish policeman who "served" the Germans.

"Officer Zeifman,'" I forcibly choked back my tears. "Why was my father arrested? What did he do?"

"Here you do not ask why," he barked. "You ask how much does it cost."

He burst out laughing then.

As if on cue, the door of the headquarters burst open and dozens of Kazet's prisoners rushed in, each screaming proposals of money. Moshe Puczic emerged from another doorway. "Form a line outside my office door," he shouted.

By the time I entered his office I was unable to control the tears. "Commander Puczic," I sobbed. "Please release my father, Henoch Wurman."

He got up from his chair. "In this place you do not cry. You pay."

"How much do you want?"

"Five thousand *zloty* for Henoch Wurman."

"I haven't got that much money. Please give me a few days and I will get the money and bring it to you."

"Out of the question. You have till twelve noon. After that it will be too late."

I ran to find Chania. The tears had formed two furrows down her cheeks.

"Chania, they want five thousand *zloty* by noon."

"How will we get it? We've got to see who can help us here. We can't get back to the house."

We ran to everyone we knew—even those we knew only slightly. Most people didn't have any money or valuables left at all—the camp administration had taken care of that. An iron band was forming around my chest. My heart beat rapidly.

Daddy! Daddy! We'll get it! We'll get you out!

Those who had the money needed it to ransom their own fathers or brothers.

At two o'clock, two trucks of Ukrainian guards and Gestapo pulled into camp.

The Jewish police led thirty-eight men and women left in the square—the rest had been ransomed—to the trucks. My father was among them. As he walked toward the truck, he turned, searching for Chania and me. We were standing together. Tears stained his cheeks. Tears stained our cheeks. We saw his lips move in a blessing upon us.

Sobbing, choking, Chania and I answered with a blessing. Then, only in a whisper: "Goodbye, Daddy. Oh—God!— Goodbye, Daddy."

The trucks drove away rapidly. We watched them till they disappeared.

That evening, as we were sitting with our dinner rations, we heard the Ukrainian guards and the Gestapo—and some of the Jewish police—having a party in the headquarters hut. "Let's celebrate! Let's celebrate!" they repeated over and over.

"Yaacov," I said as quietly as I could. "Is there any way you can make me a shirt and trousers out of dark blue?"

But could I endanger Chania's life? And how would I get around the tightening security of the factory and the camp? And then—where would I go? We all knew that outside the camp the hostile Poles helped the Germans, directly and indirectly, in capturing Jews: the "reward" of two pounds of sugar was the least of it. And often Poles murdered Jews in order to get their boots. Kovalevsky, though. There was Kovalevsky.

April 1944

Jews from Budzyn arrived at camp. Mingling with them at free time, Chania and I learned that Mother, Chaike, and Moshe were still "safe" at Budzyn. They told us, also, that Moshe could have come with the new arrivals, but had chosen to stay with Mother and Chaike.

We swelled with pride when they told us about Eliezer. Eliezer had been in Budzyn from 1942 to 1943. He knew that if he escaped, the guards at Budzyn would shoot Mother, Chaike, and Moshe immediately. So, he got transferred to a camp in Krashnik, where they needed an electrician. This wasn't difficult. At Krashnik, Eliezer secretly built a radio set. He learned that the Germans were suffering defeats at the fronts, and passed this information—with what glee I could only imagine—to friends in the camp. He also managed to organize an escape group. Somehow they got to the Lublin forests. Since he did not escape from Budzyn, his family was safe.

In the Lublin forests, Eliezer and his group organized a Jewish partisan unit. From what the new arrivals could tell us, the group had already waged heroic battles against the German forces.

It strengthened my resolve. Daddy would have been even prouder—if possible. But now Eliezer stood in Daddy's place. And I would follow in his footsteps.

I had to reach his partisan unit at any cost. I *must* get beyond that fence and join the ranks of the avengers. But how? When? And—what about Chania?

An uneasy atmosphere pervaded the camp. Each of us walked about knowing, somehow, that the end was near. All the signs were there. We knew what happened to Jews in other ghettos and camps. Each day, each hour, we waited for death. We surmised that they would probably line us up on the "parade ground" and shoot.

The guard at the camp was increased—because escapes *were* occurring by those who felt they had nothing to lose. Among the escapees were some of the Jewish police: they usually managed it when they were leading us to the factories.

The Germans increased the Ukrainian guard; they began to rely on the Jewish police less and less.

They held the Jewish supervisors responsible for those who ran away. Jewish supervisors, afraid for their lives, regularly handed over to the Gestapo Jews whom they thought were "thinking about escape." Like the Stein brothers.

The two Stein brothers planned to escape from the bricks factory. We didn't know how the authorities learned of it, but the Ukrainian police brought them to the "parade ground" just before dinner. We were all ordered to assemble on the parade ground.

Zviezina arrived in a car driven by Gestapo. He stood, again with his hands behind his back, and made a short speech to the two thousand of us. "You must know," he concluded, "that whoever tries to escape will be executed at once."

I looked at the brothers. They did not flinch. They held their heads high. They gazed at Zviezina without a trace of fear on their faces. *Like Eliezer,* I thought.

Zviezina took his pistol from the holster on his belt and shot them.

It worked—for the most part. The camp inhabitants were frightened to death. Escape plans were shelved for the time being—or entirely. Those who were determined to escape became afraid of even those closest to them.

I had not changed my mind. I would not rest until I reached Eliezer's partisan unit and, with them, take revenge on our enemies.

I consulted with Chania. We were both crying.

"Nachemia, save yourself. Don't think about me. Run if you can. Our fate here is already set. We've all been sentenced to death. We have nothing to lose. Maybe you will stay alive. Run!"

I burst into fresh tears. "Chania, it is your death warrant!"

She soothed me. "You can see what's happening. The destruction of the camp is only a short time away. One way or another I won't get out alive. Save yourself, Nachemia. You carry our name. That is why you should not consider anything but escape."

I grasped her shoulders. Chania. My Chania. She had saved me from death by typhus. At the "small" ghetto and again in camp, she had risked her life to bring Daddy and me extra food. Again, she placed my life ahead of hers.

I couldn't answer her in words. I could only nod. The tears continued to flow.

I began to plan my escape. My shoes were good, almost new. Yaacov was making dark blue clothes for me. Then I'd be ready.

They didn't suspect us. The Jewish police at the gate to camp were under orders to carry out strict surveillance on whomever they deemed the least suspicious-seeming. They knew that Chania was not suspect—because if she left me behind it would cost my life. When I passed through inspection, one said to the other, "Pass him. He has a sister in camp and won't try to escape."

It took two evenings of "free time." On the first evening, Yaacov slipped me dark blue trousers. On the second, he slipped me the dark blue shirt. I wrapped them around my waist before donning my raggedy "uniform."

Summer 1944

Nothing unusual occurred that morning. We were marched to the iron factory, forced to sing. Once there, I started my usual routine of handing the brick layer bricks, sand, and cement.

At about ten o'clock the Jewish supervisor came to our area. He was pale and agitated.

"I've just received an order," he said. His voice shook. "All Jewish workers must get back to camp immediately. The line is forming at the main gate. Whoever does not show up will be shot at the place he is found."

This was it. This was the end of weeks of fear and apprehension.

I saw that each Jewish worker, as he heard the orders, ran in a different direction. I stood still, not knowing what to do.

Then I ran. Without knowing why, I ran to the tunnels under the smelting ovens. My mind clicked into place: I knew which ovens were in repair; I knew into which tunnel I could run. The tunnel I ran to stretched far underground, then forked to narrower ditches—which were in complete darkness.

I entered the tunnel. Its sides were as smooth as glass from the heat, which had melted the metal. I could not make a sound. It seemed like miles to the ditches.

Once I reached a ditch, I sat down to think.

There was no doubt as to what was going to happen in the camp. The inhabitants would either be shot in the "parade ground" or sent to other death camps. In my mind I saw the bodies, perforated with bullet holes, on the "parade ground." I saw the blood running, over other bodies, then to the ground. "The parade ground drenched in Jewish blood," as Yaacov had said. I could hear the cries and the screams of hapless victims. *Why, God, why?*

Those who didn't die quickly enough they would bludgeon to death with rifle butts. Their faces would become featureless masses of gore. *Chania! Oh, Chania!* I felt my newly sewn outfit wrapped around my waist. I had to put it on. I thought my mind would burst.

And what about Tarlovsky? What about Hershel? Did they give the same orders at the brick factory? Were they back at camp by now? Why not just go there—why not just give up?

No! No! No!

I will not give up! I will not let the Nazi beasts slaughter me! I will not give myself into their hands of my own free will!

I sat back, overwhelmed by the force of my own will. I could think clearly again.

I was afraid to move. The smooth sides of the tunnel formed an echo chamber. It amplified the voices of the Ukrainian guards who entered the mouth of the tunnel looking for hiding Jews. I crouched against the wall of the ditch. I heard one Ukrainian say to his companion: "The Jews don't have the courage to hide there."

Then, perhaps to be sure, they called out: "Jews, come out! Nothing will happen to you!"

I held my breath. I heard bullet shots from their pistols. Then silence. They went away.

I didn't dare move. I hardly moved for the rest of the day and for what I assumed was the entire night. I knew it was a Tuesday. The following morning I heard the Polish workers coming to work, laughing and joking. Were they laughing about the extermination at camp? I picked up that the Ukrainians were still searching every corner of the factory for hiding Jews. And when they found one they shot him immediately.

One of the Poles said smugly, "Well, they're finally finishing with all these damned Jews. They've even caught some who escaped in the forests. I think we're through with 'em at last."

Another mentioned that he had seen huge newly dug pits on his way to the factory.

"Sure," the first one said, "dump 'em in. What loss?"

Why do we deserve this? I asked myself. *What have we done? Chania—what's happened to Chania?*

No answers came.

I remained in the ditch for another day and another night. By then hunger and thirst overpowered me. I began to feel weak. I steadied myself. I had to get out of the iron factory. And I would try to get to Kovalevsky. I figured the welding area, where he worked, was about nine hundred feet from where I was hiding.

The following evening I changed into the dark blue shirt and trousers Yaacov had made for me. In what seemed like an inch a minute, slowly I crawled out of the tunnel, looking to the right, then to the left, constantly ready to turn around and run to the ditch. There didn't seem to be anyone around. I suppose the guards were convinced that all the Jews had been smoked out. I began to make my way to the welding area where I knew Kovalevsky worked night shifts.

It was fairly simple to avoid the places which were lighted up. No one noticed me—thanks largely to my "new clothes." As I approached Kovalevsky's area, my heart began to pound. What if his co-workers saw me? There was no doubt they'd turn me in.

Carefully, I circled the piles of iron, wood, and coal adjacent to the train tracks. I remembered—how long ago had it been? When I was eating lunch with Kovalevsky I'd noted that these piles might be good places to hide. There didn't seem to be anyone between the railroad tracks and the buildings which bordered them. I began to breathe a little easier.

I came upon a wagon adjacent to Kovalevsky's station. I scrambled under it. I waited until what I thought was the time Kovalevsky went for his food ration in the kitchen.

It was two hours before the siren called the workers to a dinner break. Every muscle in my body strained as I watched the big lighted hall where they handed out food. I would be able to identify Kovalevsky in the reflected light. But what if he walked with another worker? I could not call him aside!

Then Kovalevsky emerged from his work area—alone. I crawled out from under the wagon and walked up to him very rapidly. He was startled.

"It's all right, Mr. Kovalevsky. No one has seen me. You're not in danger. Please—please—help me get out of the factory."

"Nachemia! My God, you scared the hell out of me! How did you—" He stared at me for a moment. "Well, never mind."

"Please," I pleaded. "They've sent my father away. I've been hiding in the ditch underground."

He nodded. "We'll get you out." He paused. "But I can't do it tonight. I've got to think. I will do what I can—you know that."

"I am so grateful—" Tears sprang to my eyes.

"Nachemia," he bent his head toward me, "it's okay. Listen, can you meet me here tomorrow night at this same time?"

"Yes."

"Look, I will try to get you something to eat from the kitchen. But if someone walks back with me, I can't. You understand?"

"Yes. I will wait under the wagon. If I see that someone is with you, I will go back to the ditch and meet you here tomorrow night at this same time."

"Good."

I had no sooner gotten back under the wagon when I heard the cry: "Jew! Halt!"

I got out from under the wagon and raced back to the ditch. I don't think they saw me; my dark clothes were a good camouflage. But they fired a few shots in my direction anyway.

Moving quietly and blindly, I bumped into a pile of woodframes which were used as dies. Then I dove into the frames and hid myself.

Someone was pulling my legs down. *Oh, God, have I escaped so far for this? Is this the end?*

I closed my eyes. When I opened them I turned to identify my murderer.

Hershel! It was Hershel!

He clapped his hand over my mouth to keep me from crying out. As we lay there, we heard the Ukrainians:

"Jew! Halt! Come out! We will not hurt you!"

"They don't know where we are," Hershel whispered. I nodded.

We didn't make the slightest move. It was at least three hours before we dared speak.

"I've been here for four days," Hershel whispered. "Tomorrow Stanislaus Konior, a decent Pole, is supposed to come and get me out."

"Can you trust him?" I asked.

He nodded. "Yes. I think so. You know I haven't eaten for two days."

"Me neither."

We lay in the woodframe pile that entire day. By some great stroke of luck no one came to remove a frame—or to inspect the pile. Each minute seemed like an hour.

When darkness had fallen I crawled out carefully from the pile of frames and made my way stealthily towards my appointed meeting place with Kovalevsky—near the wagon by the entrance to his building.

As I approached it I saw a few workers. They could turn me over to the Ukrainians! Desperately I looked around. A huge pile of coal stood nearby and I ran to it. Digging furiously with my hands, I scraped out a space near the bottom of the pile and pulled some coal over the opening— with enough room to see out. The dust from the coal choked me. And I knew I must have been covered with black—that was fine, actually. But I couldn't see the entrance to Kovalevsky's building. So I couldn't see whether and when he came out. Kovalevsky was my hope of escape. And I couldn't reach him. What was I going to do?

I waited. Later, close to midnight, I made my way back to the woodframes and Hershel. At least his friend Konior would get the two of us out, I reasoned. Whispering, I told

Hershel what had happened to me. We huddled together silently. Slowly, the darkness turned into daylight.

Konior never showed up. We remained in the woodframe pile, not knowing what to do or where to go. A horrible feeling began to creep over us: the woodframe pile was our grave.

By the following afternoon both Hershel and I had gone four days without food or drink. Incredibly, I stopped feeling hungry or thirsty. But I felt terribly weak. Bright points of light hovered in front of my eyes. Hershel said that lights danced in front of his eyes, also.

We recognized this as a danger sign. We had to get out. We had to get food. We agreed to leave the woodframe pile after dark, by ourselves, not waiting for anyone to help.

Our best chance was to get into the toilet nearest the wall which surrounded the factory compound at Kolejova Street. That evening we crept out of our hiding place and made our way to the compound. There were no lights on in the toilet. And, by great good fortune, no one came in. We hid there until we knew the late afternoon shift was leaving the factory.

There was a pile of bricks by the wall, and a tree close by. Before we made the run for the pile of bricks, we agreed that we could meet in the Rafchizna field outside of Ostroviec, near the river.

I ran out first. It was easy to climb the tree from the bricks. From there I could watch the guards—and the departing workers as they began to emerge from the gate. I lowered myself from the tree branch to the top of the wall. It was about ten feet high. The late afternoon shift consisted mostly of Poles; they were not forced to walk in two straight lines. Some straggled; most were tired after the day's work and merely shuffled along. I waited until about fifty passed underneath my vantage point.

Then I jumped.

I landed almost on top of one. "Hey," he yelled. I walked rapidly ahead. He was too tired to pursue it. I mixed among them. They didn't notice me. How could they—I was in dark clothes, my face blackened with soot. And the night was dark. I walked among them as though I belonged, hardly daring to breathe. We headed towards Ostroviec; then we were in the town's streets!

As unobtrusively as possible I pulled away from the crowd and headed for the Rafchizna field, not far from the river. I was nearly fainting. I couldn't help myself; I lay down in the field and went right to sleep.

I woke with the sunrise. I didn't know where I was at first. Then, with a great surge of joy, I realized. I crawled to the river on my stomach in order to get to the water. After drinking, I put my head in the water. Strangely, I did not feel hungry.

I hid in the bushes alongside the river, waiting for Hershel. I must have been there for four or five hours. He did not come.

I had to get something to eat. I would have to go back into the town. But I felt so weak; I swayed as though drunk. *Get into town, Nachemia; get something to eat,* I said out loud. My feet didn't want to obey. I forced them.

I was very familiar with this quarter of Ostroviec. The houses were larger than I'd seen; trees lined the streets. A middle-aged woman moved towards me, a long loaf of bread jutting out of her marketing basket.

Watching her at that moment, she appeared to be the richest woman in the world; a whole loaf of bread! I consumed it with my eyes. When she came close enough, I asked her where she'd gotten the bread.

"At Koshchelma Street, the bakery there," she replied.

"Lady, may I buy that bread from you? I will pay you more than you paid for it," I offered.

Her face darkened. "You are a Jew! Go stand in line for a couple of hours—as I did!"

Frightened, I figured out where the bakery was by the fifty or so people in line. Following them onto Koshchelma Street, I joined the end of the line.

A couple of people eyed me as I stood there. What did

they make of my dark blue shirt and trousers? Did I appear to them an escapee from a concentration camp? I stood quietly, trying to look as though I did this every day.

Suddenly the voice rang out: "Jew! That one's a Jew!"

Everyone on the line turned towards me. I bolted.

I ran down Koshchelma Street towards another street with many trees and large houses. Still running, I headed back towards the Rafchiza Field, not knowing where else to go.

Maybe Hershel would be there by now, waiting for me.

If not, I would have to decide what to do next.

FIVE

October 1944

As a full-fledged "soldier" in the German army, I had work detail in addition to kitchen duty. I went on patrol twice a week for four hours. With another soldier I patrolled the munitions sheds and the village streets.

Volka Voynowska, like most villages in the region, was set in the middle of fertile farmland—which was the lifeblood of the village. The heavily treed forest, green from the abundance of rain—I assumed it was part of the Sviento Krzeskie—was off in the distance, like a frame surrounding a pastoral painting.

I routinely wondered how difficult it would be for a partisan group to infiltrate the village.

An older peasant in the village supplied us with most of our milk and vegetables. Michel assigned me to go to his house regularly to collect the food. Again, another soldier usually accompanied me.

"So, now we've made a real soldier out of you," Michel said when he saw my uniform and haircut.

I cringed inwardly.

He looked content. I scrubbed the pots, I chopped the wood, I gathered water, I started the fires—all the harder work which he had done previously. And we worked well together; I did as he asked and didn't get in his way. Our conversations were friendly enough, but during "working hours" concerned only the food preparation and serving.

"You'd think they hadn't eaten in three weeks," seemed

to be his favorite remark about the troops as they lined up for meals.

I invariably answered noncommittally; I knew what it was like not to eat for days.

Did he ever wonder why I didn't join in that banter?

Heinz did not spend great lengths of time in the kitchen during the day. Usually he'd come to our area, look around, exchange some words or jokes, and leave.

He was obviously well liked by the rest of the troops. On many afternoons, as I rested between cleaning up from lunch and beginning preparations for dinner, I saw him engaged in conversation with the other sergeants. Often they sang German drinking songs, or folk songs, or popular songs. I could always tell his voice; it was rich and resonant.

Evenings in our quarters in the schoolmaster's house were different. I began to look forward to them. Heinz was growing increasingly friendly towards me. And, frightened as I was of being found out, I was becoming fond of him.

I liked Michel, also. I'd bet with myself—and sometimes with Heinz—as to whether we'd have to carry Michel to his pallet at the end of the evening.

Usually, by the time I reached our quarters, having packed up the kitchen area for the night and having strolled around the encampment, Heinz would be seated at the table, writing letters.

"*Ja*, he makes sure Elsa gets a letter from him every day," Michel joked, "so she doesn't run off with some handsome young swain from Hamburg."

"She's not going to run off." Heinz never even raised his head.

Heinz spoke a good deal about his father, whom he obviously loved and admired greatly.

I had the same feeling for my family, yet I could not voice them.

His family had a gasthaus on the river in Hamburg, I understood. A ferry crossed nearby. The area was stunningly beautiful, he told me. The gasthaus had been in operation for about one hundred years. His father ran the place. He was in his fifties, and also served in the civil patrol but not active military duty. The entire family worked in the pension.

"My youngest sister, Gerta, is the pet of the whole place," he once said. "There's not one guest who hasn't the greatest affection for her."

"Why? What is she like?"

"Oh—she's tall, brown curly hair, blue eyes that always seem to be laughing at a joke. Bouncy . . ."

Like my Chaike, I thought.

"Ach, Marion. I shouldn't go on about my family," he would say. "You have none. I am sorry."

"Don't be sorry, Heinz. It's all right."

It wasn't all right. But was I going to say that it was his Fuehrer's fault?

"Ach, this stupid, stupid war. If I could have gotten out of the military I would have. Those S.S. beasts are not going to conquer Europe, no matter what they think or propangandize. The German Army is being defeated on many fronts, now that the Americans have joined in."

I didn't utter a word. I gave silent thanks.

"So, we've enslaved Paris. Does that paperhanger think he's going to reign, like a king, from the Louvre? Or maybe from the top of the Eiffel Tower, eh Michel?"

Michel laughed. Michel didn't have much to say about his family. When he'd joined the service his son had taken over the butcher shop in Dresden. He had four children, two boys and two girls, but that was about all I could make out.

"How long have you been in the army, Michel?"

"Oh, let's see—six years, seven years. Ha! I thought I was too old!"

"Isn't there a time limit?"

"No. When the war is over is the time limit."

"Ha!" Heinz interjected. "Then he'll re-enlist. He's afraid if he goes back to Dresden they'll have another baby, then another—that will make—what—five? Six? Eh, Michel?"

Michel snorted and poured more rum into his glass. "I

can see Heinz and Elsa twenty years from now, Marion. With twenty children."

Heinz laughed uproariously. I never saw him when he wasn't in good spirits. I was very, very fortunate.

There were times when I thought he looked at me with a particularly penetrating gaze. Or was it my imagination? Did he wonder why I never spoke of my family? Did he accept that it was painful for me to do so?

Did he have any idea of my real story?

Gradually, I began to think that he would not have betrayed me to anyone, had he known. But I reminded myself that then he himself would be in a very bad position.

I lived well. Heinz, because of his upbringing and familiarity with fine food, liked to eat well, and we often enjoyed "meals" not available to the rest of the battalion.

"The best job in the army is that of cook, Marion," he would say. "Better than general. With food you can buy even the highest officers and get what you want or need."

He was right. His responsibility for the feeding of the troops gave him the key to all the other warehouses and headquarters.

Still, the question hovered: *How would this phase end? When would the Germans be finished off so I could get out of this new strange trap??*

I had not given up the idea of finding the Soviet troops.

November 1944

Michel received a telegram from his family; his house had been bombed and was totally destroyed. But the whole family was alive. It was routine that in such a case a soldier was given a month to go home and take care of things. He left early the following morning. He waved from the jeep.

By lunch, Heinz had pressed another soldier into kitchen service to help me—because I was doing just about everything.

Later that day he hired a man and woman from the

village to assist me with the heavier work, and told me that he'd put in for a temporary head cook. The cook never arrived.

We received orders to move from the village to a farm, "Wojnovitze," that belonged to a wealthy aristocrat. Headquarters, which included the kitchen, moved to the landowner's chateau, and nearby was a building with a kitchen already installed—including a stove, sinks, and pots. The army field kitchen was used only to make coffee. The troops consumed coffee by the gallons.

Our living quarters seemed positively luxurious. Heinz and I shared a huge bedroom with two beds, a sitting area in front of a fireplace and, luckily, a table on which he could write his constant stream of letters.

We were quite comfortable with one another by now—at least on the surface. I was certain that he wondered about me, my background, my family. I had said so little in nearly four months.

I could not even let my guard slip when I drank rum or cognac. But, more and more, Heinz's intense dislike of whom he called the "paperhanger" and his "minions" came out. I wondered if he spoke as freely to the other sergeants.

"Well, Heinz," I said late one evening, "the Bolsheviks killed my family, and the Germans are fighting the Bolsheviks. What can my loyalty be?"

"*Ja*, I understand your feelings. But I tell you, the ordinary German, like my family—decent, upright, hardworking—cannot see this megalomania, this need to enslave all of Europe. For what? Just because Germany was defeated in the last war? This man—he's insane. A madman. A beast. You can hear it in his voice."

Yes, I could. I remembered that voice screaming over the air waves the day the Germans bombed Kurov.

I said nothing.

Sometimes I walked with two other soldiers back to the old peasant's house in the village to collect the milk and vegetables. We usually left with a patrol detachment, then broke away from them in the village and made our way towards the farm.

One fall evening, as we prepared to start off to the old man's house, we saw that there were quite a few troops in a "special" detachment. Apparently they'd received orders to round up as many young men in the village as they could find to press them into civilian service on the estate—for the German army, of course. My helper and I walked with the detachment as far as the village, then broke away towards our usual destination.

"They'll bring them to the schoolhouse and then march them back to our camp," my partner said.

"How do they do it?"

"Oh—we've done it before. They go from house to house and seize anyone they think is able-bodied. We need the manpower."

How many nights in Ostroviec had the Gestapo or the Jewish police gone from house to house seizing people, I wondered. It had the feel of a nightmare.

"Hey, let's take this shortcut," I said, eager to get away from the detachment.

I felt a certain tension as soon as we entered the old man's house. A youngish, dark-haired woman sat in the kitchen. She looked very familiar. Recognition crossed her face in the instant before she turned her head away from me. *Who is she?* I asked myself. Then I remembered.

Alte Yanovaska: she had been in the ghetto in Ostroviec, and then in camp. Her brother, Itcha Birnzweig, had stolen the uniform of the Yugoslav, Betez, from the iron factory. That is how they'd escaped from camp.

In a flash I knew somehow that Itcha was also somewhere in the house. He'd probably run for the cellar when he heard our footsteps on the walk.

"Let's get out of here," I said to my partner.

We were to accompany the detachment back to "Wojncvitze," so we made our way to the schoolhouse.

Troops from our battalion stood outside the schoolhouse. Those seized were held there prior to the march back to the estate. "They must have sent more men," I observed.

Inside, about twenty men in civilian clothing were

seated in the main schoolroom. As we watched, two more were brought in and directed to seats. I looked at the taller one; I couldn't believe my eyes. Cautiously, I made my way over to him. I whispered in his ear:

"Bolek!"

He pretended not to hear.

June 1944

I hid in the shrubbery next to the river all day. Hershel did not appear. There was, I thought, only one thing to do; I would go to Kovalevsky. I knew where his house was; I had picked up letters from our family in Urzendov there while we still existed in the ghetto of Ostroviec.

I waited until just before midnight before starting for the house. He probably would not reach there until about 1:00 a.m. His rear garden was surrounded by high bushes. Two storage sheds stood near the back of the house. I stationed myself between a shed and the bushes; from there I could see anyone who entered or left the house, and I could see up the street.

All sorts of possibilities whirled in my head; what if he didn't return from the factory alone? What if his wife came out the door to meet him as soon as he approached the house? What if she were looking out the windows now, checking the backyard?

Finally I saw Kovalevsky walking up the road. He was alone. No one seemed to be stirring in the house. As quietly as I could, I ran over to him.

"Mr. Kovalevsky!" It was a whisper.

He jumped. "Nachemia! My God!"

"I got out, Mr. Kovalevsky."

He bent towards me and scrutinized my face. "When I didn't see you the second night at the factory, I thought they'd gotten you. The men in my unit told me the Ukrainians had shot a Jew hiding under a wagon. I thought for sure that was you."

Hershel, I thought.

"Nachemia, wait at the rear of my house. I will be out in about fifteen minutes."

He was a decent man, I knew. And most sympathetic to our plight—a sort of member of the underground. But I trusted no one. I took up a post at the side of the house from which I could make a fast run—if necessary.

As I waited I wondered how I would broach the subject of his underground connections. He would probably be killed—and perhaps his family as well—if the Germans found out. Would he confide in me? With my fugitive mindset, *I* didn't trust *him* enough to wait where he'd told me to.

He came out of the back door of the house with a dish in his hands. I walked to him. Did he notice my lack of confidence in him? He seemed not to. He handed me the dish of warm cooked food. It tasted like manna from heaven. "I don't know how to thank you," I murmured. He patted my shoulder. I wanted to cry.

When I finished the food I asked him about the underground.

"Mr. Kovalevsky, is there any way you can put me in contact with the partisans of the *Armia Ludova* (People's Army)?"

"Nachemia!" He drew a deep breath. "Your father told you about this."

I nodded.

"This is extremely dangerous," he said slowly.

"Yes, I know it," I responded.

"I think I can." He looked searchingly at me. "But—it may take a while. Can you come back here at this time in a couple of days?"

I was overjoyed. But where would I hide for a couple of days? Then I remembered Chechochinski's barn.

Near my uncle's fur factory there were barns of grain crops and straw that belonged to a Pole, Chechochinski. My uncle had mentioned that Chechochinski was most unsympathetic to the Germans. Perhaps he would not turn me in, if I were discovered. But I certainly wasn't going to announce myself. Again, I made my way over there in the darkness, avoiding the German patrols with a deftness that surprised me.

It took about an hour: the barns were on the other side of Ostroviec. The larger barn had two stories: I went right up to the second one. It was a sort of hayloft, and was filled with straw. I wedged a plank loose from the wall that faced the town and could see what went on through the opening. I took no more than a cursory look; the minute my body felt the straw I went to sleep.

When I awoke the position of the sun told me that it must be about noon. It was a Sunday. I don't know why, but I felt very calm.

I stayed in the hayloft all the afternoon. Chances were good that no one would be coming into the barns or the haylofts on Sunday. I surveyed the town from my vantage point very carefully, and was surprised to see that I wasn't at all far from the house of Daddy's friend, Manovski. I could see the fish pools behind his house from where I was.

Towards darkness, he and his wife emerged from the back door of their house and seated themselves in chairs next to one of the pools. She had a pitcher and two glasses in her hands, and poured drinks for each of them. I decided I would go to him.

I waited until it got a little darker before descending the ladder and sneaking out of the barn. Keeping in the shadows, I made the three hundred feet or so to Manovski's property in about two minutes.

He and his wife were facing in different directions. I stood directly in his line of sight. When he looked up and saw me, he signalled me to hide behind a shed. A few minutes later he joined me there.

"Son of David—what are you doing here?"

I described my escape. I didn't mention that my father had been taken away. For some reason, I wanted him to think that Daddy was still alive. I guess it was because I thought he would be more willing to help me.

"Mr. Manovski, Daddy tells me that your son, Kazik, is

in the People's Army. I want nothing more than to join them. Can you put me in contact with—"

"No, no, no, Nachemia! You are wrong. None of my sons are connected with the underground in any way." He shook his head vehemently.

"Mr. Manovski, I know you would not have told that to my father, whom you respect and like, were it not so."

"You misunderstood, Nachemia."

"You are a good man, Mr. Manovski. You are opposed to Hitler and his beasts, aren't you? If I could make contact with the partisans I could help defeat this scourge on Poland."

"Nachemia—" His fair skin seemed to grow paler.

"Mr. Manovski, you don't think for a minute I would tell anyone about Kazik, do you? I have so much more to lose. Please."

He looked at me for what seemed forever. Finally, he said, "Listen, Nachemia. Come back here tomorrow night at this time. Can you?"

"Absolutely, Mr. Manovski."

"I will see you then. Hide here again, behind this shed."

Suddenly he asked, "Where are you hiding now?"

"Chechochinski's grain stores."

"That is dangerous—very dangerous," he warned. "It is risky to hide on this side of town. The Germans conduct inspections here almost every day. Their horses graze in the fields right over there. They drink water from my pools . . ."

Suddenly Mrs. Manovski came round the shed holding a tray with a bowl of beetroot and some bread.

"Yulek," she called, "bring him over here so he can eat this."

I took no more than a minute to consume it all. They smiled at me the whole time.

"See you tomorrow, Nachemia."

I headed back to the barn. But sleep didn't come. My head spun. Why had Manovski told me to leave the barn? Perhaps it was true that the Germans came here often to graze their horses, to inspect the area. On the other hand, perhaps Manovski was afraid that someone might notice our meetings. My head cleared suddenly. Whatever the real story was, I knew I must leave the barn as soon as possible. I looked about me.

Hundreds of sheafs stood in the field. I waited until dark. Then I crawled into a large sheaf and went to sleep almost immediately. I hardly noticed that it was scratchy.

Towards dawn I was wakened by voices and the snorting of horses. I peeped out. Dozens of German soldiers were taking away the sheafs in carts. They were no more than fifty feet away from the one in which I crouched. I looked around. They seemed to be in one general area—between the barn and my hiding place. If I kept the large sheaf between me and them, I could possibly make it to the river . . .

Crawling on my stomach, I left the sheaf and reached the river bank. I waded across the shallow water towards an area where bushes stood about five or six feet high. On the further bank I dared to look around. A German soldier was unholstering his gun. He took aim at me. I dove between the bushes.

A few shots, and the gun was silent.

I guess you weren't worth more than four bullets, Nachemia.

Crouching low, I ran among the bushes.

Indeed, Manovski had told the truth.

About a quarter of a mile away, unharvested crop left from the previous fall stood, dried out. I plucked some of the heads, pried out the stone-like rye and chewed it. What was I going to do now? Go back to Kovalevsky.

It was a long way back. I planned to wait until darkness—my usual time of travel. But that night every nerve in my body was taut as I prowled the streets of Ostroviec. Somehow I knew intuitively I would be seized. I must return to the field, I thought. Tomorrow I'll walk through the town as if it were my routine. Other people are wearing dark clothing. I'd be safer.

The following morning, as I travelled the streets in the direction of Kovalevsky's house, I noticed men unloading sacks of brown sugar from trucks. Some of the sacks had broken open and passersby were helping themselves. I sauntered over, filled my pockets with the hard brown sugar and continued walking. I swallowed it all at once.

Within the hour there was a fierce burning in my throat. I turned back towards the river to slake the incredible sensation. I must have drunk two or three quarts of the river water. Suddenly terrible pains began in my stomach and diarrhea started. I dragged myself to the nearest dense bush. How was I going to get to Kovalevsky?

I waited. The pains got worse. The diarrhea turned to dysentery. How did this happen? I asked myself a dozen times. But I knew the answer: I had been foolish to wolf down all that sugar and drink too much river water. Who knew what was in that river? My intestines felt as though they'd been turned upside down.

I didn't have much choice. I had to go back to Manovski.

Somehow I got back to Manovski's place. When I finally succeeded in sneaking into the house, Manovski and his wife were waiting. They looked at me as though I'd just returned from the dead—which is perhaps what they actually thought. They put their arms around me.

"Nachemia! We were sure you'd been caught . . ."

Mrs. Manovski stared at me. "Wait here," she said. I nodded. I was in no shape to go anywhere.

She came back with a dark brown bottle and a spoon. "Here. It tastes awful, I can tell you, but you must take it."

She was right. It tasted like bitter herbs. They plied me with soup and hot tea. Soon I began to feel better. As I was finishing yet another cup of tea, Kazik came into the kitchen. Kazik Manovski took after his mother in appearance: he was slender, tall, blond and blue-eyed. I looked at him and looked at his father. Kazik smiled at me—a compassionate and sweet smile.

He came over to where I sat at the kitchen table and laid his arm across my shoulder. "Okay, Nachemia. My father has told me all about you. I will help you."

I wanted to weep for joy. I put my hand over his. He understood, I am sure.

Kazik was the liaison officer of a partisan unit based in the Sadlovisna forests, about thirty miles from Ostroviec. He spent ten minutes going over the route with me. He drew it on a piece of paper. "Under no circumstances can you carry this paper with you, of course," he said. He showed me how the route steered clear of German patrols. The partisans checked on the patrols very carefully. They knew where they were and when.

"The Sadlovisna forest is part of the Sviento Krzeskie forest, which is the largest forest in our part of Poland," he explained.

"Sadlovisna is right next to Kunov. First you get to Kunov, about thirty-five or forty miles from here, and then to the Sadlovisna. You just stay on this road; eventually it's called Kunovska Road; then you'll know you're near Kunov. The forest will be right in front of you."

He looked me in the eyes. "But don't go into Kunov. Go around the town. Whatever you do, don't go into the town.

"Now, when you arrive in the forest, you must go straight to Kvjatkovski, the forester. He's about thirty-five; medium build—maybe a bit stocky—"

"Ja, ja, listen to him," his father interjected. "Everyone's stocky next to Kazik."

Mrs. Manovski shushed him.

"—average height, blond. Always carries a double-barrelled hunter's rifle. Look, he's also a bit of a bully. Don't mind that. Just tell him, and you may have to repeat it before he believes you, that you want him to take you to Bzioza because you have important information for him from the P.P.R. (Polish Labor Party) committee in Ostroviec. He'll take you to Bzioza. When you reach Bzioza, give him the password: *dzik* (wild); he will answer *sosna* (pine), Most importantly, tell him that Kazik sent you. Now, let's go over this again . . ."

When I could repeat the route, Kvjatkovski's appearance, and the passwords to Kazik's satisfaction, he was satisfied. I was euphoric. At last, the chance to take revenge with my own hands. *Eliezer*, I shouted silently, *I am with you! Between us we will avenge our father, your wife, our people!*

The Manovski's sensed my joy. Mrs. Manovski wrapped up a loaf and a half of bread. "It will last the best," she said. "Do not eat it all at once, Nachemia," her eyes twinkled, "or drink river water in great quantities . . ."

We all laughed.

Darkness was beginning to fall. I took the route around Ostroviec that Kazik had described, and as he'd promised, met no German patrols. At about 3:00 a.m. I curled up under some dense bushes at the side of a stream, my bread clutched in my arms, and slept.

The following night, having gone about ten miles, I crawled into a haystack at about midnight. Kazik said that journey would take about three days. Perhaps I could make it in less?

The countryside stretched out endlessly in fields and meadows. Horses and cows grazed, oblivious to the hell that was rolling over Poland. Crops of barley and rye shone bright green. By now there were no woods to be seen, only occasional stands of beech or larch. From what Kazik had told me, I would not see forest again until I reached Kunov.

As evening approached on the following day I noticed a pit covered with boards in the middle of a field. Soil had been piled on the boards to disguise them. I waited in the nearby woods until dark, then approached the pit. I was delighted: a safe shelter!

Within ten minutes I heard footsteps approach. Every muscle tensed. Could I make a run for it? Was I going to be wiped out on my way to the partisans—before I had a chance to fire even one shot in revenge? I stood up.

Suddenly a flashlight's beam shone into the pit. A farmer held the light.

"Get away from here as fast as you can, Jew! The Germans are approaching!"

I leaped out of the pit. "You've saved my life," I exclaimed, overwhelmed.

"Go on," he answered, "run!"

I made for a pile of straw about a hundred yards away and dove into it. I pulled the straw around me. Soon I heard the noise of a military truck approaching. In its headlights, I clearly saw two German soldiers descend into the pit I had just vacated. I would never know who the Pole was who warned me. But I began to believe in miracles.

I was up with the dawn. The thickness of the forest bordering the side of the road told me that I had to be nearing the vast Sviento Krzeskie Forest—and the Sladnovisna Forest was part of it. I was cheered; I was reaching my destination. I covered about ten miles a day, but by the middle of the second day I had finished the bread and could find nothing else to eat.

By the middle of the third day I was desperate. I judged myself not far from the Sladnovisna. The partisans would have food for me—once I joined them—but, I reasoned, I had to have the strength to get there. Fifty feet off the path I spied a ramshackle wooden hut. I sat watching it for half an hour. No one emerged or entered. I went up to the door and knocked.

The door opened slowly. The peasant woman who stood there had white hair, a kind, wrinkled face, hunched shoulders.

I took a deep breath. "The peace of the Lord be with you, old woman," I crossed myself.

She smiled broadly at me. "It's all right, son. You do not have to do that. I understand you're a Jew . . ."

I got ready to run. She took my hand. "You have nothing to fear." She led me inside, closed the door, and sat me in a chair in front of the table. She got a bowl from the pantry, limped over to the stove, and ladled at least two pints of black porridge into it. Then she took a pitcher of milk from the windowsill and placed it in front of me. I ate without stopping. She refilled the bowl.

"You are so kind, old mother . . ."

"Nonsense, son." Her blue eyes looked at me kindly. "We are all His children."

I stared at her. "Yes, I know what you're thinking," she said softly. "I know you think all us Poles are against the Jews. That is not so. Those of us who still hold to the old values and ways cannot stand what is going on. Now. Some more porridge?"

When I had eaten about half of the second helping, I asked, "How far to Kunov?"

"Oh," she smiled, "about ten miles. You are headed there?"

"Yes," was all I replied.

When I finally had to leave, I said, "I wish I could stay here for a day or two."

She put her withered old hands on my shoulders.

"Now listen, my boy. You must run away from here and never come back this way again. Move as fast as you can. And God be with you."

"And with you," I answered.

I saw it about half an hour later, an old, small, weathered sign: "Kunovska Road." Elated, I stepped up my pace. About three hours later I saw the village in the distance. As I approached I saw fifty or sixty small, cream-colored houses clustered together. More importantly, I saw deeply greened woods a little distance beyond the village. I breathed a sign of relief. I was almost there!

As Kazik had instructed, I kept a fair distance from the town of Kunov. As I passed the perimeter of the town the words: *Another mile—less!* kept running through my head.

As I approached the forest, I saw horses and cows grazing in the fields. Lucky creatures! What did they know of hatred, wars, concentration camps, gas chambers, crematories?

A rider came galloping toward me out of nowhere. I bolted for the forest. He increased the horse's pace, and as he reached the edge of the trees threw a rope with a lasso after me. I managed to disappear from his sight. He looked for me for about twenty minutes; I heard his horse's hooves crushing the undergrowth.

When I was sure he'd moved away I emerged from my

hiding place and sat on a fallen tree trunk. What had I done to him? I wondered if he knew instinctively that I was Jewish—or was it only that my presence annoyed him? What was the cause of such sadism? And would it ever end?

Then I remembered the Manovskis; I remembered Kovalevsky; the Pole who had warned me out of the pit; the old woman whom I'd left only a few hours previously.

I thought of my father. My mother. My sisters and brothers. And—especially Eliezer, whom I was going to join—in spirit if not in fact. Then I stood up and continued walking toward the Sadlovisna Forest.

At first the sunlight dappled everything in the Sladnov-isna Forest; there seemed to be no shade. Gradually the spaces between the beeches and the oaks lessened; first formed partial ceilings; the undergrowth, waiting to burst into green, thickened. Once in a while a bird called or a small creature jumped from branch to branch, dislodging dried snow or dried twigs, but the only steady sound was my footsteps. I must have walked for hours. I was certain I was on the right path. Kazik had made me go over this part of the journey repeatedly. "This is where you will think you're lost," he had said.

At times I thought I was.

I jumped when three people appeared as if from no-where. Each aimed a gun at me.

"Stop there!" they said in Polish. "Arms up!"

In the brief second I looked at them I spied Polish flags sewn onto their lapels. *Bandits*! I thought.

I turned and ran. I ran about a hundred feet, tripped, and fell. They surrounded me.

"Arms up, we said." They spoke as if they were one person, their voices in unison.

Quickly, I did as I was told.

It took a while to discern that the short, fat one was a woman. They all wore caps pulled low over their eyes. They all wore civilian clothing; the woman and the shorter of the two men wore Polish military caps; while the taller of the men wore a civilian cap. The woman and the shorter man carried rifles; the taller man held an automatic. He ran his hands over my body, checking for weapons. I looked at them. The woman's brown eyes snapped at me. She was about twenty or twenty-two. The two men were thin, about twenty-five, and from what I could make out under the cap, had dark hair. Had I found the partisans?

"Okay, you come with us," the taller man finally said.

One of the men walked ahead of me; the other man and the woman walked behind. I had no doubts that their weapons were ready. We travelled for what must have been half an hour. They ordered me to sit down. So far, I had not uttered a word.

Then I became frightened. Suppose these were the anti-Semitic *Armia Krayova* partisans who'd told the Gestapo about the underground in the Ostroviec ghetto? If they were, I was as good as dead. But, I reasoned, according to Kazik, these might be the P.P.R. for whom I was searching. But then, I thought—what if they were merely forest bandits? Would they kill me?

"All right," the shorter of the men asked. "Who are you? What is your name? What are you doing here? Who are you looking for? We find no arms on you."

"Kazik Manovski has sent me to Kvjatkovski, who is to bring me to the partisans' commander, Bzioza."

"What is your name?"

"Tadek." I don't know why I said that.

The woman spoke. "You're a Jew. You came to hide in the forest. You came only to hide in the forest."

"That is not so. I am looking for Bzioza."

They moved away from me and began to speak in low voices.

The shorter one declared, "There is no need to play games, the Jew must be killed."

The woman objected. "We can't shoot him on the spot without an interrogation. Perhaps he does have an important message," she said.

The man who'd interrogated me came towards me. "Why do you want to see Kvjatkovski?" he asked intimidatingly.

"I have an important message for him and I must tell it to him."

They motioned to each other and stepped away. They knew Kvjatkovski, it was clear. I was in the right place.

"Well, then, what is the message?" the taller man said.

"I cannot tell you that. I can only tell him. And the password."

"How do we know you're really looking for Kvjatkovski? Can you describe him?"

"Yes. He's about thirty-five, medium build, average height, blond. Carries a double-barrelled shotgun."

They looked at each other silently. The woman took a small bottle from her jacket pocket and offered it to me. "Would you like a drink of water?"

I took it gladly.

"Okay, let's go," said the taller man.

It was about another hour's walk. We were in the same formation as before, but I felt much easier. We arrived at a small stream and stopped. The shorter man walked on ahead; the other man, the woman and I sat down and stretched our legs.

"More water?" the woman offered.

"Thank you, yes," I replied.

That was the only conversation.

After about half an hour my interrogator re-appeared with another man. There was no doubt as to who the other man was. He carried the shotgun over his shoulder. The other three began to talk with him as with an old friend. My interrogator pointed to me: "We caught him in the forest, not too far from the edge. He says he has an important message for you."

Kvjatkovski approached me. "Jew, you want me to hide you? Did you bring money with you?" he snapped.

"No, I have no money, and don't want to hide," I answered calmly. Then, in a low voice, I said: "*Dzik.*"

"*Sosna*," he whispered. "So?" he asked.

"Would you bring me to Commander Bzioza?" I replied.

He laughed loudly. "That was all you had to say to me?"

"Yes. Kazik Manovski said to tell the rest to the commander himself."

"Who did you say sent you?" he asked, staring intently at me.

"Kazik Manovski, of the committee of the P.P.R. in Ostroviec," I replied.

He dismissed the other three with a wave of his hand and motioned me to follow him.

We walked in silence. Birds twittered irregularly. Dried undergrowth crackled under our feet. Very little light penetrated here. The birds, I thought, can move wherever they want with no fear, can fly about carefree. But not I, I told myself. *Stop it, Nachemia*, I told myself, *You're near your goal*!

"I want to tell you," Kjvatkovski interrupted my thoughts, "and you probably know—that many Jews try to hide in the forests. And they all say they came to fight the Germans. But it soon becomes clear that the Jews are no fighters; that they are cowards and do not want to fight—only to save their heads and survive the war. We generally shoot them without ceremony . . ."

I cringed.

"Times are hard," he continued. "We can't consider anything . . ." His voice trailed off.

I knew it was best to keep quiet. But, I thought, he will not be able to make that accusation against *me*.

We came to a fork in the path.

"Now you go alone," Kvjatkovski said sternly. "Whichever way you go, you will meet the partisans, and they will take you to Bzioza."

He pointed to the right fork and warned me not to leave the path and not to look backwards. A certain fear cut through me: was he going to shoot me in the back?

So I zig-zagged among the trees; every tree was a protection against the bullet that I was afraid would fly at any moment. At one point I pretended to bump into something and fell down. When I got up I looked back. Kvjatkovski still stood there. About fifty yards later, I fell again. This time when I arose, he had gone.

I stood there for a few minutes. Why wasn't Kvjatkovski leading me right to Bzioza? Was this a trap?

In any case, I couldn't remain standing there. So I continued in the direction he'd pointed out. It was growing increasingly dark. I stopped zig-zagging and grew tired. I thought longingly about napping for an hour or so before continuing.

By now it was almost totally dark: the thick spruce and entangled ferns allowed no light to penetrate, it seemed. Idly, I wondered how the undergrowth survived without light as I crouched down next to a tree to nap.

I wasn't even on the ground when two armed men jumped from behind the trees. I leaped up as if attacked by animals.

They were about my height; one was of medium build, the other was rather pudgy. They also wore caps pulled down to their eyes; in the darkness their features were completely obscured.

Again the interrogation began: who was I? What was I doing here?

Again, I explained slowly, trying to appear confident— after all, I had already passed Kvjatkovski's interrogation.

The heavier man leaned toward me menacingly.

"Okay. We'll see. Come with us."

They found their way through the darkness as if they had cats' eyes. After about fifteen minutes we met what appeared to be a patrol.

My two escorts gave the password. They walked on either side of me as we headed toward a bunker deep in the ground, camouflaged with tree branches and bushes.

I climbed down into the bunker between my two escorts. It was large, but dimly lighted by an oil lamp, so the edges disappeared into the darkness. A table and a few benches stood in the middle; two men sat at the table. I could discern other men sleeping on straw pallets around the edges. "We found this Jew in the forest," one of my escorts announced. "He claims he has a message for Commander Bzioza."

One of the men got up from the table. He was tall; his head nearly grazed the top of the bunker. Well built, blond, strong-looking and wide-shouldered, his blue eyes radiated good nature—and determination. He was dressed in a semi-military uniform: his coat was from the Polish army; his trousers were civilian; he wore German Army boots and, on his head, a military hat with four edges and an eagle fashioned out of sheet metal. He wore a long pistol in his belt. An automatic German gun hung from his shoulder.

"I am Commander Bolek," he said. "What do you want with Commander Bzioza, Jew? I warn you—there is no place for you to hide here." He clenched his fists menacingly.

"Yes, I am a Jew," I replied calmly. "But I am not here for shelter. I am here to fight the Germans—as my brother Eliezer is doing with his own partisan unit."

"So why don't you go fight with your brother?"

"His unit is in the Rzecice forests. I cannot get there. Kazik Manovski told me how to get here from Ostroviec."

"What were you doing in Ostroviec?"

"We were closed up in the ghetto. Then they forced us into an even smaller ghetto of about fifteen houses. Then into the concentration camp, which they made us build . . ."

Bolek was nodding. He'd heard of our plight, I guessed.

"They've murdered my father." I spat the words at him. "I want to avenge myself on them! It is not true that Jews are afraid to fight, Commander Bolek—"

"All right. Androw," he called to one of the men, "give him some food. Show him where he can sleep. Tomorrow," he turned back to me, "I'll take you to Commander Bzioza."

I feasted on a few boiled potatoes. Julek pointed to an empty straw pallet and told me I could use it. I was asleep the minute I stretched out.

Morning. The air in the bunker was moist and stuffy. I climbed out and drank in the fresh air. Blinking, I looked around. Somehow glints of the morning sun cut through the thick firs, alleviating the darkness. With the branches overhanging, it was as though we were in a high-ceilinged room.

The ground beneath us was soft with fallen needles. Birds sang in what seemed like an antiphonal chorus. There was an inexplicable feeling of peace.

About twenty-five feet away a group of partisans stood around what appeared to be a low table. Then I smelled the inviting aroma of chicory: they were cooking a kettle of coffee.

I walked over to them.

"May I have some?" I asked.

My two escorts were there. They gazed at me noncommitally. I guessed I was all right with them. One of them handed me a piece of bread to go with my coffee. I smiled. He grinned back.

Suddenly I heard Bolek's voice behind me: "Okay, Tadek, let's go see Commander Bzioza."

We passed a number of camouflaged bunkers on our way. Carts were tied to trees where the ground was flat. After about a ten minute walk, we were stopped by a partisan who asked for the password; Bolek gave it to him and he responded. Not fifty feet further on, another partisan demanded the word. Again Bolek gave it to him. Yet another fifty feet, and this was again repeated.

"The security here is better than in the ghetto," I joked lamely.

Bolek looked at me and grinned.

Finally, we stopped in a clearing where about six partisans stood, seemingly lounging, but quite alert. Bolek called to one of them:

"You! Watch our friend here! I'll be right out!"

He entered the bunker and disappeared from sight. After a short while he emerged and signalled me to walk towards the bunker.

Bzioza sat at a table by himself in the bunker. When he rose I saw that he was taller than Bolek. He had dark, wavy hair, and a moustache. His shoulders were very broad. His expression was stern.

"Commander Bzioza, I am Tadek."

"Is that your real name?"

"That's my nickname."

"Who sent you to us?" His eyes were demanding. There would be no lying to this man.

"Kazik Manovski, liaison officer of the Ostroviec."

"So?"

"Commander Bzioza, I came here of my own free will. I'm not seeking shelter or a hiding place. I'm here to fight. The Germans murdered my father. Maybe my mother and sisters, as well. My brother, Eliezer, heads a partisan unit in the forests of Rzecice. I, also, want to be a partisan. It is my revenge!"

Bzioza stared intently at me—I felt he stared *through* me—for a long while. *Well, if he's gazing into your soul, he knows you're telling the truth*, I told myself.

"Okay," he finally said. "Wait outside."

I clambered back up the ladder. No one told me I had to stand, so I ambled over to a tree trunk and sat down. The six partisans guarding the bunker never took their eyes off me. I was confident.

I don't know how long it was before Bolek emerged from the bunker. "Okay, Tadek. Come with me." I tried to read the expression on his face: was I accepted? Was I rejected?

We walked over to a nearby bunker. Inside was a sort of clothing supply. Determining my size from the worn shoes I had on, Bolek gave me a pair of shoes. He pulled a decent pair of trousers from a hanger. "Your jacket is still good," was all he said.

I was ecstatic. "Commander Bolek! You've accepted me! I'm a member of your unit!"

"When you've learned how to use a weapon, you are. Now listen. You never go more than three hundred yards from the bunker without my permission, do you understand?"

"Yes, sir."

"Good. Now let's teach you how to shoot." He called one of the guards over.

"Teach our newest member how to use a gun, Wladek."

"See," Wladek held his gun toward me proudly. "See the swastika on this gun? I killed a German and got his gun. Many of us have gotten our weapons that way. You will, too. It's the only way to get weapons and ammunition."

"The *best* possible way!" I exulted.

Wladek grinned at me. "Yes. You will be a good fighter."

I wanted to kill a German right then—whether it meant I got his gun or not. But first I had to learn how to do it. And if it was the last thing I ever did on earth, I would do it.

Wladek was pleased with me. I was pleased with myself. At last! A partisan! I was a partisan!

"Tadek, you learn fast," he said as I copied his movements.

"That is because I want to kill fast."

He clapped me on the back. "Don't worry, Tadek. You'll get to do all the killing you want with us."

Action began that day.

In the afternoon Bolek assembled a group, including me, in his bunker. "Stand around the table and look at this map," he ordered. It was a map of the area. That night groups of us were going out to determine what time the German munitions trains crossed the bridge over the river at the edge of the forest—and when and if a motorcycle detachment accompanied the train along the road. He divided us into the groups.

I was beside myself with excitement. I could not believe it: two days before I was in a death trap, an outlaw—anyone could have done as he wished with me. Today I was a partisan—a fighter.

I was the happiest man in the world.

I saw myself avenging my father, my people—and proving that Jews were not cowards.

I learned almost immediately that I was not going to begin shooting quite yet. I was assigned to a patrol group— which was not to come into contact with the enemy. Patrol groups were to check the possibility of bombing the bridge, to time the passing of the train, to provide cover to the other two groups, to check the movement of the Germans in the area.

My patrol group was to remain in the forest, near the main road and gather thick tree branches and bushes with which to block the road where the motorcycles travelled. Oh, well.

Bolek went over the mission in detail. The first two groups left the bunker. Then Bolek introduced me to the two other men in my group.

Maniek was about my height, thin, with dark hair and intense dark eyes; Stach also had dark hair, but was stocky and powerfully built. Instinctively, I felt secure with them. Once outside the bunker, Maniek and Stach checked their weapons, then filled a bag with food and water bottles. I was the only one without a weapon.

"Don't worry, Tadek," Stach said. "You'll have one soon."

We took advantage of the remaining daylight to move in on our target. As darkness fell movement became slower. Other patrols stopped us from time to time; we were allowed to pass when we gave the word. Gradually, the oaks and firs gave way to beech, larch, and birch. As it became totally dark we reached the road that ran along the edge of the forest.

"Okay, let's check it from here," Maniek breathed, and climbed the nearest tree with almost amazing agility. "Good view," he called softly from a branch about ten feet above us.

Stach and I began to tear off branches and bushes from the nearest trees. We dragged them to the edge of the road. We would build a road block the next time we returned; this was a surveillance operation.

We stopped suddenly. The sound of approaching motorcycles was unmistakable. Stach and I climbed up trees immediately to get a good view of the road.

"Won't they see us?" I called softly.

"Not if you keep your mouth shut," Stach replied.

Motorcycles with sidecars, all emblazoned with swastikas, drove up the road. Each sidecar held two German soldiers. They drove very fast.

We hid in the tree branches, waiting. After an hour or so we heard the train whistle. So—the motorcycles had come to ensure that the train would pass over the bridge safely—as Bolek had thought. Stach, Maniek, and I remained in the trees. It wasn't too long before we heard the motorcycles return from the direction in which they had originally gone.

Then we climbed down from the trees and, as Bolek had instructed, waited for the other groups that had been lying in ambush position—one near the bridge, the other across the road.

By the time we got back to our base in the forest, sunlight shone through the treetops, and the place was alive with refreshing odors. Our eyes were nearly shut with exhaustion and, although not one shot had been fired, I was content. After all, this was a preparation for the real combat, which was only a couple of days away.

And I felt close to Maniek and Stach. Stach amused me. He had an extraordinarily colorful vocabulary with which he described the German Army. Maniek was more reserved, but no less anti-German. Each seemed to accept me without question as one of them. They, like the other partisans, knew I was Jewish, and, instinctively, I knew I was safe with them—if for no other reason than both Bolek and Bzioza had accepted me.

Maniek was impressed with Eliezer's exploits. "He's routed a few Nazis, has he?" he asked.

"Yes. His unit is almost completely Jewish. They have good reason to destroy whatever Germans they can."

"So have we, Tadek. So have we." Stach looked right into my eyes. "Polish farms, Polish industries, Polish resources—everything has been stolen from us—even our lives."

"Stach, I am a Pole, too," I answered.

"Yes you are, Tadek. No one questions that, except—*them*!" He spat the last word.

Bolek assembled us again a few days later. Now the mission would be done in earnest: the traps would be set for the motorcycles; the bridge would be mined; the guns would be fired.

"Now it's not guaranteed that the train will cross the bridge at the exact time it did a few nights ago," he exhorted us, looking from one to the other. "Don't any of you become impatient and begin firing before you can actually hit the train. Remember, too, that they put carriages filled with sand right in front of the locomotive so that the munitions carriages won't be damaged by sabotage. So let a couple of carriages go by before detonating the mines."

We buzzed with excitement as we left the base. I was exultant: I, a seventeen-year-old Jewish boy, was going to fight the German military machine; to wreak revenge for the spilled blood of my father, my uncle and—who knew?—perhaps my mother and sisters and brothers.

Maniek carried an automatic German gun on his shoulder and a few magazines of bullets and hand grenades on his belt. Stach carried a German rifle and a few hand grenades. I was not armed. I broke off a thick branch and held it on the way to the site. It would have to do for the moment. Stach and Maniek were quick to assure me that I was not the only partisan unarmed; others had not yet had the opportunity to obtain guns.

"Listen, Tadek. You'll get your weapons, don't worry," Maniek said as we made our way through the forest and past the other patrols. "It was a couple of weeks—nearly a month—before I got mine."

"That's true, Tadek," Stach chimed in. "You're lucky, you know, to be sent out on a mission so quickly. You'll probably have your weapon by the end of the night."

Yes. My own weapon. I began to walk fast, as though marching in formation.

"Now, don't run," Maniek interrupted my vision. "It would be a pity to tire too soon. We need all the strength we've got for later on, for running. For throwing."

About halfway to our destination we rested on a felled tree and wolfed down some bread and water. By the time we resumed walking the forest was in complete darkness, except for the lights in the sky: a million stars were soon there, and the moon was almost full. They lighted the way and, we felt, nature was on our side. For it was important for those mining the bridge to have sufficient light to place the explosives properly. The one drawback to the radiant sky was that because of the light the German cyclists could notice the roadblocks before they ran into them.

Maniek, Stach, and I piled the branches and bushes as thickly and as rapidly as we could. It took about two hours. Satisfied with our handiwork, we climbed up the trees to watch the road. The other group took up their positions on the other side of the road, ready to fire on the cyclists. They were instructed to let no German come out alive.

We sat in the trees for one full hour.

"Thought these Nazis were so damned punctilious," Stach growled.

"You know what Bolek said," Maniek rejoined.

"Yeh, well. I know what happened. The captain or whoever he is probably got some sauerkraut stuck in his asshole and had to—"

"Sst! They are coming! They are coming!"

The motorcycles had darkened their headlights—probably as a precaution against the Soviet planes that bombed freely at night. They drove slowly. I counted six.

Silently, we climbed down the trees and took up positions by the road. I lay closest to Maniek; Stach was about thirty feet away. Maniek adjusted his automatic and inserted a magazine of bullets. He handed me two grenades.

"Listen to me: pull that little cap off with your teeth. Take aim—fast!—and get rid of it before it blows up in your hand."

This time, each motorcycle had two soldiers—one driving, one in the sidecar. A machine gun was mounted on each sidecar. They approached in single file.

The first one crashed into the road block and flipped over. Those behind, moving more slowly, tried to avoid the barrier and turned off the road into the ditch.

"*Zuruck! Zuruck!*" The shouts filled the air. The partisans on the other side of the road began firing at them. The Germans ran about like cockroaches in a bottle. Maniek and Stach opened fire.

One German extricated himself from underneath a motorcycle and fired at us with an automatic pistol.

"Tadek! The hand grenade! Let him have it!"

I stood up, ripped the cap off with my finger and flung it at him. The German and the motorcycle went up in flames.

By now some of the other cyclists had recovered their senses. They began shooting at us and at the group across the road.

Maniek and I crawled to the cycle that had flipped over. The machine gun was smashed. A few yards away lay a dead German soldier with an automatic pistol on his shoulder; not far from him was another with a rifle across his neck. I swooped down, grabbed his pistol—and some cartridge boxes. Satisfaction seized me. I had my own weapon, just as Maniek and Stach had said. Maniek took the rifle.

The skirmish lasted no more than ten minutes. All the German cyclists lay dead—as Bolek had ordered. We took all their weapons, ammunition, boots, overcoats—any military equipment that could be of use to us. Our two groups backed into the woods and sat, waiting for the bridge and the train to explode.

It was at least an hour before we heard the whistle of the freight train.

"Bye, bye Adolf," someone said.

"You wish!" came the answer.

The first explosion shook the ground. As the others followed, the area lit up as though it were midday. The cars loaded with ammunition blew up one after the other—each with a tremendous roar and higher-leaping flames. They must have been seen for several miles. We smiled. We clapped each other on backs and shoulders.

No one was hurt in our group. None was tired. Excited, exhilirated, exuberant, we started back to the base—and Bolek.

I was happier than anyone. I hadn't been this happy

since before the war broke out in Kurov. I patted my automatic pistol as if it were a living thing.

Maniek was pleased with me. "Good work, Tadek! Your first battle—you were like a veteran fighter. Your aim with that grenade was perfect." Some of the other group looked around at us. "We can be glad we've got him," he said to them. "And," he continued to me, "you got your weapon. On your first day—see? You'll kill many, many Germans with it. You're more eager than we are—I think," he added, scrutinizing me more closely.

Dawn was glowing when the three groups reached the base. Bolek was waiting impatiently. He directed us all into his bunker and brought out a bottle and glasses from a wooden box.

It was polish *bimber* that the farmers made from potatoes, not real vodka. It had an unpleasant taste. When I inhaled the bitter pungent odor from my glass I immediately lost any desire for it. The others drank it hungrily.

Each group commander reported to Bolek on the operation. He became increasingly pleased: no losses; excellent results. By the time he got to our group he was all smiles.

"And you can be proud of Tadek," Maniek told him. "He's courageous, disciplined, efficient. And eager." Bolek chuckled at this.

"And look," Maniek pointed to the automatic, "an excellent weapon. On his first night!"

Bolek clapped me on the shoulder. "Show Tadek how to use this toy, Maniek."

November 1944

I left the schoolhouse in a total quandary. How could I help Bolek?

"How long will the Poles stay in the schoolhouse?" I asked one of the German officers.

"We don't know exactly—probably not more than a day or two.

SIX

November 1944

I returned to our room in the chateau exhausted and upset.
It was hours before I fell asleep.

Bolek! I had to save Bolek! Those men in the village
weren't being rounded up to serve our battalion—they were
going to be deported, I knew. *The answer will come*, I said to
myself before I finally dozed off.

As soon as I could get away from the clean-up after
breakfast, I got into my full uniform and headed for the
schoolhouse. The men were still seated inside, not knowing
for what they were waiting.

I approached Bolek and ordered him to come with me.

"I'm taking this Pole to work with me in the kitchen at
the estate," I said to the soldier at the door. "My assistant
hasn't shown up and we need someone to keep the coffee
kettles full. When we're finished I'll return him."

The soldier knew who I was; there were no questions.

Bolek seemed confused, nervous. "Keep silent," I mumbled in Polish. "Just come with me."

Neither of us spoke on the way back to the estate.
Doesn't he recognize me? Doesn't he remember? I asked
myself over and over.

In the kitchen I ordered him to fill the kettles with
water. He obeyed. He looked very agitated.

"Bolek, don't be afraid," I said finally. "I'm 'Tadek.' "

He looked at me long and hard. "But what are you
doing with the Germans?"

"They don't know who I am. I got here accidentally and I had no other way. They think I'm a *Volksdeutsch*—I told them I am." I filled him in on what had happened since the Germans had bombed us out of the Sadlovisna forest.

It took a long time, but he finally began to believe me.

"Listen, Tadek. You must pull Janusz Mazur out of that schoolhouse as soon as possible. He is with us."

All of a sudden Heinz appeared in the kitchen with the menu for lunch and dinner. "I see you have a new helper," he smiled.

"*Jawohl*!" I replied. "The workers didn't show up today because of the search, so I took this one from among the Poles detained in the school. But I must have one more to help in cutting up wood. Afterwards I'll return them."

"Of course," he nodded. "Go on now and get another," he replied.

When Heinz had left I asked Bolek to describe Janusz Mazur.

"Short, dark, wiry," he said. "Sort of like Maniek, only short."

I practically ran to the schoolhouse. Inside I announced, "Janusz Mazur is to come with me." A man of about twenty-five, fitting Bolek's description, stood up, looking panicked. "Come," I said calmly.

There was a different soldier at the door. He didn't want to let him leave.

"Get your sergeant," I told him.

He looked at me. I stood my ground. He stepped outside and turned the corner of the schoolhouse. Janusz and I could have left then, but I wanted this to seem perfectly legitimate.

"So?" the sergeant approached the door.

"Sergeant, my superior, Sergeant Klockmann of the headquarters company, asked me to obtain a helper in the kitchen for today. He specifically directed me to come here and obtain one of the Poles rounded up last night. Otherwise there will be no lunch." I tried to speak authoritatively.

That did it.

"*Ja*, so take him," the sergeant said.

I tried to calm Janusz as best I could on our way out of the village. "It's okay, Janusz," I said. "Bolek is waiting for you."

That seemed to frighten him even more. He eyed the cross-paths and alleys frantically as we walked along the main road. *My God, he's going to try to run!* I realized.

"Janusz, don't try it. You'll be shot on the spot. Please!"

Inside the kitchen, when he saw Bolek busily filling the large kettles with water, he visibly relaxed. No one else was about, and Bolek walked over to us and put his arm around Janusz's shoulder.

He said jovially, "Listen, Janusz, believe me, this 'German soldier' is one of us. He's saved us. But while we're here in this army camp we must do whatever he says."

Janusz nodded hesitantly.

After a while we stopped for a breather, and Bolek told me what had happened after the raid. "Once we got out of the forests we each went in a different direction. We headed for the villages nearby the forests. By God, if the village I landed in wasn't under siege! They took every male over thirteen away. Janusz and I hid in a cellar. And here we are."

"Hey, Tadek, tell Janusz what you told me about how you wound up in German uniform. I want to hear it again."

"Okay, but first—you must call me 'Marion' around here."

" 'Marion'?!" His eyebrows shot up.

"That's who I am to the German Army."

"You've got more names than—oh what the hell, Marion." He winked at Janusz. We all grinned.

I repeated my adventures for Janusz's benefit. By the time I was describing my hair being cut, Bolek was laughing uproariously. Meanwhile, an idea was forming in my head.

"Listen, Bolek. With my position here, it would be very easy for us all to escape . . . We could look like I was returning you to the village; no one would stop—"

"No," he rejected the idea. "You're more use to us while you're working with the Germans—think about it. Stay on your post. At least for now."

That evening, as I supervised the serving of dinner, I learned from the talk between the soldiers that the gendarmerie had taken the detained Poles out of the village and transported them away on trucks. I couldn't wait to get Bolek and Janusz alone after clean-up.

"Get out of there as soon as possible," I said. I told them what I'd learned.

We decided to wait until it got dark. I knew exactly when the patrol came around our area, so we could time it to the minute.

Just before they disappeared into the dark, Bolek put his arm around my shoulders. "Tadek, you've saved our lives. You will hear from me soon, I promise. For now, our hearty thanks. I am proud you are part of my group. Just hold on for now."

They disappeared into the darkness.

The following week a woman of about twenty or twenty-two came into the kitchen. She looked around to make sure we were alone.

"I am Kazia; Bolek sent me," she whispered. "You are to hire me to help you. I will work in exchange for just food."

I immediately began to show her around the kitchen, pointing out what her chores would be. She set to work at once.

In the middle of the morning Heinz came into the kitchen. He looked right at Kazia. *Well*, I thought, *who wouldn't look at her? She is beautiful*! And she was. Shiny black hair, sparkling black eyes—which missed nothing.

"Heinz, this woman came in from the village looking for work in exchange for food. She seems like a good worker. I certainly need the help, with Michel gone and no one reliable . . ."

Heinz continued to stare at her. *Did he suspect something*, I wondered? I began to feel uncomfortable.

Kazia looked up at him from the corner where she was peeling potatoes, smiled briefly, and went back to her work.

"Marion, what happened to that man and woman we hired?" Heinz asked quizzically.

"They disappeared after two days, Heinz."

"And those two men you had here last week," he scratched his head, "probably made a run for it—how do we know she won't?"

I lowered my voice as if I didn't want her to hear. "I think she really needs the food," I mumbled. Then, "After all, Heinz, that's how you got me."

He laughed. "All right, Marion. Use your judgment." He turned and left.

Kazia was constantly on the alert. And she worked diligently—Heinz could have no complaints. She was in the kitchen promptly at 6:00 every morning and didn't leave until we'd finished cleaning up after dinner. She never began a conversation, except with me, but always responded pleasantly when someone spoke to her.

Once she confided to me, "The most important thing is that they've issued me the certificate." The certificate, issued to civilians working for the German Army, ensured that she could move about freely and would not be deported to Germany for forced labor.

She spoke only Polish, but I was certain she understood German. She wore a cross around her neck, and frequently used the words "Saint Mary" and "Jesus" in conversation. But I was absolutely sure she was Jewish, struggling for her life, like me.

One morning, appearing in the kitchen, she whispered to me, "Bolek wants you to meet him tomorrow night in the village."

I thought fast. "No, Kazia, that is dangerous. You must tell him. If he's recognized, they'll deport him immediately— or worse. Tell him to come here, after dark, between 7:30 and 8:00, and meet me behind the kitchen building—this one. The patrol won't be here until 9:00."

Even in the dark I recognized Bolek's wide-shouldered frame the following evening. He put his hands on my shoulders.

"Tadek, we've reorganizd the group—in the Lagov woods. Janusz, of course, is with us."

"That's wonderful news!"

"Tadek, you are still a member of this group and, as such, under my command."

I was overjoyed: he was going to order me to leave with him for the Lagov woods right then. "I can leave right now!" I exulted.

"No, no! You are *much* more valuable to us here. Now listen," he said as he noticed my disappointment, "what you must do is get the password each day and tell Kazia. She will get it to us and we can get in and out of here without trouble."

Of course—I would be much more help to the partisans from inside the enemy camp than out.

"You're right, Bolek."

"I know. Will you do it?"

"You know I will."

It was easier said than done. I didn't go on patrol every day and couldn't obtain the password directly. Also, as far as I knew the password changed at 6:00 p.m. every day—and that was when Kazia left.

I began to casually discuss the password at mealtimes. It wasn't too long before I learned from a couple of the men who worked in the staff office that the password was actually decided upon by 4:00 in the afternoon but not given out until 6:00.

"So," I said to my informants, "by the time you get here for dinner at 5:00 you know the password for the next day."

"*Ja.* So?"

"Well. There's a girl down in the village . . ."

Both grinned broadly.

I continued. "Well, it would be *very* convenient if I knew the password so I could get back into camp here without trouble at all—well—at any time."

"It sure would," drawled the less talkative one, "but we're not supposed to give it out . . ."

"Not even for a few extra cigarettes at dinner?"

"Well . . ."

It worked.

Not long after I'd been obtaining the password on a regular basis I asked Kazia to whom she was passing it on.

"It is better that you don't know, Marion," was all she said.

Perhaps it was.

In fact it was better for me not to think about the whole situation. I was starting to feel more and more as though I were walking around in a trance, that this was not reality.

I was fighting the enemy—Hitler's beasts—enabling the partisans to infiltrate the battalion in order to carry out God-knows-what plan.

And I was betraying Heinz.

July 1944

Exhausted, our attack groups slept most of the morning following the destruction of the munitions convoy. By noon we were awake and gleefully going over and over the night's exploits in increasingly elaborate detail. We had killed all twelve motorcyclists. We had destroyed most of the thirty-five-car military train: those cars filled with sand had not been totally destroyed, we'd guessed.

Bolek showed up around 2:00. "There have been quite a few soldiers in each train car killed," he said. "Of course, all the ammunition has been destroyed."

We cheered.

"Let's not get careless now," he warned. "They'll probably find us."

It didn't take long.

We were just stretching out on our straw pallets in the bunkers that day when we heard the sound of planes overhead. At first it was hard to tell if they were German or

Russian observation aircraft. Then bombs exploded—one right after the other. The forest shook.

"Stay inside the bunker!"

The raid lasted almost two hours. Crouched inside our bunker, Maniek, Stach, and I tried to joke while the bombs dropped steadily.

"Do you suppose they're going to get smart and find the bunker?"

"Who said the Nazis were smart?"

"It's that they've got poor eyesight—with all that beer they swill."

Suddenly it got quiet—except for the sound of faint hissing. After about half an hour we climbed out of the bunker. Huge flames, like torches, leaped to the sky from different parts of the forest. The hissing sound was that of the burning leaves and branches of trees. The nearest fire to us was about fifty feet away. Eye-stinging smoke was beginning to fill the air. A few of the group began to cough.

Kurov, I thought.

Bolek called us together. "This is to be expected," he announced. "It is the reprisal for our action last night. This time they didn't get us.

"Now we must liquidate the base. Destroy what you can in the bunker. We will retreat—each of us will take a different route. Get shelter where you can."

He clenched his fists. "But first—we'll probably have to fight our way out. My information is that the Germans have readied a large group of infantry to destroy us here. Well, we're ready for that—we'll shoot them with their own weapons, whether they know it or not. Until then, we must work fast. Destroy the bunker. Load the equipment into the wagons and harness the horses and have them ready. Throw the tarpaulins over the wagons—the plain ones won't be as suspect 'outside.' Tonight we sleep under the trees. And hope it doesn't rain."

As he spoke, I looked around. Every single face—male and female—was set in determination and anticipation. It dawned on me that I knew only two—Stach and Maniek—but felt that everyone there was my good friend.

"When the battle is over, each of us will get out in his own way," Bolek continued. "Head for the Lagov woods. Remember. We will each be on our own until we reassemble in the Lagov woods—however long it takes."

Dawn began with another German aerial bombardment of the forest. More trees leaped into flame.

Then came the artillery and machine-gun bombardment. "Christ, they've surrounded the forest!" someone yelled.

"They'll have a helluva time getting the tanks and armor in here!" another man angrily answered.

The partisans had constructed obstacles of tree trunks and branches across the forest roads and wider pathways. But this time they didn't stop the foot soldiers. There seemed to be thousands of them.

They were Russians! They were the troops—under General Vlasov—that had gone over to the Nazis! We saw it by the insignias they wore on the lapels and armbands of their German uniforms. And heard it by the commands, which were shouted in Russian.

"Rotten cowards," Maniek growled beside me. "Won't even send their own men in—they send the Russians. They're afraid of us, Tadek, that's what."

We fought ferociously. We battered them. They were fighting in a cause not really their own, while we fought for life.

The Germans managed to send reinforcements almost continuously, but they weren't familiar with the forest and couldn't judge from where our attacks would come. We suffered losses—but we slaughtered hundreds of them. The bodies strewn among the underbrush increased by the hour.

Stach, Maniek, and I stayed close to one another. And we formulated a strategy: if a Vlasov discovered one of our positions, the other two would open fire on him. It worked. A group of Vlasovs approached Stach's position. Maniek, stationed opposite Stach, opened fire on them. They didn't know where or whom to shoot. Stach, Maniek, and I began firing at them. We got them all.

Not too long after that, ten men armed with rifles and hand grenades approached my position. I opened fire with my machine gun. Stach threw a hand grenade at them.

The hand grenade burst into fire. The thick smoke made it difficult to breathe. We had to find other positions.

"It's okay, Tadek," Stach chortled, "we'll get the bastards just as well from one position as the other."

The battle lasted the entire day. The shooting finally stopped as darkness fell. But we couldn't tell whether the Vlasovs had left the forest. And, once again, the forest was an inferno. Each of us hid as best we could.

The thick, beautiful forest—where at times I felt as though I'd been walking through a cathedral or temple—seemed a sea of blackened stumps.

We couldn't leave that night: we could fall into a trap set by the Vlasovs—or the Germans. At the first light of dawn we began our retreat—every nerve alert to Vlasov's minions.

It wasn't long before the planes reappeared. Then we knew that there were no enemy soldiers remaining in the forest; they wouldn't bombard the forest if their troops were still there.

But we couldn't get out. It was clear that the troops had surrounded the forest and were trying to smoke us out with bombs. So we wasted another day.

After night settled in, we literally crawled out of the forest. The moon was only a sliver. The forest thinned out to thin strands of beeches and larch at its edges. We were familiar with the best places to hide. We buried our weapons where we knew they would be safe.

Maniek, Stach, and I were still together. It was understood we'd head for Opatov, their town.

"When it gets light, we can move," Maniek observed. "No one will follow us."

We slept on the ground, each of us taking a turn to

watch the area. I wondered why I didn't feel sore from the lack of straw—or a mattress.

"You're getting tough, Tadek," Stach grinned. "You're a true partisan now."

I grinned back at him. Did they understand how happy—how proud—I was to be one of them?

We headed out cautiously toward the fields. Stach and Maniek knew the area intimately; they'd grown up around it.

We cut through fields green with barley, through orchards where the fruit was just beginning to bud and where some was already ripening. "Early pears," Maniek commented.

At night we slept under bushes.

Maniek's father was a shoemaker in Opatov, he told me. "He hears what's going on through the customers that come to his shop," he said. "Besides, we have an apple, pear, and plum orchard on the edge of town."

Stach nodded. "Good fruit," he grinned.

"No wonder you know about what's ripening," I remarked.

Stach lived in Opatov with his wife and child. As we got closer to the town he confessed that he was going home for a while.

"I've had enough," he said determinedly. "I don't think I'll be back with you."

Maniek and I said nothing.

We reached Opatov on the third day. It was old—and ugly: squat, two- and three-story buildings, thrown together with no apparent rhyme or reason, seemed to jar the bucolic countryside.

"I know a shortcut," Maniek said.

We tramped through the yard of the ugly brick and concrete town hall, which the Germans had confiscated and where, Stach told me, they had installed their own commisar.

"Careful," Maniek hissed.

We were.

At twilight we reached the orchard. Streaks of coral cut through the sky. Suddenly the stillness was shattered by wild barking. I froze; I was certain that the Germans had tracked us.

"Oh, it's all right," Maniek assured us. "That's our watch dog—he guards the orchards." Maniek rushed toward the sound of the barking—which immediately stopped when the dog scented Maniek. It was a large, long-haird, and black and white mongrel. And it was overjoyed at the sight of Maniek. He scratched the dog's head and patted its shoulders.

"Good Rexi, good boy. You missed me, eh?"

Rexi's frantically waving tail answered.

"Listen," Stach turned back toward us, "I'm going to say so long. I'm going to head for my house."

Maniek said, "Are you going to join in when we regroup in Lagov?" He looked into Stach's eyes.

"Yes, I guess so," Stach said hesitantly.

"So now you'll just rest a bit, then?" Maniek continued.

"Yes, I'll see you." Stach started to walk away. He suddenly walked back and put an arm around each of us. "After all, we work so well together. It would be a shame to break us up."

Maniek and I slapped him on his shoulders. "Get home safely, Stach. Be careful. And we'll see you soon."

He turned to go. "Of course. Haven't I been so far?"

Maniek turned to me as Stach disappeared into the increasing gloom. "Tadek, listen. The Germans search the houses here routinely—"

"I know what you're saying," I interrupted. "Your whole family would be in trouble if they found me. Where can I—"

He pointed toward the dog. "See Rexi's house?"

I looked. The structure could have housed two dogs Rexi's size. In other days living in a dog's house would have been unthinkable. But these were different times. Besides— could it be worse than "Kazet"?

"I built it for him," Maniek said.

"You really love that dog.

"I've had him since he was a puppy. Anyway—I think you'll be safe there."

I nodded. "Yes. I agree."

"I'll probably have to help my father in his shop during the day, now. But we get a lot of traffic through there and I can bring you news. Now listen, I'll be out to see you—tell you what's going on and bring you food."

"Okay, Maniek. Thanks."

He patted the dog. "Watch over him, Rexi."

I crawled into the house. In spite of its having seemed large from the outside, I couldn't stretch my legs out fully. Rexi slept half in, half out of his house. But it was piled deep with clean straw. I curled up and fell asleep instantly.

A knocking sounded on the wall next to my head. I jumped awake, knocking my arms and legs on the sides of the dog house.

"It's all right, Tadek. I'm Maniek's mother," a low, sweet voice called out.

Rexi sprang out, leaping about.

I crawled out after him. The woman, about sixty, straight as a tree with warm blue eyes, placed a pail of food about five feet from the house. She smiled at me.

"And this is for you," she said as she handed me two thick slices of bread spread with amber-colored honey, and two rosy apples.

"Listen, Tadek," she went on, "you must be careful. There are many Germans around this section. Not that you must stay in the doghouse all day—but just be careful. And watch out for the neighbors. Poles—but not much better than the Germans."

I chose to stay in the doghouse most of the time. Rexi kept coming back, licking my face and hands and urging me to follow him outside into the warm sunshine. I scratched his head and patted him. It wasn't long before we became attached to one another.

Maniek's mother returned at dusk with more food. Again, she put the pail of Rexi's food a few feet from his house. Then she pretended to inspect it and put some food for me just inside.

"How are you doing, Tadek? You should get out and stretch your legs."

"When it's dark. Thank you. Where is Maniek?"

"He'll be around soon. He's helping my husband in the shop—trying to pick up news."

I looked around. How beautiful the orchard was, like a still life painting with deep purples and yellow greens. Apple, pear and plum trees were separated into sections. Beneath them soft, early summer grass grew profusely. Some apples were already ripening, and I could see the beginnings of others on some of the pale branches. The setting sun turned the leaves to orange-gold. I couldn't wait to get out and walk underneath them.

After dark I roamed all around. Rexi trotted contentedly beside me, glad for the company.

Just before dawn I washed in the river, and took a long drink of the delicious, coursing water.

The next morning Maniek's mother brought me a couple of books along with breakfast. "So you don't go crazy in there," she smiled.

Maniek didn't come to me until the fourth day. He was clearly agitated. He crawled into the house with me. The two of us were twisted like pretzels.

"It is very dangerous for you to stay here, Tadek," he sighed. "One of the neighbors has asked my father who it is going round the orchard at night."

My heart sank.

"Wait," he said, "I'm not saying you must leave. But here's what we must do. After dark we'll dig out a bunker on the other side of the orchard, cover it with boards, spread earth on the boards and disguise it as a cabbage patch. We'll camouflage the entrance."

Nodding, I wondered how I would ever thank him. Tears sprang to my eyes. "I don't know how—" I said.

"Let's not mention that," he said abruptly.

At about 10:00 that night he arrived at Rexi's house with two shovels. He knew exactly where to make the bunker. We spent about three hours digging it out. We gathered some boards from an old fence on the edge of the property; Maniek went back to one of the buildings and returned with two huge bundles of straw which we spread inside the bunker. We stuck pipes in either end for air circulation, and planted cabbages in the earth above the boards. It was nearly three in the morning when we finished.

There was just enough room for two people to sit or lie down inside the bunker.

It was like a grave.

"I'll be joining you here, Tadek. The Germans are grabbing young Poles in Opatov left and right and deporting them to Germany for hard labor."

"I wonder if they'll grab Stach," I mused.

We looked hard at each other.

Maniek appeared quite often at the bunker. His family usually managed to bring food once a day. But there were times when they could not arouse suspicion, and then I went for two or three days without anything to eat. When that happened, I would leave the bunker—after dark—and gather what I could of what was ripening in the fields. Rexi usually accompanied me.

Except for the heightened tension, my routine was the same as it had been when I occupied the doghouse. This went on for weeks. I became more confident.

August 1944

One morning I loitered at the river bank. It was a glorious morning: the fresh air seemed to vibrate. The green on the ground and in the trees was a joyful, intense green. It felt wonderful.

Suddenly two German soldiers appeared out of no-where. Their uniforms showed that they belonged to the *Luftwaffe*. It was too late for me to run. I'd have been killed instantly.

They pointed their guns at me.

"Raise your hands!" one yelled.

The other searched me for weapons. He found the German-made military field kit in my pocket.

"Where did you get this?" he asked in German.

"I don't understand you." I spoke in Polish.

"Come with us."

They marched me to the German military police post. There they filled out a form. I read it over their shoulders: they wrote that a Polish informer had told them a Jew was hiding on Maniek's property.

Suddenly another officer, tall, menacing-looking, entered the room. He approached me. "Are you a Jew?"

I pretended I didn't understand. "I am Polish, Polish," I cried over and over.

This exchange didn't last long. The tall German repeatedly beat me with his fists—my face, my stomach, my chest. I felt the blood trickling down from my nose and forehead.

"Where are your identity papers?" he demanded.

"I know nothing," I answered. "I am Polish."

He turned abruptly and picked up the telephone. I sank onto the bench, every muscle trembling. He called someone into the office.

A tall, blond, blue-eyed well-built man wearing a brand new military police uniform, entered. He saluted the officer.

"Two *Luftwaffe* caught this Jew and brought him here," the officer snapped. "But the Jew denies this and insists he is a Pole. Now you question him in Polish and tell me if he is a Jew or a Pole."

The young military policeman turned to me. "What is your name?" he asked sternly.

"Thaddeus Kowalski," I responded.

"Where do you live?"

"In Kloda village."

"Where is that?"

"Near Kurov."

"What are you doing in Opatov?"

"Looking for work."

"Where did you get the German military emergency kit?"

"I found it."

"Are you a Jew?"

"No—I am pure Polish."

The policeman turned to the officer. "His accent is pure Polish," he said. "I believe he's a Pole."

The officer wasn't satisfied. He grabbed the telephone again. "Send in the doctor!" he barked.

The doctor wouldn't be in until tomorrow morning, he said to the young military policeman.

Clearly disappointed—and angry—he ordered the policeman to lock me up in a detention cell until morning. "Then we'll see whether he's a Jew or not!"

We crossed the yard to a low structure used to store farm equipment. Inside a long corridor divided rooms with locked doors on each side. Stopping at one of them, the policeman opened the huge lock that hung there. The room was completely empty—as if it were waiting for me.

"Are you hungry?" the policeman asked.

"I haven't eaten all day." I looked into his eyes and saw sympathy. I was amazed.

He left.

A few minutes later he came back with a slice of bread. "It's all I could find," he said apologetically.

He turned to leave, then said in Polish, "Don't be frightened. Be strong."

I couldn't believe my ears as I heard the lock turn on the door. Wasn't that policeman a Hitlerite? And why did he tell the officer that he was sure I was not a Jew? I'm sure he knew I was. Why did he improve on my answers as he translated them into German? And why did he bring me the bread and reassure me?

I couldn't find an answer.

The room was about twelve feet wide and twenty-four long. In the middle of the high ceiling was a small opening which admitted some air. There was also a small window on the outside wall through which I probably couldn't even stick my head. The furnishings consisted of one broken chair. I sat on it gingerly.

I had struggled for life for so long. I had fought so stubbornly. I had been saved so many times from certain—and uncertain—death. And now I had fallen into the clutches of the murderers—just when it seemed my salvation had arrived. The Germans were losing on all fronts. Surely the end of the war was approaching. Was I going to die?

I thought about the happy years of my childhood in my parents' beautiful home; of my brothers and sisters; of the toys, the games, the mischief we pulled in *cheder*: all cut off in the cruelest fashion.

Now I didn't know who in my family was still alive. Possibly I was the last of them all—perhaps even the last Jew from Kurov left. And tomorrow that would come to an end.

It grew late. The moonlight appeared shrouded in fog. I finally fell into a deep sleep.

I was in my old home at my writing table where I used to prepare my lessons. Suddenly my father seemed to appear at the door of the room—tall, handsome, smiling. I wanted to stand up, go to him, but was unable to move. He did not approach me. From the doorway, he said, "Why are you crying, son?"

"Daddy, I cannot get out of this place. Help me, please."

"Son, go to the door; there you will find a key and you'll be able to get free."

I tried again to stand up, but I seemed rooted to my chair.

Then my father disappeared. I screamed wildly and woke. Dawn was breaking, and light eked in my cell. I felt confused: what did the dream mean? Should I begin to believe in dreams and miracles? I never had. The miracles that happened to our forefathers, that Mother used to tell us about, were they true?

I went to the door. I didn't find a key. But as I examined the door I found that it was suspended on only two hinges and that it was not supported by any framework. I also saw that there was a rather large space between the door and the floor. I shoved my hands under the door, lifted with all my strength, and pulled it off its hinges, so that it rested only on the outside lock. I pulled the door towards me and slipped out into the long, empty corridor. I ran to the exit door at the end. It was locked from the other side.

I crouched against the wall in the corner near the door and waited.

Soon, I heard the door unlock from the outside. An old woman entered, apparently to get food from storage. She ambled back down the hallway, leaving the door open. I slipped out. About twenty feet from the building, there was a stream. Carefully but quickly I made my way down to it.

A military policeman stood on guard. He seemed interested in something far across the field. I slipped into the water. On the other side thick bushes grew. Still unnoticed by the guard, I dove into them.

SEVEN

November 1944

With Michel gone, I was pretty much in charge of serving the meals. As Heinz had said a number of times, it was the best job in the service. One could get anything one wanted with the promise of food. Or cigarettes.

I stood next to the kettles supervising the distribution of lunch. I noticed the two "Heivies" towards the rear of the line. "Heivies" were Poles who volunteered to serve German military units. They wore German uniforms, but instead of the swastika, they wore the HIW insignia—hence their nicknames. They were not issued weapons. They usually cleaned the barracks and officers' quarters, and did other work the German soldiers preferred not to do. They were given food and shelter, and a small stipend. I was, in effect, of higher status than a "Heivie."

As these two came closer to where I stood, a chill ran down my spine. I recognized them. And they recognized me—I could see it in their faces.

They handed me a note for four servings for the officers. I didn't raise my eyes; I busied myself with the note, and tapped my assistant of the day on the shoulder to show him. Then I heard it:

"He is a Jew," one of the Heivies said to the other.

Both turned and looked at me sharply.

I began to sweat. I felt as though I couldn't move— then I had the feeling that my feet were going to collapse under me. I felt the world stopped at that moment, and I was suspended in it. *Hold on, Nachemia, don't lose your head*, I said to myself reassuringly.

I looked at them coolly and continued to supervise the servings. My heart pounded against my ribs. *Escape. You must escape, I told myself. But where?*

All the ways were blocked. I was a mouse in a maze.

At about 3:00, Sergeant-Major Emil Werner came into the kitchen. He and Heinz seemed to get along well—but then Heinz got along with everyone. In a gathering, Heinz and Emil usually tried to top each other's jokes. Emil was about Heinz's height, but he was pudgier than Heinz. He had nondescript brown hair and eyes. He was always amiable, and never failed to greet me with a smile. Not tonight.

"Where is your superior?" he snapped.

I froze momentarily. "He will be here soon, Sergeant-Major Werner."

"Hmph!" He sounded displeased, irritated.

Yes. I rubbed my eyes. His had been one of the names on the food slips the Heivies had passed to me at lunch.

After a few minutes, Emil barked, "Well, where is he? I have something very important to discuss with him."

"I am sure he will be here in a few moments, Sergeant-Major Werner."

Kazia entered. Emil threw her a black look. Behind her back, she looked at me—then looked again. It must have shown on my face. I knew what the "very important" matter was that Emil wantd to discuss.

Heinz finally arrived.

"Heinz, I have something of the utmost importance to discuss with you. For your ears alone," Emil said sternly.

Heinz looked at him and then at me quizzically. Emil had never before refused to discuss things in front of me. Heinz led him into a small room adjacent to the kitchen. He left the door ajar.

I crept close to it. Kazia came up behind me. "Marion, what—"

I shushed her. Then I heard Emil's words—each a hammer blow across my chest:

"Heinz, I know for sure that Marion is a Jew."

"How do you know this?" Heinz replied coolly.

"The two Heivies that work for me recognized him. They knew him well, they say. He lived in the ghetto in Ostroviec. They know they are not mistaken. Heinz, this is absolutely outrageous; a Jew wearing a German uniform, working for the *Wehrmacht*."

My heart sank. Kazia patted my shoulder. Then Heinz spoke. I couldn't believe what I heard:

"Listen, Emil, my advice to you is that you occupy yourself with *your* unit, not mine. The affairs in my unit concern me and me alone. In any case, I don't see why you would want to believe those Polish swine. They're *all* liars and self-seekers, as far as I can see. I am Marion's supervisor, not you. I am responsible for him, you are not."

"Heinz, what in hell's the matter with you? Are you harboring a Jew in your unit?" Emil spat the words out. "What if I report *you*?"

"You will regret it, Emil. Never threaten me. Never!"

They kept arguing. It seemed to go on forever. I was paralyzed with panic.

Finally the door flew open and Emil stalked out through the kitchen. He slammed the outside door behind him as he left.

I was shaking all over. My brain throbbed. *Escape! Escape!*

Where? Where?

"Kazia," I managed to croak, "I have to get out of here."

Suddenly Heinz emerged from the other room. "Marion, how are preparations for dinner coming?" he asked quietly.

"Fine, Heinz. On schedule."

"Good. Now tomorrow send someone into the old man for milk and vegetables right after breakfast, okay? We're going to have to see about more meat, as well. And while we're at it," he winked, "some more wine and cognac. No sense living in a state of deprivation."

"All right, then," he started toward the door and patted my shoulder. "See you later."

Kazia waited a few minutes. Then she came over to me, put her hands on my shoulders. I was amazed again at how beautiful she was. I stared at her, unable to speak. "Listen, Marion—Tadek," she said softly. "Nothing is going to happen to you as long as Heinz is here. Didn't you hear how he refuted Emil? Didn't you see how he acted toward you just now—as if nothing is wrong? He puts no stock by what that Emil says. Obviously you have nothing to worry about."

I shook my head. "Kazia, no. I am afraid. Very afraid. Look at me trembling. I must get out of here. Kazie, listen. Ask Bolek what I should do, will you?"

She seemed to hesitate but then nodded.

I was afraid to inquire about the password that afternoon. Every time a soldier looked at me my blood ran cold. *They know, they all know*, I thought.

I served dinner in a trance. That night I got to our room early and pretended to be sleeping when Heinz came in.

As soon as Kazia appeared in the kitchen the following morning, I asked her if she had seen Bolek—or the liaison officer to whom she handed the password. She had not. My heart began to pound. *Only Bolek can help you now.*

Two days passed. They were the longest of my life. I tried to remember when I'd felt this badly before. I knew: it was when Chania and I ran around camp trying to raise money for my father's ransom. It was the same feeling of panic, fear, despair.

Every time Heinz approached me I was sure he was going to say, "You've betrayed me. You are a Jew." But he never did. I tried to smile, to joke with him, to act "normal." It took all the control I had.

On the third day Kazia relayed Bolek's instructions: "He says you are not to move for the time being. If it becomes clear that you're in danger, *I* will tell you where to flee—he will tell me."

Emil did not come near our unit again.

After about a week Peter Wagner, a soldier whom I

knew only slightly, came up to me. "Headquarters commander wants to see you. Now."

This was it, I thought trembling.

"Look, I'm right in the middle of lunch preparation," I replied as casually as I could. "I can't really leave now."

"You have to," the soldier prodded. "The commander says so. Those are my orders."

I looked at him.

"It won't take much time," he said decisively.

"Well, what is it?" I tried to gain some time.

"Oh, it's just that we need someone who speaks Polish and German. This Pole is in the commander's office complaining about something, but nobody can understand him. Come on now," he said calmly.

I felt better.

But only momentarily. What if "the Pole" was one of the Heivies?

"Okay," I finally said. "Let me just give some instructions here."

I walked over to Kazia. "Kazia, they want me in the commander's office. I'm not exactly sure what it is, but if I disappear—well, tell Bolek what happened."

She looked up at me. Her eyes were like a startled deer's.

I put on my uniform, buttoned it, and we left.

At the commander's office, I saluted with the usual *Heil, Hitler.* "I am at your disposal," I said simply.

"Private Schmidt, please find out what this Pole wants." The commander pointed to a gray-haired peasant of about fifty who leaned on a walking stick in the corner of his office.

I approached the peasant and asked him, in Polish, what was the matter.

He was from Ruda Koshcielna, he said. Jews, two men and two women, had attacked him, robbed some of his animals as well as other food supplies, he told me. They'd told him they'd kill him if he didn't give them food. He said that he knew exactly where the Jews were hiding and would be able to indicate it to the Germany army.

I translated for the commander. But I made a slight change. I reported that a group of bandits had attacked him, and he would be happy to point out their hiding place.

"What does he think we are, the local police?" the commander snapped. "Tell him we have no time to go chasing after bandits. And tell him he'd better not complain about bandits robbing his food supplies. If he were meeting his quota to us, there'd be nothing left for the bandits . . ."

I translated this for the peasant, who looked around fearfully. "And," I added to him, "I think you'd better go as fast as you can and don't return with these dumb complaints."

He limped out of the office awfully fast. A huge weight lifted from my chest.

"Okay, soldier, you can go now," the commander snapped.

I practically skipped down the stairs. But not before I heard him grumble to the others in his office, "Damn stupid Polacks . . ."

Kazia was very nervous by the time I reached the kitchen. "Oh God, Tadek, I was sure you were detained." Tears sprang to her eyes.

I told her about the old peasant and his "bandits." We both laughed uproariously. Watching her dark, pretty looks closely, I was convinced she was Jewish.

"Marion, come over here." Heinz smiled reassuringly. "We haven't shared any fine cognac for a long time."

I moved toward the table. He was right. He must have wondered why I was always "asleep" when he entered our room. I couldn't go on doing that.

"Excellent French cognac," he said as I got to the table. "Here, wait. Here's another glass."

I noticed that the bottle was about a quarter empty. Heinz had had a couple of glasses before I'd arrived. "Hey," he said, "what do you think of this letter?"

He began to read the letter he was writing. It was obviously to Elisabeth. "The war is near an end. We will be together again soon." I noticed tears forming in his eyes. I felt that I too might begin to cry. I was *very* fond of Heinz by now—and not only because he'd saved my lfe when he'd defended me to Emil. He was a good, decent human being. I started to comment on the letter when he interrupted. His next words ripped through me like a bolt of lightning.

"Tell me the truth, Marion. Are you a Jew?"

I was stunned. I gazed at the cognac in my glass. An eternity passed. Then he said, so quietly I wasn't sure I heard:

"I know, Marion. I've known for a long time. But you are not a Jew, a Pole, a German, or a *Volksdeutsch*—whatever—to me. You are a human being, like me. I am not a Nazi. I shit on them. I know what *Scheiss Hitler* has done to the Jews—to your own family, probably. He is a criminal. He has brought Germany to disaster.

"It's okay, Marion. As long as I'm alive, you are okay. I know how lonely and forlorn you must be. I promise you, on all that's sacred to me, that as soon as this war is finished— and it won't be long—I'll take you to Hamburg, to my home, to my family's gasthaus. You'll be content there."

I couldn't move from my chair. Neither could I utter a sound. Yet I knew he understood my silence. I stared at him.

After what must have been a long while, I rose. I felt tears falling from my eyes. I wobbled to my feet.

"Good night, Heinz."

"Good night, Marion," he said gently.

I lay awake a long time. A decent German soldier. Was it possible he existed in this den of wolves? Did I dare believe him? Did I have reason not to? Was it possible that a German could be a human being as well?

When I finally fell asleep I dreamt of Leon.

August 1944

Once on the other side of the creek at the edge of Opatov, I broke into a run. I knew they'd begin to search the area as soon as they saw the unhinged door.

I cut across the fields, not exactly sure where to go, but trying to head east toward the Vistula River. I avoided the field where animals grazed, because there would be herdsmen nearby. I followed the creek as far as I could. It soon became a river.

The ash and lindens were bright green with midsummer. Rye and barley crops were beginning to burgeon. The grasses were tall. Wildflowers bloomed. A soft breeze blew.

I stopped by the river to drink where it curved around a hill. Suddenly a blond boy of about seventeen appeared over the hill. He carried a stick; he was apparently a shepherd. There was no way to run.

"Good morning," I said as warmly as I could.

"Good morning," he said amiably, then—"*Amchu?*" (Jewish?)

I stared at him. My tongue was paralyzd. He approached me, put his hand on my shoulder, and whispered in Yiddish, "Don't be afraid. I'm also a Jew."

"Why are you soaked from the waist down?" he continued.

I hesitated.

"Well, come with me." He gestured with his crook.

I followed; *I could always turn and run*, I reasoned.

We walked for a quarter of a mile to where the fir and beech trees thickened considerably. He suddenly turned into an especially dense growth of trees, lifted a small beech tree, and exposed the entrance to an underground bunker.

The floor of the bunker was covered with straw. It was roomy. There were some clothes stacked in one corner. He gave me a faded pair of blue pants and some shoes.

"Now," he said, "I am Leon Chernikowski, once from Opatov. But not anymore. The Germans drag us off regularly. My home now is this bunker. It is now yours, also."

I stared at him. "You—you—" I stammered.

"It's okay. Listen. I have a girlfriend in Opatov. She's Polish. Her name is Krisha. She's also beautiful. She helps me out. Tells me what's happening outside. She comes here in the evenings. So you'll meet her. Meantime, you rest. I'll go back to the animals."

That evening, Krisha came to see us. The three of us sat in the fields as darkness fell, and we shared our adventures.

Krisha's blonde hair streamed halfway down her back, a smile played constantly on her lips and her blue eyes shone with good nature. She and Leon leaned on each other's backs as we sat in the field. Clearly, they were lovers.

"Tadek, I am delighted that you and Leon are going to share the bunker. It makes me less scared for him, knowing someone else is there with him. And don't worry—I'll bring food for the two of you," she reassured me.

I couldn't believe my luck.

The days passed quickly. Sometimes I helped Leon with the cows during the daylight hours. Other times I carefully explored the countryside, trying to map out the best way to reach safety. Maybe safety was with the Russians— who were, after all, fighting the Germans. How could I reach them?

Krisha was our prime source of news. Soon it was good news.

The Soviet army had reached the Vistula, which divides Poland into two halves and divides Warsaw into two sections: Praga on the east and the main portion of Warsaw itself on the west. Praga was by now almost completely under Soviet control—as was the entire eastern bank of the river. The Soviets had made a bridgehead at Sandomierz.

"They've apparently stopped there," Krisha told us. "They've dug in—just like the Germans. They're fighting each other with loudspeakers now—each side telling the other to surrender. It goes on all day and all night."

August 1944

The Nationalist Polish underground organizations had begun their revolt in Warsaw. "They are sure," Krisha said, "that the Soviet army will help them by furnishing them with weapons. Then the Soviets will attack the Germans, giving us the military help we need to defeat them."

The revolt had broken out under the orders of the commander-in-chief of the *Armia Krayova* (National Army), Genral Komarovski (Boreh), and the representative of the Polish government-in-exile in London, Yanovski.

Another week had passed when Krisha rushed across the field and hurriedly climbed into the bunker. "Mikolayi-chik, the Prime Minister of the Polish government-in-exile, has flown to Moscow to meet with Stalin and Molotov," she said, her eyes twinkling. "He's going to obtain military help for the rebels and to assure the turning over of the liberated Polish areas to the representatives of the Polish nationalists. Poland is going to be freed!" She kissed Leon.

But it soon became clear that Moscow had no intention of handing over the rule of Poland to Polish nationalists—or anyone except themselves. They wanted to establish a government in Poland that would be completely subordinate to Moscow and that would create a pro-Soviet Poland. Mikolayi-chik's mission was futile.

Meanwhile, the "National Army," untrained and poorly armed, was managing to sustain the revolt against the tens of thousands of well-trained, well-armed soldiers from the German regular army, the S.S. Corps, and the brigade of criminals. About twenty thousand were killed, and twenty-five thousand wounded.

"Yes," Leon said dejectedly, "and the Bolsheviks are sitting back, letting us and the Germans bleed each other to death. Then they'll walk in and take over."

Days passed. I had been with Leon and Krisha for almost three weeks. We cried the evening Krisha reported the Germans' revenge on the Poles: the destruction of Warsaw. "They bombarded it from the air and from the ground. Then they deliberately set it on fire." Her hair swung as sobs shook her. "The whole center of the city is gone."

Leon put his arms around her. I patted her shoulder.

We sat there in silence for a long time. Dear God, we

had thought the war was coming to an end—that the Hitlerite beasts were being routed at last—and now Warsaw was ashes and rubble.

Five days later, Krisha came into the bunker carrying a bottle of wine. "The Soviets have crossed the Vistula," she cried out. "They've liberated Warsaw from the Nazis. And they've established their own government. Let us celebrate." Krisha bent to kiss Leon.

That's when I decided I would have to reach the Soviets, come what may. If necessary, I would fight in the Soviet Army against Hitler's beasts.

"I've got to get to Sandomierz," I said with sudden iron determination.

"It's about twenty miles from here," Leon answered. He shot me a sideways glance.

"That's not far."

Two days later, at midnight, we sat up waiting for Leon. Several hours later, Krisha was in tears—as I nearly was. By then we couldn't even speak about it. We finally decided to part; she went to her family's house, I went to the bunker. I sat there and let the tears flow. Leon had become like a brother to me. Was he on his way to a labor camp in Germany? Had he been shot by now? Still waiting, I went to sleep for ten or fifteen minutes, then woke with a start.

Suddenly I heard someone approaching—the police, I was sure. They'd probably tracked me down as well as Leon. I was lost.

And then I heard Leon's voice. He was at the secret entrance. "Open up, Tadek," he called in a firm, confident voice.

Joyfully I opened the concealed panel. Leon jumped down. He stammered out what had happened:

"This morning I was standing in the fields, tending the animals as usual. All of a sudden two policemen approached me. They arrested me and hauled me off to the military quarters. Probably the same place they took you," he said heatedly.

"Anyway, they called some doctor in. Sonofabitch

pulled my pants down and, for whatever reason, decided I was a Pole."

I wondered if the doctor was a decent human being like the young policeman who had translated for me at police headquarters.

Leon continued. "Well, anyway, they took me to the local schoolhouse. There were dozens of guys our age there— all set for deportation to Germany, and you know what that means." He shook his head meaningfully. "And—there were quite a few Polish guys I knew in the hall and I was sure they'd inform the Nazis that I'm Jewish—to get themselves off the hook, of course. But they didn't. Probably too frightened to open their mouths." He reached for a potato.

"Anyway, they'd put straw on the floor for us to sleep on," he continued. "When they all went to sleep, I inched over to the window. Then I pulled it open. We were on the third floor. I held onto the woodwork and climbed down to the second floor. Damned near slipped off a couple of times, but jumped from the second floor to the ground. I don't know whether anyone saw me, but I ran like hell. And here I am. Got anything to drink?"

I poured what was left of Krisha's wine.

We stayed in the bunker for several days after that. Finally, we went back to our old routine.

"What are you going to do, Tadek?" Leon asked as we stood outside the bunker breathing in the heavy summer air. It was almost August.

"Sandomierz. I've got to get to Sandomierz. To the Soviets. I'll fight the Germans with them." I felt defiant.

"How do you know they'll protect you?" Leon asked in a low voice without expression.

I clenched my fists. "They will. They have to be better than the Germans, don't they?" I paused. "Leon—come with me."

"No, I can't." He shook his head. "I have some Gentile friends in Opatov. They'll let me hide in their cellar."

"How do you know they won't turn you in?" I asked, remembering my family's experiences.

"No—they won't. They're really good people, Tadek," he insisted. He looked at me. "But how are you going to get to Sandomierz?"

"I'll walk," I said determinedly.

November 1944

The following morning Heinz made his usual perfunctory visit to where we were serving breakfast to see that everything was all right. I couldn't look him in the eye. He could be shot because of me.

Gently, he put his hand on my shoulder and turned me towards him. He was smiling. "What good meal are you preparing for us today?" he said.

EIGHT

December 1944

I felt the tension in the air almost as soon as I woke up. Orders were being shouted outside. I washed and dressed as quickly as I could.

"Heinz, what's going on?" I asked anxiously.

"I don't know, but I'll find out as soon as I get to staff office. You go get breakfast ready."

"Okay," I stammered.

Kazia didn't show up in the kitchen. And I knew that unless I got some help the meals wouldn't be on time. I grabbed two privates, told them to watch over the kitchen, and started out for the village: I would ask the *soltys* for a couple of people to help.

Dozens of field gendarmes blocked the roads. They were going from house to house—obviously in a search expedition.

I turned back immediately. I wasn't about to come into contact with gendarmerie. I headed for the staff office where Heinz had his official post.

"Heinz, the woman has not shown up yet—I guess she couldn't get past the gendarmerie on the roads—and unless I can get a couple of assistants the meals won't be ready on time. Can you send a soldier to the *soltys* for two assistants?"

"Of course, Marion." He grabbed a form and wrote down an order. He called over a soldier standing nearby.

"Okay. I'll be in the kitchen," I waved at him.

"See you later," he murmured.

I thought about asking him if he'd found out anything but decided against it. He hadn't volunteered any information and I didn't want to arouse his suspicions. I headed back to the kitchen. Maybe I'd find out from one of the troops.

The gendarmerie kept the roads blocked and the peasants in their houses for two more days. Kazia returned to work on the third day. She slipped into the kitchen, and, satisfied that no one else was there, broke into a broad smile.

"Kazia, what—"

"Tadek, don't you know what happened?"

"No, what—"

"Listen. They've stolen a truck full of arms from the base in the village! Bolek's group. They entered the base at about two in the morning, dressed in German uniforms—"

I interrupted her with a tight hug. "Kazia, Kazia, this is wonderful."

"Let me finish," she smiled. "They got into the munitions store without a shot being fired."

"They had the password."

"Of course. Thanks to you," she murmured.

"Kazia, Bolek was right: I *am* more help to him here than out there."

She nodded enthusiastically. "Here is the best part: the guard not only let them in—he helped them load the truck!"

We giggled endlessly over that, stopping only when someone else entered the kitchen.

Later that evening, Heinz brought it up himself.

"Marion, I guess you've heard by now what happened," he said while he was writing still another letter.

"*Ja*. Some underground broke into our munitions store and stole a truck?"

"Full of arms and munitions! How in hell did they do it?" He sounded bemused. Was it possible he was not entirely displeased at this? Was I reading too much into his tone of voice, his raised left eyebrow? Was I putting it together too closely with his vehemently expressed attitude towards Hitler and the Nazis?

"What do they say?" I countered.

"Someone said they gave the password!"

My insides shrivelled. What in God's name would he do if he knew who'd given the password? *Calm yourself, Nachemia*, I told myself.

"Don't you think that's impossible?" I said, My heart was pounding.

"I would have thought so," he said. "Well, look, they got away with it. And they've disappeared into the air!"

By the time we arrived in the hall many of the officers, commissioned and noncommissioned, were there, drinks in hand, milling about. The lighted candles on the tree glowed softly but insistently.

Heinz pressed a glass of rum in my hand. "Enjoy yourself, Marion!"

I managed to wend my way to a corner. Was anyone looking at me for too long? Had Emil told any of the others that he "knew" I was a Jew? *They probably won't really notice me here*, I thought. I did my utmost to keep a pleasant expression on my face. But I couldn't understand their high spirits, their happy noise, their joviality; weren't they aware that they were being defeated daily on all their fronts? Weren't they aware that their kingdom was toppling?

"*Achtung!*" the lieutenant called out.

The orchestra stopped playing. Everyone got up. A slick-haired general, accompanied by a few senior officers, stalked into the hall. We all raised our right hands in salute, and called "*Heil, Hitler!*"

The general and his entourage walked to the head of the table. Someone poured him a cognac. He raised his glass.

"To the health of the Fuehrer, Adolf Hitler—*Sieg Heil!*" he intoned.

Everyone in the room responded with the same gesture and shout—I among them. My heart bled. I silently mouthed the words: "*Heil Henoch Wurman!*"

Then the orchestra broke into *Deutschland, Deutschland uber alles.*

Everyone sang. I moved my lips, but no words would

come. Heinz caught my eye from across the hall. *I'm not betraying you, Heinz. I'm moving my lips*. He looked at me with compassion. I fought back my tears.

The men resumed their eating and drinking. A barrel of rum, and bottles of cognac and other liquor were on the tables. As more liquor was consumed, the singing became noisier. Folk songs. Cabaret songs. Dirty songs. Popular songs. Christmas carols. I heard Heinz's voice rise above others . . . *Stille nacht, heilige Nacht* . . .

Towards midnight, the songs got faster and raunchier; groups of officers began linking arms and moving to and fro with the rhythm of the music. I stole out of the hall.

At dawn I had to wake Heinz.

"Marion," he rubbed his eyes tiredly, "where did you disappear to? The general wanted to thank the cook for the tasty food. And I couldn't find you."

"I—was tired," I stammered. "I came to bed."

He looked at me intently. "I know, Marion," he said quietly.

December 31, 1944–January 1, 1945

"Nothing fancy, like Christmas. No major preparations," Heinz smiled fleetingly. "Just a sort of—private party. It's a tradition—for certain people on the staff."

I nodded. *Not Emil, I hope.*

New Year's Eve arrived. At about 10:00, twenty sergeant-majors and other noncommissioned officers came into the kitchen. Silently I served them cognac. Within ninety minutes they were all blind drunk. I stepped outside for a breath of air.

There is a silence and a clarity about a snow-covered countryside like no other. The deep snow that covered everything magnified the stillness. Voices from other quarters in the encampment wafted over to where I stood; some raised in discussion, some raised in song.

I took a few deep breaths of the fresh, clean air, then I returned inside.

The food was all gone. But the liquor was still in abundance. Well, it was New Year's Eve. One of the officers decided to go outside. The suggestion was met with cheers.

I could hear their merry shouts and joking. Many had removed their jackets, but ran around as though it were spring or summer. They were so drunk they apparently didn't feel the cold.

"Heinz, can you walk?"

"Of course I can." He had difficulty standing on his feet. "C'mon—don't you want to greet the new year?"

"Yes, sure. Let's go." I put my arm around his back. He wouldn't have made it otherwise.

The others were singing lustily when we got outside. "They'll wake the whole post," I said to Heinz. I don't think he heard me.

Suddenly he slipped from my grasp and fell into a huge snowbank. He lay there absolutely still. I pulled his arms. He didn't move. I grasped his shoulders and pulled. He didn't move. I got hold of his legs and dragged hard. He didn't move.

"Heinz! Heinz!" It was useless. He was in a stupor. And he was going to freeze to death if he stayed there.

I ran over to a group of sergeants who were singing at the top of their lungs. "Heinz fell in the snowbank! We've got to get him out!" They didn't even hear me.

I ran to a couple of noncommissioned officers, standing by themselves and laughing.

"Please come," I prodded them. "He'll freeze. You've got to help me get him out." My words didn't register.

I ran over to another sergeant, leaning against the building, and tapped him on his shoulder. I was getting desperate. "Heinz is going to freeze to death. Please help me get him out of the snow."

"Wha—? Go 'way," was his bored reply.

Finally I ran into a barracks. I went straight to the guard. "Sergeant Klockmann has fallen into the snow and can't get up. Please—we must get him out of the snowbank."

The guard looked at me suspiciously. Then he seemed to decide that I was telling the truth. "Okay," he finally said.

He woke a couple of soldiers and explained the situation.

"I know," a stout fellow with a low voice said, "let's get a horse and sled and take him to his quarters. Between the four of us we can do it."

Heinz was a dead weight. The four of us struggled mightily getting him into the sled—and again when we got him to the room we shared. He never even opened his eyes.

Heinz slept for two full days. On both days I went to staff office and reported to the commander there, "Sergeant Klockmann will be late this morning."

On the second morning the commander laughed. "*Ja, ja*, we know," he said.

Heinz finally woke up after dinner. He had absolutely no recollection of what had happened.

"You were mighty heavy, I'll tell you that," I joked.

"Marion," his voice was heavy with emotion, "you saved my life. The others were too drunk to know what they were doing. They'd have left me. I owe you my life."

I looked at him for a long time. Finally, I spoke. "Well, Heinz. That makes us even, doesn't it."

It was January 12, 1945 when the Soviets attacked.

The estate on which we were encamped was about three miles from the front line. By mid morning the order from the German General Staff reached us: leave Vojnovitze and retreat westward, away from the front.

"Marion, get some help to distribute the 'iron rations' (dry commodities)—enough for five days," Heinz told me. "And see that the carts are loaded with our equipment as fast as possible."

"Yes sir."

I was taken by the efficiency with which the platoon prepared for retreat: every loading of the carts, every gathering up of equipment, every strapping on of arms, was accomplished with the precision of a clock.

We were divided into units, with a unit commander for each. The commanders appointed guides to stand along the road and watch for their units. "Marion," the commander said, "you are a guide."

Willi handed me an armband. "See," he said, "they can't lose you—and you can't lose them."

I looked about. The kitchen unit's carts bore the same insignia as my armband.

Automatically, the units lined up. Each manuevered right into position for march formation.

"We will take the main road to Suchedinov and camp there for the night," the platoon commander announced. "The guides will now go out and space themselves at mile intervals along the road. Watch for your units; units watch for your guides. Guides may join the units once you've met up with them."

Kazia rushed up to where Heinz and I stood. "Am I to go with you?" she asked plaintively.

I shook my head. *Yes, Kazia, I know. I also have nowhere to go.*

"Of course," Heinz said.

The platoon moved out of the estate with the military precision for which the Germans were famed—and feared.

"Marion, a wagon will drop you off about three miles down the road," our unit commander told me. "You stand there until you see the wagons of your unit approach. They will know they are on the right road when they see you. You may join them then. See you in Suchedinov."

"Yes sir."

As the wagon full of guides moved out of the estate I observed the platoons still stationed outside the village also moving into precise formation, preparing to join the headquarters battalion. All wagons were neatly packed. The troops stood at attention, ready for anything. *No wonder they've been victorious up till now*, I thought.

As planned, we reached Suchedinov by evening.

We were back on the road by nine o'clock the following morning, heading for Kielce. No one commented on the burnt-out villages that appeared from time to time along the sides of the road. No one commented on the signs that stood on the sides of the forests and warned, in German: "Do not enter forest; partisans!" I smiled to myself as I read these signs.

A tall blond officer drew his horse alongside our wagon. "The retreat goes well."

Heinz nodded.

Almost at once Soviet reconaissance planes appeared in the sky. They circled our lines several times, warningly.

Utter panic broke out. Soldiers yelled. They drove the carts to the trees and tied them there, then ran. Formations broke as the soldiers dove into the heaped-up trees lining the road.

I caught Kazia's eye. She seemed in high spirits.

Someone tapped me on the back of my shoulder. I jumped. It was Heinz. "Marion, we have to get out of here," he cried. "It's going to be hell in a couple of minutes. Come on." He motioned to me.

I signalled to Kazia to follow us. We dove into the nearest tree clump and fell into a deep ditch full of snow. Kazia cradled her left arm. We peeped out from our snow-filled foxhole. There were still a number of carts and horses— and soldiers—stuck in the middle of the road. Small bombs from the planes rained on them. As each bomb struck it burst into flames. The sound of gunfire crackled. Soldiers and horses tried to leap away from where the bombs struck; many didn't make it. Carts caught fire. Horses caught fire and whinnied with terrible noises. Soldiers screamed.

Finally, the Soviet planes disappeared. Bodies, many with the garments burned off, littered the road and the sides of the road, as did the corpses of horses. The sickening odor of charred flesh burned our nostrils.

Now the air was rent by shouts, groans, screams, and the neighing of horses who were still alive. We waited for about twenty minutes, then crawled out of the ditch and onto the road to help the wounded. Carts lay on their sides or upside down, their contents strewn across the road. Blood stained everything—especially the snow. Tanks burned with a flame that was bright even at midday. Many of the wounded were caught under the dead bodies of their comrades: they shouted for help. I recognized a few of the dead. Surreptitiously, I looked for Emil's body, but couldn't see it. Heinz, tears streaming down his face, called me over. He looked intently at me. *He's wondering what I'm thinking.*

"Let's see if we can find our equipment," he said.

We found it. It was completely destroyed.

Only then did we notice that Kazia was still holding her left arm. She was wounded. Heinz pulled out his field emergency kit and dressed the wound. "You'll be all right," he said kindly.

Kazia's eyes were wide and anxious.

"Well," he said, "let's try to reach Kielce. Perhaps another battalion will meet us there."

About a mile down the road we sighted a peasant driving a carriage. He was about thirty, with large brown eyes and sand-colored hair. He seemed oblivious to the surrounding disaster, but when Heinz stopped the carriage he leaped out of it in fright.

"It's all right, we're just trying to get to Kielce. We'll sit in the back. Drive," Heinz said. The man never took his eyes off the road.

By nightfall we reached a village of about fifty or sixty houses. It didn't appear that there were many people about.

"They're probably afraid of the bombings and are hiding in the woods," Heinz commented. "Let's stop here for the night. We're not going to make it to Kielce."

We looked around for a sign bearing the name of the village. There was none.

"Do you know what village this is?" Heinz asked our recruited driver.

The peasant shook his head.

"Okay, go on," Heinz dismissed him. We watched as he urged his horse into a fast trot.

We walked toward the largest house. It stood empty. The wood stove in the center of the room was still burning.

Primitive but charming hand-carved table and chairs stood under one window; two beds lined the opposite walls. A small room off the main room contained a bed and scarred maple dresser.

We looked around more closely. Milk and cream chilled in white clay pitchers on the windowsills. In the pantry, chicken, vegetables, and fruit were laid on chopped ice.

"Kazia, do you feel well enough to be cook tonight?" Heinz asked. "Marion and I have to gather our strength." His eyes twinkled.

Kazia smiled and nodded.

Somehow Kazia managed to find the housewife's store of spices. The meal—chicken scented with rosemary, vegetables with onion and dill, and boiled potatoes—was delicious.

"We'll let the lady have the largest bed," Heinz gestured gallantly toward the small room after dinner. Kazia smiled again.

I wondered if Heinz thought about whether she was Jewish. If he did, he never mentioned it.

"Well, Marion," he commented as we prepared for bed, "it's not the same accommodations as on the estate—but times are tough right now."

We laughed.

Footsteps scraped and crunched in the snow and voices were raised raucously. Light streamed through the shutters. We looked out. Soldiers were milling about the village huts. Many were going from small house to small house, searching for food. We dressed quickly.

"Good thing we got here first," Heinz muttered.

We went outside.

"What's going on?" Heinz asked the nearest sergeant.

I looked around. They all seemed to be sergeants or noncommissioned officers. I recognized quite a few from our battalion; the survivors.

"Haven't you heard?" came the response. "General staff ordered all officers, sergeants, and non-coms to assemble in this God-forsaken place to await orders."

"Ah well, we just thought we'd beat you to it," Heinz laughed.

"*Ja.*"

This was my opportunity to sneak off and get to the Soviets, I thought. If I can just tell Kazia quickly . . .

I couldn't. Heinz didn't leave my side. He took me with him to the assembly point where we were to receive orders from the General staff. At about 10:00 a car arrived in the field. I couldn't help thinking: *How many times have you stood in the middle of a field waiting for a car to arrive— whose occupants would then demand everything you owned in the world, including your life.*

Men in uniform jumped out of the car, ran around to the trunk and took out a large easel. They set it up about ten feet in front of us and unrolled a large map of the area. Then a general emerged from the car.

"*Heil Hitler!*"

"*Sieg Heil!*"

"Let us go over the stages of retreat," he said, producing a pointer. He turned to the map which had been set up on the easel. Many towns in the area were circled in red. "These towns circled in red are already in the hands of the Bolsheviks," he said.

A palpable shudder went through the assembled men. I studied the map intently.

"We have withdrawn from Kielce, Skarzysko, and Konsk," the general continued, pointing out each town as he mentioned it.

We were encircled by the Russian Army.

"We must break through. We can do it. There are six divisions in this area; we must concentrate near the town of Opoczno"—he pointed to it on the map—"and break through the ring heading west. Further orders on this operation will come through your division commanders. First, you must get the six divisions together.

"For now," he began to fold the pointer up, "blow up all tanks, armor, and trucks when they run out of fuel. Destroy anything you cannot take with you. And burn or blow up all the houses in the towns and villages you have abandoned."

"*Heil Hitler!*"

"*Sieg Heil!*"

The tension was unbearable. This was to be a literal battle of life or death. I hoped it was death for the Germans—except for Heinz. The unit commanders began to shout orders:

"Check which tanks and trucks still have fuel in them!"

"Destroy the carts and horses! We'll be moving too fast for them."

"Field gear and rations only!"

"Let's get this place burning; we'll get the others as we go along."

Heinz had gone to confer with other sergeants about march formation and field rations. I stood there, looking about me. It was their Armageddon. It was my day of liberation. Before long, I would be a free man for the first time in more than five years.

Once outside the village, we turned into what appeared to be another highway which branched off that leading to Kielce. Again, no one commented on the burnt-out villages we passed, nor the charred remains of German jeeps and trucks which occasionally blocked the road, forcing us to march around them.

We were skirting the Sviento Krzeskie Forest, I knew. I wondered how many partisan units crouched in its depths—as mine once had. More signs in German occasionally dotted the road: "Danger—Partisans"; "Bend down behind wagons"; "Do not go into the forest."

"How far is it to Opoczno?" I asked Heinz.

"I'm not sure—but I don't think we'll reach there by evening." He sounded thoughtful.

"Well, we didn't do too badly last night," I quipped.

He grinned at me.

Towards darkness, we came to a tiny village of about ten scattered houses. Again, no sign told which village it was.

"Do we camp here or burn it?" a bald-headed sergeant

asked, pulling his scarf higher up around his nose. Laughter ensued.

"Well, what shall we do?" another voice called out.

Suddenly we were bombarded. Russian *Katiushas* darkened the sky. They flew every which way, striking the fields indiscriminately. It was the scene on the road to Kielce all over again—only no horses screamed; they had been shot by their owners.

I ran and ducked into a clump of fir trees about a hundred yards away. I could see Heinz looking for me. I didn't move—or make a sound.

Heinz, I have to do this, I pleaded silently.

For the next half hour, the bombardment continued. Then abruptly it stopped, leaving blood, smoke, charred flesh and corpses in its wake. Heinz emerged from his hiding place and began to look for me. He approached a few other men, whom I saw shake their heads.

Heinz, please understand. My lips mouthed the words.

Slowly, the remaining troops gathered in loose formation. I could see Heinz's erect, graceful stance among them. He still looked around, searching for me.

"We'll go to the next village," he called out with firm dignity. They began to move away.

I waited until darkness fell. Parting the trees, I climbed out of my hiding place and jogged over to a hut. Inside softly lit lamps threw soft golden light onto the snow.

A weather-worn man and woman, perhaps in their thirties but looking older, and two children sat around the central stove, talking quietly. As I approached the circle of light they jumped to their feet.

"It's all right," I said in Polish. "I'm one of you." They looked dubious.

"I bring you no harm," I said. They looked at one another. "May I have something warm to drink?"

The woman moved toward the cupboard. Suddenly three German soldiers burst in; one was a captain. I saluted and displayed my armband, showing my status as a guide.

"What are you doing here?" the captain snapped.

"I'm waiting for my unit to show them the direction they have to go," I answered.

"Well, then, get outside and wait for them," he barked. "Your place is not in here. You must stand on the road. Now—out!"

I rushed out of the hut. There was a small shed nearby and I crouched down behind it. After about twenty minutes the three soldiers emerged.

As soon as they were out of sight, I went back inside the hut. The family was very agitated by now.

"Don't be afraid," I said patiently. "I'm not one of them." I jerked my thumb towards the door through which the Germans had left.

They still looked dubious.

"Will you give me something warm to drink?" I smiled reassuringly at the woman. She smiled tentatively, got up and moved toward the cupboard. She took a kettle from a shelf and set it on the stove.

"I'm not a German," I said, "I'm a Pole. In fact, I was in a partisan unit before I got into this uniform."

They stared at me.

"It was an accident. I just stumbled onto a German Army battalion. I'm telling the truth."

They seemed to visibly relax. So far not one of them had uttered a word.

"Now listen," I went on, "the Germans are going to set fire to the village tonight. I know this for a fact: orders from the high command."

"Are you sure?" the man spoke at last.

"I am positive. I heard it with my own ears. You must leave here as quickly as possible. Take with you what you can. All I ask of you is one of your coats and hats."

He got up, went over to a tall cabinet, and came back with a black cap and shapeless black coat.

"You must cross to the other side of the river; there are no Germans left there."

They packed a few belongings into rucksacks, strapped them to their backs, and we left the hut together. The fire was still burning. I thought of the still-burning woodstove Heinz, Kazia, and I had enjoyed in another nameless village a few nights ago.

The man was familiar with the route to the river and we crossed without mishap. No sooner were we on the other side when the village burst into flame. Orange-red light lit up the blackness. The five of us watched for about ten minutes.

"My God," the woman exclaimed softly, "you were right."

"Yes," I replied, "they are much more efficient destroying innocent folk than their enemies on the battlefield."

I turned to the man. "How far to the next village?"

He gestured with his hand. "About three hours' walk."

He knew the way through the white, hushed woods. Planes began to circle the area, their roar breaking the stillness, but as we got deeper into the forest the sound became muffled.

"Tell me," I said to the man, "why are there no signs telling the names of the villages?"

"Oh, we took them down. We don't want the Nazis to know where they are. Same with the roadsigns. You notice there are no roadsigns along the roads? All of us in the villages around here want to confuse Hitler's soldiers. So we take down the signs."

It was rough going. After a couple of hours the children began to weep with weariness. The man put his arm around the boy's shoulders; the woman took the little girl's hand.

"We must go on," she crooned to the little girl, "otherwise the Germans will kill us."

It was about one in the morning when we arrived at a village of widely scattered houses. The seventy or eighty houses appeared large and sturdy. Clearly, this was one of the more prosperous villages.

"I guess the sign for this one has also been removed?" I asked the man. He nodded.

It was buzzing with people.

"I see many from other villages," he commented. "Probably those which the Germans have set on fire."

I deliberately lagged behind the family and entered one of the larger houses, where dozens of people were milling about. I made my way to an empty corner. In the shabby hat and coat the peasant had given me I didn't attract attention. I prayed no one would look down and see my German military trousers and boots.

My body pleaded for sleep, but I couldn't give in. I had to be alert in case this village were bombed and panic broke out. I stared at the opposite wall as I took in the conversations.

"I tell you, the Bolsheviks are already in Konsk," a tall, burly peasant stated.

"That's only about ten miles from here," another put in.

"That's right. And they'll be right here by morning. Probably with bombs."

"Why are they bombing *us*?" a stooped older woman cried. "It's the Nazis they're after."

"Ah—they don't care who they get!" spat the young blond man beside her.

I left the house at dawn. It was bitterly cold. I wished I still had my warm German Army overcoat. A half-smile came to my lips.

Shots and explosions rent the sharp morning air. I was exhausted, hungry, and thirsty. And so the cold cut through me like a razor. But I couldn't think of that. I had to find the Russian Army. This was the moment: I would go to them, not wait for them to come and deliver me—they might entrench themselves in their positions as they'd done six months ago on the Vistula.

Some peasants were emerging from other houses. I approached the nearest one.

"Which way to the highway to Konsk?"

He stared at me, suddenly wide awake. "You want to go to Konsk?"

"Yes. Which way is the highway, please?"

"Are you crazy?"

I merely shook my head as I looked into his incredulous eyes.

"All right," he shook his head continuously. "Go on up here. You will come to the Konska Road in less than a mile. When you reach it, turn east—that's left. It's about nine or ten miles."

He was still shaking his head as I walked toward the road he'd indicated.

Konska Road was strewn with the corpses of German soldiers and the carcasses of dead horses. They were piled upon each other and upon the charred remains of carts, tanks, cars and trucks which lay splattered in the middle of the road and on either side.

Please, God, let Heinz not be among them.

I was torn between searching the face of each dead German and keeping my eyes straight ahead as I navigated around the charred, bloody, nightmarish mounds of flesh.

As the morning wore on, Poles appeared on the highway, scared, weary; were they all going to Konsk also? I wondered. A dark, bearded man came up alongside me. "Where are you headed?" he asked.

"Konsk."

"The Bolsheviks are holding it."

I nodded. "I know."

"So why are you going there?" He rubbed his grimy eyes.

"Well, they're routing the Nazis, aren't they?"

"Yah," he spat, "but they'll enslave us just as the Nazis have."

"Listen," I said. "Do you think it's safe for us to be walking along the highway like this? I mean—couldn't the Bolshevik planes return and bomb *us*?"

"What can we do? We've got to get to shelter and food."

"Yes," I interrupted, "but we could cut through the fields."

He shook his head vehemently. "Are you crazy? They've mined the fields. We'd be blown into pieces. You can't see the mines in the snow."

We stayed on the highway.

This time it's freedom, I whispered to myself. *It can't be otherwise. Why else have I survived for so long?*

And then in the distance we heard the rumbling, un-mistakable sound of vehicles approaching from the direction of Konsk. It must be the Soviets—or could it be the Germans? I wasn't sure, and there was no place to hide along the road.

There were about four cars. They were moving so fast that those on the road virtually leaped to the sides. They went by at high speed—and I couldn't tell to whom they belonged.

I resumed walking. The lack of sleep was really begin-ning to tell on me. More jeeps approached—about five or six. Again, cars went by at high speeds. Again I could not tell whether they were German or Russian.

This occurred three times. My companion had some-how disappeared. Suddenly, as a squadron of jeeps ap-proached, one turned directly toward me and stopped inches away. I still could not tell who they were. My heart pounded as three soldiers armed with automatic rifles jumped out and pointed the rifles at me. I saw by their uniforms that they must be Russians: they shouted at me in a language I didn't understand.

From the movements one of the soldiers made with his automatic, I realized they wanted me to raise my arms. Then I understood one word: "German . . ."

Of course, they thought I was a German. They saw the military trousers and boots under the short peasant's coat. They probably thought I was a deserter. I was going to be shot.

"No, no, no!" I shouted in Polish. "I am a Jew. A Pole! *Yevrei* . . ."

The soldiers began to search me. When they saw the rest of the military uniform under the coat they were certain I was a German.

"*Jestem Polak! Jestem Zyd! Jestem Yevrei!*" It became a chant.

When they completed their search and found no weapons, they stopped and stared at me. I continued to cry: "*Jestem Polak! Jestem Yevrei!*"

They ordered me into the jeep with gestures. I jumped in.

The jeep turned around on the road. We headed to Konsk. *Soon, Nachemia, soon*, I calmed myself.

Konsk was a little smaller than Ostroviec. The small houses looked huddled together in the snow. Like Ostroviec, there was a large market square, on which the wooden cross of the country church glistened in the sun. I looked for the synagogue, but couldn't see one in the streets through which we drove.

Soldiers, tanks, military cars, and jeeps were everywhere. All bore the Russian red star. The soldiers wore long, light beige military overcoats and fur hats, which made them seem tall and commanding. Loudspeakers, which had been installed on the roofs of many houses, blared Russian songs and marches.

We pulled up in front of a large, white building which must have been the municipal building and was now the military police station. Inside, some soldiers clustered near a scarred wooden desk. They spoke a Russian dialect similar to Slavonic Polish, so I was able to grasp most of their words. They were eyeing my trousers and boots. I kept repeating:

"I am a Jew. I know only Polish and Yiddish; I don't understand Russian."

Finally, I saw the staff sergeant behind the desk nod and turn to the soldier next to him, ordering him out. The room became silent. The soldiers sat staring at me.

The soldier who had been ordered out returned with an officer. The other men in the office saluted him. He walked right over to me. He was about my height and had dark brown eyes and hair. "*Amchu?*" he said.

My head spun. *I am saved! I am saved!*

Then the officer began to interrogate me in Yiddish.

"Where are you from?" he asked sternly.

"Korev."

"Who are your parents?" The officer stood over me menacingly.

I took a deep breath. "Henoch and Sarah Wurman. I have two brothers and two sisters: Eliezer—who is the leader of a partisan unit—Moshe, Chania and Chaike—Chayale."

"Where are they?" His voice rattled sharply in my ear.

"They took my father out of the Kazet concentration camp and sent him to Firley. I haven't heard about my mother or sisters or brothers."

"Now—how did *you* get into German military uniform?"

I told him everything. How I'd escaped. The people who'd been kind to me—and those who had not. My part in blowing up the German munitions train and motorcycles. My stay in Opatov and capture by the Luftwaffe—I told him of my dream about my father, and how I escaped from the cell there. My meeting with Leon Chernikowski. My determination to reach the Soviets at Sandomierz and my stumbling upon the Seventy-second Fusiliers.

His brown eyes filled with tears. But he was a soldier, and there were other soldiers present watching the two of us. He continued interrogating me.

"I know that you have encircled this area," I told him. "At the village outside Kielce a general in Hitler's army gave orders that they were to break through the encirclement near Opoczno and continue west."

He turned to an officer seated at a desk and asked him for a map.

"Show us on the map," he ordered me.

As I found Opoczno on the map, the other soldiers in the room gathered around us. The captain spoke to them rapidly. He was relating the German Army's operation plans to them.

He motioned to me to be seated on a nearby bench, onto which I sank gratefully. He turned to the others and told them my story. Two of them stared searchingly at me, then back to him. At the end of his recitation, the officer seated at the desk got up and shouted orders into another room.

In less than a minute, a tall, swarthy-skinned major walked into the room. His stern face was encased in black hair, and he had a black moustache. Everyone stood up and saluted. I thought it best to stand up and salute also. The officer looked at me quizically.

Three of the staff began talking at once. They took him to the map and pointed at it. From time to time the officer turned and looked me straight in the eyes.

I felt the tension break about a second before the attitude toward me changed palpably. Their suspicions had turned to sympathy.

Still, I was kept in detention. I was shown to a small room with a window. I was to keep to the building. I couldn't go anywhere without a guard—even the bathroom.

Hang on, Nachemia. Freedom is here, I thought, calming myself.

Later the captain tapped me on the back as I stood at the window of my "room" looking out into the main square of the town. Memories of the town square of Ostroviec were crashing through my head like waves in a storm. *No more Jewish blood staining cobblestones*, I thought. *No more searches at 2:00 a.m. No more cries of "Jews out!"*

I turned to the captain. "Stout fellow!" he bellowed, grinning from ear to ear. "You have given the commander *very* important information. We've already begun to track them . . ."

Have I signed Heinz's death warrant? I wondered guiltily.

But, I comforted myself, I had avenged my people: my father, perhaps my mother and brothers and sisters, my uncle, probably my cousins—and my people in general. I had done something against the Nazi murderers.

The captain saw the strong emotions cross my face. He patted my shoulder. "I know, Nachemia," he said. "I know what you must be feeling. Listen, I'm proud of you," he beamed.

I looked in his eyes. "Thank you, captain," I murmured.

But they still kept me in the room, under guard. I was

well treated, and well fed. But I kept asking myself, why were they detaining me?

Didn't they trust me?

Well—I didn't trust anyone; I could see their point.

The room wasn't locked up all the time. Snatches of conversation drifted toward me as the soldiers passed down the corridors. I learned that Ostroviec had been liberated. Were any of my family still there? I had to get out of here and find them.

Sometime in the middle of the third day Captain Lonka came into my room. "Nachemia, you are free."

I jumped up and clasped his shoulders. "I know, I know," he responded.

His eyes glistened with tears.

"Captain Lonka, could I go to Ostroviec?" I pleaded.

"Ostroviec?" His voice had a touch of sharpness.

"Yes. To look for my relatives who may still be alive."

"Oh. Yes." He shook his head agreeably. "I don't see why not. But listen, I'll go with you. You don't have any documents, you know; you may run into trouble."

"When can we start?"

"Tomorrow," he answered soberly. I guess my face fell. "Look," he said, "meantime, you come into my room and rest on a decent bed. We'll give you better food."

I followed him. His kindness touched me deeply. He had a large bedroom; its window overlooked the city. He saw me eyeing the chintz wing chair which stood invitingly in the corner.

"Yes, go on over and make yourself comfortable," he said kindly. "Let me see what I can get from the kitchen."

Soon he was back with a steaming dish of hearty beef stew, rice, and tea. It was delicious. "Officers *do* eat better than prisoners," I quipped.

His laugh filled the room. We spoke well into the night about my travails since the war had broken out.

"Hasn't Poland always been anti-Semitic?" he asked me.

"Yes," I said sadly. "I remember, well before the war,

the anti-Jewish campaigns. There was a priest in Kurov, a Christian priest, who regularly led a band of youngsters who thrashed us on our way to *cheder*. No one stopped them."

"There is anti-Semitism in Russia, too," he said soberly. "How strong, I don't know. It seems that this whole stupid war was just an excuse to accelerate anti-Jewish feelings."

"You know, the non-Jewish Poles call themselves 'pure Poles,'" I said.

"I know," he responded. "We have our 'pure Russians,' too."

We looked at each other.

Abruptly we changed the subject.

"You know nothing of what happened to your family—except your father."

I paused, considering. "They probably killed my older sister, Chania, once I escaped from the concentration camp," I said. "If one member of a family escaped, they killed the remaining members in the camp . . . Mother and Chaike—I don't know. Moshe—I don't know." My thoughts became agonizing; I turned away.

"Is anyone left?" he inquired.

"Perhaps Eliezer—he may still be leading his group against the Germans. I haven't heard."

"What about *your* partisan group? What's his name—Bolek?"

"Bolek, right. The last I heard he and his group stole the truckload of munitions out of the encampment on the estate. Thanks to my having given them the password through Kazia."

"I guess you haven't heard from Kazia."

I shook my head sadly. "No. Not since you bombarded the retreating battalions on the road to Kielce."

"Ah. She probably perished in that."

My eyes wandered to the window. I said softly, "I'm wondering about Heinz. A good man. A decent man. I am torn: I gladly gave you the information about the attack at Opoczno, but by doing so I may have been responsible for his death."

I felt the tears rise to my eyes. "You know, Captain Lonka, he could have been shot for sheltering me as he did. He was a *very* good man. He hates Hitler."

"Who doesn't?"

"The S.S., the Gestapo, the—"

"Yes, Nachemia, but they are as perverse as Hitler himself. And stupid to let themselves be taken in by his mad rantings." He shook his head. "Now you're wondering if you haven't gotten Heinz shot."

"Yes," I whispered. "That is exactly what I'm wondering."

"Come on, we can't have you going out in those rags," Captain Lonka greeted me early the next morning.

I trotted along behind him through the old, musty building, down two flights of cobwebbed stairs to the basement. He pounded on one of the doors. The soldier who opened it saluted.

"Take his measurements—not to the millimeter, there's no time—and outfit him."

Once again I was transformed into military garb—this time a long Russian overcoat and a fur cap.

As I'd done five months before, I studied my reflection in the mirror. There was no shock, no stomach churning, no tearing questions. I was happy—and slightly amused.

As if reading my thoughts, Captain Lonka quipped. "You look good, Nachemia. See—you should have joined up with us first—somehow that *kufaika* (overcoat) and hat suit you."

I turned to look at him. "Well, I tried to, you know," I responded.

We both laughed. The soldier looked from one to the other questioningly.

I remember the date exactly: it was Saturday morning, the eighteenth of January, 1945.

"Now, some breakfast, and we go," Captain Lonka said reassuringly.

We ate in the dark-wooded dimly lit dining room with the rest of the soldiers and officers. It seemed to take an eternity. Lonka smiled at me over tea.

"Okay, I've got a jeep waiting for us," he finally said.

It was bitterly cold outside, but I felt it only on my face: the Russian Army uniform took care of the rest of me. What do the rest of them think, I wondered as we climbed into the jeep.

The jeep made its way through the crowded streets of Konsk and finally onto the road towards Ostroviec. Snow covered the buildings and trees. Even with the devastated villages that marred the landscape, the countryside looked absolutely beautiful to me.

NINE

At midday the market square was deserted. The snow on the streets had been trampled to slush. Ostroviec was a study in stained whites, discolored browns, and dingy grays. There seemed to be no visible damage to the town.

Where were the people? I wondered.

"Okay, Nachemia, here you are," the captain gestured.

I turned to my new friend. "Captain Lonka, I can't thank—"

He cut me off. "Do not thank me. For what? For helping a brother? That is what we're supposed to do, Nachemia. All of us. You be well."

"Go with God, Captain Lonka."

We clasped hands. We embraced. I climbed out of the jeep. The driver turned it around, heading back towards Konsk. Lonka and I waved at each other until the jeep turned a corner, vanishing from sight.

I headed toward the old Jewish section, down Church Alley. At last I saw someone: a tall, thin woman, covered almost completely by a brown shawl, walked ahead of me. She carried a heavy basket and moved very slowly. As I came closer to her I heard her talking to herself in Yiddish. Suddenly I tensed, listening:

"If I at least knew where Nachemia's grave is . . ."

I grabbed her arm. She jumped. "Who are you?" I asked.

Turning towards me, she moved the shawl away from her face.

"CHANIA!"

She dropped the basket.

"NACHEMIA!" *Oh my God! Oh my God! You're alive—"* Then the words stopped. We embraced fiercely. We stood there a long time in the middle of Church Alley, crying wordlessly. The tears froze on our faces.

We stepped apart and stared at each other intently. She had braided her long, dark hair and had wrapped the braids around her head. She had become so thin, her eyes were enormous in her face. We stroked each other's faces. The past five years etched in our eyes.

She broke the silence. "Nachemia, you've grown taller since—" Her voice broke and abruptly she changed the subject. "Come, let us go to my quarters." She bent toward me again. "What are you doing in Russian uniform?"

"I'll tell you my story, Chania. And you tell me how you're still alive."

We slowly walked towards the old ghetto.

"Ostroviec was liberated only four days ago," she told me as we climbed the stairs to her rooms. "When I came back from the forests, where we'd been hiding I went straight to Uncle Matityahu's house. Of course, Poles had taken it over. But the Russians were providing for Jewish survivors, and I went then to the City Hall and they assigned me these quarters. There is a kind of public kitchen the Red Cross set up about five blocks from here where we eat. I guess that's where everyone is right now."

She looked at me, still incredulous. "Nachemia, I can't believe it's you. Tell me—"

"Not yet, Chania. Tell me first how you survived. I was sure they'd kill you—when I escaped from the iron factory."

"Your coat—your Russian coat, little brother." She took off her shawl and held out her hands for my coat, then placed them both in a small closet. She came back and we embraced again. "Come," she said, "let us sit here." We sank into an old sofa.

I looked around. The room was small; the faded sofa and two stained chairs had seen better days. A sink took up one corner; a wood-burning heater another; a table and cabinet, or cupboard filled the rest of the space. I could see an iron cot in the next room. How different it was from the well-furnished home of our parents.

The windows let in a pleasant amount of the thin winter light; Chania's large blue eyes glistened when she turned toward me.

She began. "The day you escaped there was a lot of confusion because, you know, they shot all the Jews they rounded up from the Goering factory. They hadn't gotten us out of the brick factory, yet, though. At around noon the Ukrainian guards arrived at the brick factory and gave orders to all the Jewish workers to assemble by the gate of the factory.

"I had a bad feeling. I left my station and hid in a water ditch almost under the building. But I was not the only one there; two other Jewish girls, whom I knew, were already in the ditch. The water was filthy: it was mixed with the clay they used to make the bricks. We stood in it up to our necks until it was very late. The whole time we heard the shouting of the Ukrainians and shots. We trembled with fear. But they never found us. When it was pitch black we climbed out of the water and ran for the forests.

"Way into the woods there were other Jews—about our age—who had also managed to escape. We stayed together. We thought then that liberation would come any day. The Germans were being defeated on most fronts. At first we sat and waited. It was freezing. We took turns going back into the surrounding villages for food."

"How did you get the food?"

"We begged—or we . . . stole.

"After a couple of weeks we realized that liberation was still a way off. So we organized into a sort of partisan group." She smiled. "Like Eliezer."

"And me," I said.

"You, Nachemia?"

"Yes, yes. But first—tell me the rest."

"We dug out bunkers, managed to get straw to line

them. We spaced them far apart so that they would not discover us all at once, if they came into the woods.

"Shifra Weinberg—do you remember her from Ostroviec? She was here before we arrived. Blonde, brown eyes—we worked at the brick factory."

"Yes, I remember her. She had a brother—Joseph."

"Well, Shifra and I became close. Often we'd go to the villages for food together.

"One of those times we went into a small village called Ruda Koshcielna."

"What!" I interrupted Chania excitedly.

"Ruda Koshcielna," she answered. "Why? What does that mean, Nachemia?"

"A lot!" I felt as if electricity was coursing through me.

"Nachemia, are you all right?" She bent towards me.

"A miracle," I began to cry. "A miracle."

"Nachemia—?"

"Chania, tell me. Tell me what happened in Ruda Koshcielna. Then I've got to tell you something."

"What? Were you in Ruda Koshcielna?"

"No. But I was nearby. Did you go to the house of a peasant—about fifty, with gray hair, who limped?"

"My God, yes! I will never forget that peasant. He carried a walking stick, he limped so badly. There were four of us—Esti, Beniek, Wohlek, and me. His house was at the edge of the town, and the lights were on inside. There was a small wooden barn, a stable, and a chicken coop. We split up into two groups; Esti and I on the right side of the house, where there was a side entrance, and Beniek and Wohlek on the other. Beniek and Wohlek had rifles. They hid behind the stable. Suddenly a dog began to bark; we all jumped. But he was chained, or else we would have been ripped to pieces."

I was at the edge of my chair by now. She paused and looked at me questioningly. "Go on, Chania, go on," I urged.

"Well, the peasant must have heard the dog's barking, and he came out the side door. It was too late for us to run away or hide: the dog was behind us, the peasant in front of us. He started to scream "What do you want?' and we told him we wanted to buy food. He raised that walking stick and began to hit me with it. He was screaming 'Dirty Jews. I'll kill you!" I thought the whole town must have heard it. I fell. Esti screamed. Beniek and Wohlek came from behind the stable with their rifles pointed at him. They took his stick away and helped me up. I could tell right then that I'd hurt my arm. Beniek and Wohlek ordered the peasant back into his house, and we followed him. His wife was scared out of her mind. I told them to give us something to eat, that we were starving. The peasant slyly said he'd go out to the coop and get some eggs, but we were too smart for that. Beniek ordered him to sit down and not move. Wohlek accompanied his wife.

"No one said a word until Wohlek and the woman returned from the chicken coop with a basket full of eggs. Esti and I headed straight for the kitchen; we took the woman with us, to fry the eggs. Heniek went to the basement and brought up a pot of milk. There were about twenty eggs. It was a royal treat. The old man sat there scowling the whole time, of course. After we'd gorged ourselves on the eggs and milk, we found two empty sacks and filled them with bread, vegetables, fruits, and cheeses.

"Then we got ready to leave. We told the peasant that if he told the authorities we would come back and shoot him and his wife. On the way out we took a couple of chickens out of the coop.

"Now, Nachemia—" her eyes glistened, "tell me the miracle."

I nodded. "Well, Chania, the bastard *did* go to the authorities. To the *Wehrmacht*, in fact."

She gasped. "How do you know?"

"How do I know? I was there—in the *Wehrmacht*—"

"Whaaat—?" she asked.

I smiled. "They called me over to headquarters, where he was, because they needed someone to translate from Polish to German. Of course, I was scared. Anyway, there he was, kind of stocky, gray hair, leaning on a walking stick."

Chania's eyes were as round as saucers.

"The commander asked me to find out what he wanted.

I turned to him and asked him in Polish what was the matter. He said that in the middle of the night two men and two women, all Jews, had come to his house and demanded food, had threatened to kill him if he didn't give them food. He said he'd had no choice but to fill two bags with food for them. He didn't mention the eggs and milk," I chuckled.

"What did you say to him?" Chania breatheed heavily.

"Well, I translated for the commander. But I changed his story a bit. But—I was frightened that perhaps the Pole understood German."

Chania grabbed my hand. "Did he?"

"No, I guess not, but I was *very* nervous. The peasant was insisting that he lead the officers to where the Jews were hiding. He said he knew. Believe me, I was sweating like mad. I hesitated in facing toward the commander, for fear he would see my nervousness, so I turned my back toward him while I was interrogating the peasant.

"Finally, the officer said—I guess he was getting tired of the whole thing—'What does this peasant want?' I half-turned, so I could see both the Pole and the officer, to see if the peasant understood German. He didn't seem to comprehend."

"Well, what did you tell the officer?" she asked mischievously.

"I told him that the peasant came to report that thieves had come to his house and had stolen food from him and ran into the forests. That he wanted us to send soldiers there to find the thieves. Well, the officer got angry. He got to his feet and shouted, that I should tell 'this Polish swine'—" I broke off as we both laughed—"that the *Wehrmacht* has no time to go chasing after bandits, that we were fighting a war. Then he told me to tell him that if he were giving the rations he was supposed to to the army the thieves would have nothing to steal."

Chania was laughing gleefully by now.

"Anyway," I continued, "then I told the peasant what the officer had said—and added a few words of my own: 'Get lost, and don't come back here again.' And for an old guy with a limp, he moved very fast."

Again we laughed. Then I got serious. "I watched him get into his horse and wagon outside the commander's post, and thought that if I'd had a rifle I'd shoot him. I thought of Zivja and Ester—how a Pole had gone to the gendarmerie and revealed their hiding place in the Christian's house. And how the gendarmerie took them to the graveyard and shot them to death—Zivja begging them to shoot her and let the baby live. God, Chania, I could hear the shots that killed them, could almost see the blood."

"Nachemia, don't cry." She grabbed my arm.

We sat in silence for a while.

"Nachemia," Chania said quietly, "you know, you saved my life."

It was true. Had anyone else been called into headquarters that day, he would have translated the old peasant's words verbatim. I felt, then, that I was protecting my fellow Jews. I had no idea in the world that I was protecting my own sister.

"Thank God, Chania," was all I could manage to say.

"Nachemia, you were in the *Wehrmacht* . . .?" She prodded.

"Yes," I nodded positively, "I will tell you, Chania, I promise. But first you must finish telling me about you."

"Oh, all right," she sighed.

"One time a peasant woman invited us into her house and served us a warm meal. It tasted delicious, Nachemia. Anyway, as we were eating, we happened to notice two men in the next room—they were in their twenties, I guess—and they were studying a map. Shifra and I looked at each other: since when do peasants study maps? Who were these two? We whispered to each other; we decided they must belong to one of the underground groups—and maybe it was the *Armia Krayova*. We had to get out of there quickly. We thanked the old woman and got up. She went to the pantry and brought out a loaf of bread, wrapped it up, and gave it to us.

"We were about a hundred yards away from the hut when one of the men came running out after us. We ran as fast as we could but he caught up to us. We were sure we were as good as dead. But—God was with us. The man said, I think, 'Don't be afraid. My name is Heniek. My friend is Stash. We know you're Jewish. You're safe with us.' We found out later that he was an intelligence officer in the Polish National Underground. Anyway, he warned us that it was dangerous to go near the Nationalist underground bases."

Chania smiled. "He was a Godsend, Nachemia. We were so lucky to have run into him. He arranged to meet us regularly near the little village and to give us news of where and where not to go, which villages to avoid. Our group in the woods provided him with information we gathered from our people who visited other villages and even Ostroviec. So you see we had our own underground network."

She leaned back and smiled. Somehow these past couple of years had heightened her beauty, etched the structure of her face more clearly.

"In May, it was decided that Shifra and I had to go into Ostroviec. We hadn't been in the town for ten minutes when a Pole recognized Shifra. Before we knew it two policemen were upon us. They arrested us and took us to the German gendarmerie, and *they* took us to the Gestapo."

"Dear God . . ." I whispered.

"Yes, I was sure this was my death. The Gestapo took us into separate rooms. They beat me with their fists and with sticks, trying to get me to say I was Jewish. I kept repeating that I was a 'pure Pole,' that I was Catholic and— that I didn't know the other girl, that we just happened to be walking together. Oh, Nachemia—they put me into a cellar that was totally black and left me for what must have been hours—"

I put my arms around her and rocked her.

"Chania, Chania." Tears filled my eyes.

"—but I would not give in," she sobbed. "They brought me up from the cellar. The Pole who had turned us in was there. He told them he didn't know me, but knew Shifra for sure—remembered her from Ostroviel. He told them her name. Shifra was in the other room. I managed to see her through the doorway. They had beaten her, too. Her face was covered with black, blue, and red marks."

"Suddenly the Gestapo in that room grabbed her and dragged her out to the yard. Nachemia, my heart stopped, I swear it. I heard her scream the same instant I heard the shot—" her voice cracked "—I kept my face absolutely immobile. Oh God! It was so hard to—" she stopped as the tears ran down her face.

We sat silently for a few minutes. Again, I held her tightly in my arms.

"Anyway," she finally said, "they let me go. I went right back to the forest. I didn't stop for food. We lived there from then until now—four days ago. Somtimes we were close to starvation. Sometimes Heniek was able to get us a little food—but never enough to assuage our hunger. My clothes became rags. Sometimes I couldn't wash for days—once it was for weeks.

"And we moved deeper into the forests; dug new bunkers. Sometimes on Heniek's advice. The men were able to get a few weapons—guns—from the underground, so we weren't entirely unprotected. But there was constant fear. Even today, I don't know why or how I survived the run from the labor camp into the woods; survived the Gestapo's questioning and torturing." A gasp escaped her lips, and I stroked her hair which had come loose from the braids she wore. She paused, trying to calm herself.

"It got very cold by the end of November," she went on.

I nodded knowingly.

"When the liberation came, a group of Soviet soldiers came to the village and told us we could return to Ostroviec. Our clothing was almost in tatters by then. We were close to freezing. Some of the group had frostbite—I never got it, thank God. Anyway, they guided us back to Ostroviec, to the center where the Russians provided for us. First I broke off and went to Uncle Matityahu's house, but then I went back to the center. Well, that's how I got these rooms. They gave us food and clothing and—" She got up suddenly overcome by emotion and turned away. "Look, Nachemia, I can make tea on this little wood heater. Why didn't I think of that before."

Her hands shook as she opened a cupboard, took out some tea, and got a small scarred pot which she filled with water. Then, as if calmed by the small tasks, she came back, served us, and began to speak again.

"Almost as soon as I got into Ostroviec I began asking about you, and Mother and Moshe and Chaike. Someone—I don't remember who, now—told me that you'd fallen into the hands of the Gestapo."

"The *Luftwaffe*," I said.

"The *Luftwaffe*?"

"Yes."

"How did you escape?" Her eyes widened.

"Daddy helped me."

"What, Nachemia?"

"Chania, I have lots to tell you."

Chania's eyes filled frequently with tears as I told her my story.

She was silent for a long time after I'd finished describing Lonka's driving me to Ostroviec in the jeep. At last, she said, "That Heinz. A truly good and beautiful human being."

"There is no doubt of that. I pray daily that I did not—" I swallowed hard "—sign his death warrant when I told the Soviets that the battalions were headed for Opoczno. He was—*is*—my savior, Chania. Have I betrayed him?" I muttered half to myself.

"Nachemia, listen. No. I don't think so. I think someone like Heinz will survive—as you have."

"Please, God . . ."

"Yes."

People on the streets stared at us as we made our way to the City Hall where the offices of the Russian organization aiding surviving Jews was located. They must have been asking themselves, what was a Bolshevik doing with this woman?

About a block away from the public kitchen, a tallish, well-built man in civilian clothes strode toward us. Seeing him, it was as though I'd been struck by lightning. That warm, sensitive face. Suddenly five years rolled back and he was patting my shoulder in the barracks of Kazet while I wiped the blood off my face where Puczic had struck me. Abek Fridenthal!

I stared. He approached Chania, smiling perfunctorily at me. Obviously, he didn't recognize me.

"I've just come from one of the villages near the forest," he said to Chania. "Iche-Meir Birenzweig—remember, he stole Betcz's uniform and escaped—and Alte, are there. They said they saw Nachemia in a German Army uniform. He's alive, Chania. He—"

I couldn't keep quiet any longer.

"He sure is, Abek," I interrupted.

He looked at me for the first time. He stared. Then he gaped.

"*Nachemia?*"

I grinned.

"*Nachemia!* Oh my God!"

We threw our arms around each other.

"Come with us to the kitchen, Abek," Chania said. "Nachemia will answer the questions you want to ask—like how he got into Russian uniform."

"But in abbreviated form, Abek," I said. "My throat is getting sore."

I don't remember what we had to eat in the public kitchen, but I remember that, with Chania and Abek on either side of me, it tasted wonderful.

As we were finishing our dinner, a short, well-groomed, Russian officer strolled to our table.

"Another Russian soldier, I see," he said.

"A Jewish one," I replied.

"As I am."

"What?"

He extended his hand: "Misha Rosov," he smiled. "I am assistant to the Russian Commander in Ostroviec."

"Nachemia Wurman," I responded, pumping his hand. "I've just arrived from—well, all over Poland, but most recently Konsk."

He was about thirty-five, quite dapper. "May I sit down?" he asked.

"Of course. This is Abek Fridenthal, and my sister, Chania Wurman."

We chatted a long time. Misha came from Moscow. He was well educated, played the violin, he told us. Chania and I exchanged glances. We both thought of Eliezer.

I noticed that his uniform had quite a few medals. He saw me looking at them and shrugged.

Misha included all of us in the conversation. He discussed the Committee and its relation to the Russian command with Abek. "Chania," he said, musing, "do you cook homemade Jewish food?"

Chania's face lighted with a soft smile. "Yes," she breathed. "My mother taught me well."

Impulsively, I said, "You must visit us, Misha. Chania will cook you a meal that will tear your heart out."

Misha broke into a huge grin. "I am going to take you up on that, Nachemia."

"I hope that includes me," Abek laughed.

We had a new friend.

Neither Chania nor I could get any information about the rest of our family in Ostroviec—not even Moshe and Gershon, Uncle Matityahu's sons. But we learned that Krashnik had been liberated about five or six months previously and that the Jews who had belonged to the partisan groups in the area, or had escaped the camps where Mother, Moshe, and Chaike had been incarcerated, had gathered there.

We decided I would travel to Krashnik and learn what I could.

"Maybe Eliezer is there."

Krashnik was about sixty miles east of Ostroviec. I set out on foot. It was bitterly cold and I was thankful for my

Soviet uniform. The Vistula was frozen solid—which was fortunate, since all the bridges over it had been destroyed. I just walked across.

The snow had frozen to the branches of the trees and to the vegetation that had remained in the fields, so that it appeared as though everything wore a mantle of lace. I drank it in; I had been unable to see such details on our forced marches from the ghetto or from the concentration camp to the factory. Now—it was beautiful.

Occasionally, because of my uniform, I was able to hail a peasant driving a cart and demand that he take me as far as he was going towards Krashnik. I averaged about five miles on each ride. I disclosed my true identity only to one peasant; the others must have wondered at a Soviet soldier who spoke such perfect Polish.

My journey took three days.

Before the war, Krashnik had a Jewish population of about five thousand people; now there were virtually none. I went to the center of the city which, like Ostroviec, was still intact. I stared at every face I saw. Where were all the Jews? And where were those whom I'd heard had been partisans in the area and had come to Krashnik when it had been liberated?

Finally I recognized one Jew. I stopped him. He was very nervous.

"*Amchu?*" I said.

He looked lingeringly at me, then at my uniform.

"*Jesten Yevrei,*" I smiled.

He relaxed. "My name is Leon Brener."

"Where are all the Jews in Krashnik?" I asked.

He hesitated. "There are only about one hundred of us left."

"Any from the partisan groups?"

"Some." He nodded positively.

"Do you know Eliezer Wurman, leader of the partisan group in the Rzecice forests?" I queried.

"I've heard of him, but I don't know him. I don't know

what happened to him. But wait," he brightened. "I know someone who was in that partisan group."

"Can we go and see him now?" I asked.

He looked at me, questioningly.

"Eliezer is my brother. I am Nachemia Wurman."

"God bless you!" he exclaimed. "Eliezer has done great things for us."

"Yes, Eliezer is a great man," I replied.

It was bitingly cold as we wended our way through the streets to an older section of the city.

We climbed three flights of stairs in an old, weathered building that seemed only slightly less cold inside than out and knocked on a dark, scarred, wooden door. A youth about eighteen answered.

"Hersh," said my companion, "this is Nachemia Wurman. He is Eliezer Wurman's brother."

Hersh Brenner, thin, wiry, with a shock of dark hair, grapsed the epaulets on both my shoulders. "Bless you, bless you, brother of Eliezer."

Overcome, I embraced him. "You were in Eliezer's group?"

"Yes, yes. And proud to be under his leadership."

"Yes," I said simply.

"Come in, come in. Let me make us some tea. It's warm in here."

And it was. The room, sparsely furnished, nonetheless seemed welcoming. I removed my overcoat. Hersh beckoned us to sit as he brewed the tea. He pointed to my uniform questioningly.

"Don't worry. I will explain later what I'm doing in Russian uniform," I grinned.

When it was finished, Hersh brought us each tea in steaming glasses. We sat for a while in silence, sipping the delicious hot liquid.

"Tell me, Hersh," I finally said, "about my brother.

He began:

Eliezer was originally sent to Budzyn about three miles from Krashnik, with Mother, Moshe, and Chaike. He desperately wanted to escape and join the partisans, but knew that they would have killed the rest of his family immediately. So he set about getting himself transferred to another camp, "Krashnik."

As it turned out, certain of the inmates in Krashnik, who probably knew him through his *Betar* activities in Kurov and who heard he was in Budzyn, figured that Eliezer could help them organize an escape. They went to the camp "management" and suggested that a radio workshop be set up in the camp—and that there was a highly talented electrician in Budzyn who could run the shop.

Perhaps camp "management" had the idea of a radio repair shop themselves. In any case, Eliezer was transferred from Budzyn to Labor camp. The Germans began to bring radio sets into the shop almost as soon as it was opened. And while no Jew was allowed to listen to a radio, Eliezer had someone stand outside the shop so he could listen to the news as he worked on the radios. That's how he learned that the Germans were suffering more and more defeats. And he passed the news on to those he trusted.

There were Jews who could not be trusted. They would turn on their own to curry favor with the Germans. They would not have hesitated to report that Eliezer was passing news from the front on to the others. The very thought must have been extremely painful. But Eliezer had a sort of sixth sense about whom he could trust.

The guards must have gotten wind of something, however; they began to wait for the repairs inside the shop. There was no listening to the news, then.

It didn't take Eliezer long to figure out what to do. He surreptitiously accumulated bits and pieces of various radio sets until he had enough parts to build a small set of his own: it was about four by five inches and about the thickness of cardboard. It could only be heard with the help of earphones—and Eliezer somehow managed to acquire a set. He built a hiding place in the planks on his bed—which was on the top level of the barracks.

My bed had also been on the uppermost level in the

barracks in Kazet. I could still feel Puczic's fist crashing between my eyes, the blood gushing down my face, my father's pain as he watched helplessly.

In any case, those who had suggested Eliezer's transfer to the camp "management"—including Hersh—could be trusted absolutely. And they kept the news to themselves. They were overjoyed to learn that the Nazis were suffering not only from the allies but from the partisans. It strengthened their determination to escape camp and join the partisans.

They were able to contact the partisans through the underground. Members of the underground came into the camp on supply errands. Certain signs, certain signals were exchanged; communication was established. There was a partisan force in the woods of Lublin, not far from the camp.

Eliezer, with painstaking secrecy, began to form a resistance movement in Krashnik. They were as frightened of betrayal by the turncoat Jews as of discovery by the guards, and it seemed to take forever to organize. Eventually there were sixteen in the group. The goal was to contact the partisans in the Rzecice forest who were part of the *Armja Ludowa* ("People's Party"). It was one of the groups supported by Moscow. But first, they had to get out of the camp.

The way came through a Ukrainian who guarded the front gate. Ivan Kasian's parents had been murdered by the Germans and he hated them. Not only was he sympathetic to the Jews, he was a member of the underground.

One day Ivan approached Eliezer, who was initially suspicious—especially when Ivan mentioned the radio set Eliezer had secreted underneath his bed. In fact, Eliezer was sure Ivan would tell the Germans about it. He waited for the axe to fall. It didn't. Finally, Eliezer's sixth sense came into play: Ivan could be trusted.

So Ivan became the liaison to the partisans. He routinely escorted the transport of materials from town to the camp, and Eliezer arranged that two of the resistance group go with him on certain trips. In town, with Ivan's help, they were able to establish contact with the partisans. They received crucial information and exchanged radio parts (from Eliezer's shop) for guns and hand grenades. Ivan was totally dependable.

Late in March Eliezer decided that the time had come to break out of the camp. With Ivan's help, he got the impression of the inside of the padlock on the front gate in wax, and was able to get a key made.

After dark on the agreed-upon evening, the resistance group concealed itself around the area of the front gate. Eliezer strolled up to the gate, took out the key, and unlocked the padlock. The other fifteen stole from their hiding places, pushed the gate open, and left. Ivan acted as though nothing was amiss. The group made it to the woods by the time he sounded the alarm.

The Germans mobilized rapidly: horses, bloodhounds, a jeep or two. But Eliezer's party had gotten too far a head start.

They met up with a patrol of partisans in the part of the forest that bordered Rzecice village. Eliezer gave the password, which he had obtained from the liaison in Krashnik, and the partisans led them to the main bunker. There, all the radio parts smuggled out of the camp lay on a table. The first thing Eliezer did was assemble a radio. As soon as it was working they began to receive instructions from the Soviets as to which German units to attack, which transportation to destroy, what other sabotage was to be done.

There were many Jews hiding in the Rzecice forest. No partisan group wanted them because the men didn't want to separate from their wives and children and because they were essentially unarmed. The guns and rifles they carried usually didn't work, but when they brandished them in the villages they entered in the quest for food, most of the peasants fell for it. Some even managed to obtain cows and cattle with these nonfunctioning guns.

Eliezer managed to place the children and the elderly with sympathetic peasants in surrounding villages. Those that could work became "unpaid labor"; those that couldn't merely hid. He distributed weapons the Soviets dropped to teenagers of both sexes.

The group soon grew to thirty. Guided by the Soviets, they attacked the Germans where they least expected it—and usually managed to rout them. After a while the Germans sent Lithuanian, Ukrainian, and Hungarian troops into the forest to fight the partisans. The partisans had considered themselves merely a bunch of draggle-tailed guerrillas; after a while they were quite proud of their accomplishments.

It wasn't long before Eliezer became the leader of all the partisan groups in the forest. By then word had reached us in Ostroviec. He commanded about ten thousand fighters. His code name was NILI—the first letters of *Netsach Israel Lo Yeshaker* (There is always hope for Israel).

By the end of July, 1944, the Soviets had crossed the Bug and came close to Lublin. The Germans decided to liquidate Krashnik and transfer the able-bodied to camps on the other side of the Vistula. Those in the camp who got wind of this got word to Eliezer through the underground. Eliezer smuggled a letter to his friend, Yeshaayahu Markowicz, through the underground: "Be ready. We are coming."

With Ivan's help, the underground obtained a few guns and hand grenades. The plan was to halt the transfer by launching an attack, with the help of the partisans, as the Germans led the Jews to the railway station. There would be time, in the general confusion, for the Jews to escape into the woods.

But when the day came, the partisans never appeared.

The Germans retreated and dug in when the Soviets reached the Vistula. The partisans were ordered to attack German transportation and garrisons and cause general panic and disruption—which would make it easier for the Soviets to move in and totally destroy them.

Eliezer, as commander, was not obliged to go out into battle. In fact, his lieutenants tried to talk him out of it. But he geared up.

The German unit targeted for attack on a certain day was near a grove. The Nazis washed themselves and gathered water for the unit's use in the nearby stream. Eliezer and his men got to the grove and hid in the shadows, waiting. The idea was to kill them off quietly, so as not to alert those who had dug into the trenches. The partisans were armed only with knives, daggers, and ropes.

It was hours before the Germans began to appear. When they did, Eliezer and his men attacked, and the Germans were taken by surprise. But they had guns—automatics. It was a pitched battle. It lasted all night. Eliezer and his men were outnumbered, but they were fast and fierce. Dozens of Germans fell.

But Eliezer was killed. It was three hours before the liberation.

Leon, Hersh and I sat there, not moving, for a long time. I thought of the joyous times I'd had with Eliezer. I'd have given anything in the world for him to slap my rear end and call me a spoiled brat, as he used to in Kurov.

"A great man," Leon had said to me when we'd met a couple of hours before. Yes. He was.

Finally, I broke the silence. "Hersh, I also was a partisan. The First Brigade of the First Battalion in the Sladnovisna woods. Under Commander Bzioza."

He looked at me: my thin body, my Russian uniform, my tear-ravaged eyes.

"Now tell me about you, Nachemia," he said softly.

Ten

*The cold seemed to whip right through the buildings in
Krashnik. I was constantly grateful for my Russian uniform
with its oversized fur hat. I stayed there with Leon for three
days. We went to the Jewish aid centers that had been set up
and met with those Jews who were still there.*

We were thirty miles from Lublin, which had been
liberated in July, 1944, six months before while I was still
hiding out in Leon Chernowski's bunker outside Opatov. It
had become a gathering place for survivors from the bunkers,
ghettos, forests, and death camps from all over Poland. Institutions and committees had been set up to aid them. Jews
registered in a central office so that their relatives and friends
could check to see that they were still alive.

Quite a few Russian soldiers were in Krashnik. I wondered if any knew of the bombardments of the German
battalions that had made for Opoczno—where I had become
separated from Heinz.

As I stood in line at the central registry on my second
day in the town, I noticed a Russian soldier speaking in Polish
to one of the other men waiting in line. I approached him.

"Excuse me," I said in Polish.

Surprised, they both looked at me.

"I heard you speaking in Polish," I said to the soldier,
"so I thought I could speak to you. Do you by any chance
know what happened to the Nazi troops that retreated to
Opoczno last month?"

"We bombed a lot of Hitler's army," the Russian smiled

smugly. "Why do you want to know?" He suddenly stared at me sharply.

I swallowed hard.

"Oh—some friends, who were dragged into service for the Nazis, were in that retreat. I was wondering—"

"Friends?" The Russian stared at me. "Well," he finally said, "as far as I know, those who weren't killed were taken to labor camps in Siberia." He turned away abruptly.

"Thank you," I said lamely.

I wanted to know what remained of my family.

I had to get to Lublin.

Leon and Hershel gave me five hundred *zloty* and as much food as would fit in my bag. And they gave me the addresses of survivors whom they knew were from Kurov, although they didn't know their names.

I had to walk some of the distance from Krashnik to Lublin, but luckily sometimes I was able to hitch a ride. My Soviet uniform helped.

The sides of the road were cluttered with burnt German army trucks, jeeps, and tanks. There was an awful stillness about the way they lay, immobile, on their sides—some upside down, some right side up, blackened, abandoned. The deep snow which still covered the countryside made the charred metal vehicles look even more ghostly and grotesque.

"So may Hitler's carcass blacken and rot," said one wrinkled old peasant who gave me a lift on his cart.

"Yes, yes, yes!" I rejoined.

I saw the glistening cathedral spire while we were still a couple of miles from the city. The cathedral, built in the sixteenth century, was the largest in Poland. Lublin itself was built in the tenth century. My father had taken me on a trip to Lublin when I was about ten, and I still remembered the ancient-seeming houses, sturdy and substantial, the majestic cathedral, the sprawling university, which had seemed huge to me. And the *Yeshiva Chachmei Lublin*—the largest, most prestigious academy of Jewish studies in Europe. Before the war, Lublin had a Jewish population of about forty-five thousand—one of the largest of any Polish city.

As we made our way inside the city itself, I looked around. I was surprised. Lublin had hardly suffered any war damage at all. That pleased me—perhaps because of my fond memories of the trip I'd taken there with Daddy.

"Where are you going?" the peasant driving the cart broke into my reverie.

I started for a moment, then answered, "Oh, Lubartovska Street, thanks."

I remembered Lubartovska Street also. Daddy had friends there. I looked at the addresses I'd been given in Krashnik: Number 8, Number 10, Number 12 Lubartovska Street. I was sure there I'd find people from Kurov.

The houses on Lubartovska Street seemed older and more weathered than I remembered them. Perhaps they had taken on the same color as the slush underfoot. I came upon the houses on my list: all three-storeyed, with wooden beams criss-crossing the structures. For whatever reason, I approached Number 10 and knocked on the front door. The thin, tall man who opened it looked at me and drew back in amazement. I froze to the spot, speechless. That face—thin, with bushy eyebrows, humorous yet deadly serious, belonged to only one person in the world. We both gaped for several seconds, unable to utter sounds. Then shouts burst from our throats:

"YOSEK!"

"NACHEMIA!"

I embraced my childhood friend. We wept unashamedly.

The other people in the house, afraid something had happened, ran towards the front door.

"It's all right, it's all right," we managed to tell them.

"Come in, Nachemia. My God, come in." Yosek put his arm around my shoulder and led me down the hall and into the kitchen of his apartment. Standing in front of the stove was his father. I flew to him:

"Mr. Zukerman! Thank God, you're alive. Mr. Zukerman!"

"Nachemia! My God, Nachemia."

We embraced.

For a few seconds we just looked at one another. Both Yosek and his father had aged. Before the war, Mr. Zukerman was only forty; now he looked sixty. His moustache had grown long and gray; his face was lined and somber.

"Nachemia," he asked quietly, "your family; is anyone else still alive?"

I looked at him sadly, "I don't know."

"Nachemia," he began to choke up. "Henoch—your Daddy—he's not—?"

I shook my head slowly. I could not have spoken a word at that moment.

Mr. Zukerman turned toward the stove and wept.

"Eliezer, too," I finally managed to say.

"Oh God, oh no," he sobbed.

"But Mr. Zukerman, Eliezer died fighting. He headed the partisan group in the Rzecice forests. He is a hero." I don't know how I managed to choke out those words.

Yosek put his hand on my shoulder. "Maybe we all are, Nachemia. Eliezer more so than others."

I nodded, unable to speak.

"Your mother—your sisters and brother Moshe?" Mr. Zukerman finally managed to say.

"Chania is with me in Ostroviec," I answered softly. "I . . . don't know about Mother and Chaike and Moshe. I came here hoping to learn something about them."

"Yes, yes, the information center," he said. Then he turned to his son. "Yosek, we must start dinner." Suddenly, he looked back at me. "Nachemia, what are you doing in Bolshevik uniform?"

"Let me help you with dinner, Mr. Zukerman. And I will tell you."

After dinner, it was their turn.

"Well, you know, we didn't leave Kurov when you did.

We were told by Shumel Chanisman that you'd all gone to Russia. Had made it to the Russian border."

"That was to get away from that anti-Semite, Ulrich," I said. "Daddy told Mr. Chanisman to tell everyone."

"Yes, Nachemia. He was absolutely determined to hang the six of you—and Eliezer if he'd ever caught up with him—from gallows in the square. He was furious when he heard you'd gotten out of his grasp.

"Well, anyway, three years after you left—it was 1942— they had what they called an *aktsia* in Kurov—"

"God, I know what *that* is," I interrupted him.

He nodded sadly. "All the Jews were rounded up and sent to the death camps. Well, they sent Yosek and me to Sobibor, near Chelm. The gas chamber was ready. We thought it was the end."

I looked at Yosek.

"Well, by some chance, they picked Yosek and me to be cooks. I don't know why we were so lucky. They usually selected a few out of each transport to remove the dead, to sort their clothing, to ferret out the good boots, to scw clothing and boots for the S.S. and the Ukrainians. But not to be cooks."

"Yes, I know what a good job that is, as I'll tell you later," I grinned.

"And the camp was partitioned off: one section was not permitted to know what was going on in another. I guess they didn't want anyone to get an idea when their turn at the gas chamber was up. Well, here's how we got around that. We slipped a note into a pot of food which we knew was going to be taken to another part of the camp specifically for the Jews. The next day the reply came back inside the pot: 'All persons kept here are gassed and buried. We three hundred Jews here are the workers who bury them.' I wept when I read it.

"Sobibor was deep in a forest, camouflaged from public view. The sections were partitioned off with barbed wire fence, and there were mines along the fence areas—oh, yes, and a deep stream, with an electrified fence all around. There was a sentry post every forty feet.

"We learned, through the passing of notes, that they'd opened another gas chamber in another section. Heinrich Himmler came down himself to watch its first 'test'—" his voice broke "—three hundred women. Afterward, Himmler—" Mr. Zukerman stopped to regain control of his voice, "—distributed medals to the S.S. men there that day."

"Let me put on water for more tea," Yosek jumped up.

"Yes, son, good," Mr. Zukerman nodded.

"Anyway," his voice regained some of its force, "new transports of Jews arrived every day. One time they found four revolvers in the pockets of the clothes of Jews who were sent to the gas chamber. One of the revolvers had a note tied to it: 'Brother Jews. Do not let yourselves be fooled and misled by the bandits. We come from the Belz extermination camp. Tens of thousands of Jews have already been killed there. They planted a forest on the spot.'

"There were Russian Jews in this transport," Mr. Zukerman continued. "They gave us new life. 'We shall not wait for death,' they said, 'we have to do something!' "

"But what?" I asked gravely.

He responded warmly. "Ah—this is the good part. In October, 1943, there were about six hundred Jews in Sobibor—you know, servants: they waited on the Nazis; they had talents like being electricians, which the Nazis put to use."

"Like Eliezer," I cut in.

"Yes, indeed," he smiled. "Tailors, carpenters. Well, this Sasha, a Russian Jew who had been a lieutenant in the Red Army, was the leader. They planned a revolt. First, kill the head of the camp. Then, cut the power off. Secretly they sharpened knives and axes. The signal was that Sasha lick his lips with his tongue. At roll call at three in the afternoon, Sasha gave the signal.

"The ten Jews who worked in the tailor shop sent a message to the head of the camp, Obersturmfuehrer Nieman, that the clothes he'd ordered were ready and he should come and try them on. He arrived, would you believe, riding a white horse. Anyway, when he took off his jacket—with his pistol belt—and slipped his arms into the new jacket, one of the

Jews hit him over the head with an axe—from behind—and another stabbed him through the heart. Then they signaled Schwartz, who handled the camp powerhouse, that Nieman had been killed. Schwartz cut off the power in the camp. Meanwhile, they wrapped Nieman's body in a quilt and stuffed it under a bed. The lights failed; the telephones were out.

"Meanwhile, a second S.S. man and his adjutant were fitted with new boots. They axed them as well. Then they stuffed their bodies behind a cabinet in the leather shop. Then the head of the leather shop called the chief of the gas chamber section; he told him that he should try on his new boots. He got axed, too. It was wonderful! Another S.S. man came into the leather shop: the Jews there showed him little bags of gold coins, which had just been found, and as he examined them the axe came down on his head, too."

Yosek broke in. "Seventeen S.S. men in forty-five minutes—without a shot or a sound."

"I wish the prisoners had been able to get such retribution from the beasts at Kazet," I interjected.

"I know," Mr. Zukerman continued, moistening his lips. "There was another roll call at 5:00, and the six hundred Jews came out into the courtyard. Sasha stepped out from the crowd and announced that there was no roll call but a revolt. Then the Jews brought out the seventeen rifles and revolvers they'd taken off the S.S. men they'd killed. They shot the Ukrainian guards. One S.S. man came running. A youngster—no more than thirteen—threw salt in his eyes and snatched his revolver. Nachemia—our spirits were so high by then.

'Then we all charged the Ukrainian guards," he said, his voice pitched low and serious. "We cut through the wires with the axes. They got three hundred of us—but three hundred escaped. They ran into the forest. But the Poles slaughtered those Jews. Only thirty-five really escaped." He stopped and glanced at me. There were several moments without speaking.

"Go on, go on," I prodded.

He leaned forward in his chair. "Yosek and I ran to Kurov. We didn't get there right away. We hid for months in the forest and the fields. We were afraid to go to peasants' huts—we didn't know whether they'd turn us in or what."

"Now Papa, you've got to tell him—" Yosek said excitedly.

"Yes, Yosek." He smiled. "Nachemia, Yosek also was a partisan."

I looked at my old friend. I remembered the time we'd glued the rabbi's trousers to his chair in *cheder* in Kurov. He looked back at me with unabashed affection. I wondered if I had aged as much as he had.

"Well, not me," Mr. Zukerman was winding up his story. "I continued to hide until the Russians arrived. As soon as I heard that they had liberated Lublin I made my way here. Yosek got here about two months later."

I looked around. There was a glow in the room, the glow of spirits who refused to give in to all the forces hell could unleash. A long silence ensued.

"Yosek—more tea," Mr. Zukerman finally said.

Later that evening, Yosek explained, "Nachemia, Lublin is not a paradise for us Jews, you know. There are Polish bandits—hooligans—you remember when we were attacked on our way to and from school in Kurov?—who are just as bad as the Nazis."

"Yeh, I ran into them, too," I said. "But, Yosek, I also met up with Poles who were God-fearing, decent people."

"Me, too," he said. "But still, we keep double locks on the doors."

I looked at him questioningly.

"Well, the bastards attack Jews at night—rob us, kill us."

At the sound of a knock on the door, we both jumped. "I must answer it," Yosek said.

He went to the front door. "Who's there?" I heard him call.

I couldn't quite make out the answer from the other side of the door. Apparently, Yosek was satisfied, for he opened the door. "You will *never* believe who is here," I heard him say to the visitors.

I stood up. Didn't I know those voices? Just then they came into the kitchen.

"NACHEMIA!"

"MR. CHANISMAN! YOSEL!"

"Oh my God, I don't believe—"

"You survived!"

"I thought all the Wurmans were—"

Mr. Chanisman looked seventy years old—I knew he was Daddy's age—about fifty. He had gotten terribly thin—and seemed shorter. A memory of his digging into his pockets for candy for Moshe and me flashed into my mind. Lines now criss-crossed his face. And Yosel, Moshe's pal. He couldn't have been more than nineteen; he looked thirty. We fell on each other. Crying and laughing.

Mr. Chanisman held me at arms' length and looked searchingly at me. My emotions overwhelmed me. *Soon, soon, Nachemia, you will realize the toll this hell has taken on all of us.* "Nachemia?" He said my name like a question. I knew what he was going to ask. The tears started down my cheeks before he framed the question.

He knew, then. "Henoch?" he whispered.

I couldn't answer. Daddy and he were like brothers. I wished I did not have to tell him. He stared at me and knew. I saw him crumple, sink into himself before my eyes.

"Henoch. HENOCH!" He broke into sobs. "How?" he finally managed.

"We were in Ostroviec, with my uncle," I choked out the words. "They sent all the Jews to the labor camp they built outside the town. One day, they just came in and—" my own voice broke "—rounded up Jews. They told me the ransom for Daddy. Chania and I ran around the camp to everyone we knew—even those we didn't know so well—trying to get the money. We couldn't. Daddy was taken off in a wagon . . ."

"Oh God, oh God," Mr. Chanisman moaned.

"That was . . . the last we saw him."

Suddenly he straightened up. "No, Nachemia. He is alive. He is alive in you. You have lived to see this day! You are Henoch Wurman's son. You carry his name—and him—in you."

I wept uncontrollably.

"What about your mother, your sisters?" he asked.

"Chania is with me in Ostroviec," I somehow managed to say. "I don't know about Mother, or Chaike or," I turned to Yosel, "Moshe. I came to Lublin to learn what I can."

"Yosek, more tea," Mr. Zukerman commanded. "And don't we have cakes or something?" He turned back to me.

"Now tell me what happened, Nachemia," Mr. Chanisman said. He stroked his chin thoughtfully.

Finally we all went to bed. But I didn't sleep long. I guess my army training had set my inner clock. I was awake by seven.

After breakfast Yosek took me to the Jewish Committee's information center. Its offices, like those in Krashnik, were located in the City Hall. People stared at us: Yosek in civilian clothes, I in Russian uniform.

"Bet they think I'm taking you to jail," I quipped.

"Maybe they think *I'm* turning *you* in for misconduct," he shot back.

A slow grin spread over his face.

"Like drinking all the tea in your house?" I smiled.

Yosek turned back to scan the street. "Ah—here it is," he gestured.

The Soviets had taken over City Hall. Men in uniform swarmed about.

"You're right at home here, Nachemia," Yosek chuckled.

"In more ways than one," I chuckled.

"Are the Russians supporting this—this aid to Jews, the clothing, the shelter, the food?" I asked.

"Not entirely," he shook his head. "The Jewish Agency of Palestine and the Jewish Distribution Committee in the United States contribute an awful lot to this. Thank God for them. There are thousands of us who've been totally stripped of everything we ever had."

"Yes, literally," I gulped. "But, Yosek, they're losing—the Germans are being defeated. Between the Russians and the Americans—they cannot go on."

"Yes, Nachemia, you're right. But what have they left in their wake? Death—and living death. Families ripped apart—for what?"

"Purity of the race," I responded sarcastically.

"Ach," he said soberly. "Oh, look—here's the registry. Now what you do is go in and register your and Chania's names—that lets anyone who wants to know check that you two are alive. Then you can check the lists of others who've registered here—and look for anyone you know: if they've written their names in the books it means they're alive. And usually the people in charge can give you directions as to where people are—or have gone."

"Okay," I agreed.

The registry was old and battle-scarred. Gray. Everything seemed gray. Even the shallow stairs I climbed up were worn in the center.

"I think it's the first door to your right, Nachemia," Yosek called. "Listen: I'll meet you back here in an hour or so."

"Okay," I waved.

The first room to the right was small and cluttered. It seemed to be the registry. About fifteen people stood on line. It felt too warm. I took off my hat and unbuttoned my overcoat. After a couple of minutes I took the overcoat off and held it over my arm. People turned to stare—what was a Russian soldier doing standing in line to register with the Jewish Committee? they must have been thinking. But I expected that.

As I stood, I kept hearing the word *Bhricha*. It was whispered. *Bhricha* means "runner." What were they talking about? I wondered.

One woman waiting on the clothing distribution line never took her eyes off me. I kept looking straight ahead, stealing only occasional glances at her. She seemed to be about forty-five, short, thin, black hair overlaid with gray. Who was she?

Suddenly she was at my side. Her eyes impaled me. "Your face seems familiar," she said thoughtfully. "You remind me of someone."

I don't know why I was abrupt with her. I replied, "I'm sorry—I don't know you."

Why did I do that? I asked myself. It's not as though I was still in the Seventy-Second Fusiliers waiting to be discovered.

She wasn't fazed. "Tell me please," she continued, "where were you during the war?"

"Ostroviec," I said crisply.

She was about to ask another question, but I turned to her: "Where were *you* during the war?"

"I came out of the death camp—Majdanek, near Lublin."

"How did you survive the gas chambers?"

"A miracle," she sighed.

Why was she so insistent on talking to me? I wondered.

"They had regular roundups of Jews in Lublin," she continued.

"*Aktsia,*" I offered.

"Yes, you know," she patted my arm. "Anyway, they got me in 1942. I was sent to Budzyn. I don't remember how long I was there before they—"

Budzyn! I broke into a cold sweat. Mother, Chaike, Moshe! I opened my mouth but nothing came out. I swallowed hard a few times. She continued her story.

"From Budzyn I was sent to Majdanek. Not long after my transport arrived there, the Russians bombed the camp and the surrounding area. But, I tell you, it didn't stop those beasts from stuffing people into the gas chambers. They—just didn't choose me for the gas, that's all. Then the Russians marched in and freed us—there were only about a hundred of us left."

I was gaping at her.

"Are you all right?" she asked.

My mind raced backwards. "Budzyn, you were in Budzyn?" I finally managed to whisper.

She nodded "Yes."

"Sarah Wurman—did you know—?"

"Sarale? Yes. Are you Sarale's son?!"

I could only nod.

"Nachemia?" her eyes glowed.

"How do you know my name?" I gaped at her.

"Come over here with me."She led me to a bench along the wall of the room. "We must talk, Nachemia."

"Almost as soon as I arrived in Budzyn they assigned me to the kitchen," she began. "Your mother was there. Right away we got along. Ach, I liked her so much. Our souls met— you know? I'd had no one, but she told me a lot about her family—your father—" Her voice broke.

I blinked to keep the tears back.

"Oh, Nachemia, did they—?"

I nodded, unable to speak.

"I'm sorry, child," she said softly. "She spoke of you, your two sisters—Chayale was there with her; I don't know what they had her doing, but she wasn't in the kitchen. Oh, wait: I think she was in the sewing shop. Moshe was, I think—"

"Working with the electric?" I asked.

"Yes, I think so," she mused. "Anyway, your mother always spoke about you, Nachemia, always. You are her youngest. Ach, did she love you! You know, whenever she talked about you, she would say, 'Nachemia will come through this. I know it.' She paused for a moment to look at me intently. Then she gave a half smile. 'You know, you resemble her."

I had gone cold. "What do you mean, 'She *did* love me?' What happened—?"

She did not answer. Suddenly her silence made me realize what the answer was going to be, and she saw it reflected in my eyes.

"Nachemia, Sarale, Moshe and Chayale were in the first group that was sent to Auschwitz from Budzyn . . ."

I bowed my head. I made no attempt to stop the tears.

She put her arm around my shoulder. "I know, child, I know," she murmured. "Sarale was like my sister. We were sisters, as far as we were concerned. And look, maybe they survived. You know, a lot of camps were liberated by the Russians . . ."

"Yes. Maybe," I said through my tears.

"Come, now. Don't you want to register? If they're alive they'll be able to find you and your sister."

I wrote down my Ostroviec address and gave it to her.

Then I registered along with the long line of displaced, isolated survivors all hoping some of their families had not been killed.

True to his word, Yosek was waiting outside the office in an hour. "What is it, Nachemia?" he said with one look at my face.

I told him what the woman had told me. "I don't even know her name," I suddenly realized.

Yosek was silent for about half our walk back to his apartment. Then he said quietly, "Nachemia, are you keeping in mind what she said last? That perhaps they survived to be liberated? You know, there *are* survivors of Auschwitz—even Auschwitz."

"Yeh," I said bitterly, "but very few."

"Yosek," I said as we neared his apartment. "What are *Bhricha*? I heard that name at the registry."

"Not now, Nachemia," he muttered. "I'll tell you when we're inside the apartment."

That evening, more people from Kurov called at Yosek and Mr. Zukerman's apartment.

"This is the busiest teapot on Lubartovska," Yosek joked.

I had only a slight recollection of these people from Kurov. But I queried them about the town.

"I would like to visit Korev at least one last time," I said resolutely. "I grew up there."

"Nachemia, do not go back there," one woman exclaimed. She was about my mother's age, I guessed, but her hair was almost completely white. Her brown eyes were sad.

"But that is where I went to school, where my father was on the city council, where—"

"It is *very* dangerous for Jews to go to Kurov!" her husband exhorted. "And especially you."

"Why? Is Ulrich still commisar?" I joked.

"No—but listen. The Poles owe your father lots and lots of money. They don't want to repay—you know that. Some of them in Kurov were worse than the Nazis. Were they to learn a Wurman is still alive they might kill you to avoid paying you back."

My lips tightened. "Well, how could I make them pay me back? I mean, I have no power to demand the money."

"Yes, you do. You could go straight to the Soviets and demand reparation, and those Poles know it, Nachemia. Listen to us—don't go."

There was a protracted silence. Finally, quietly, I said, "I must go."

We argued for about an hour. My determination increased. I wanted to see the scenes of my childhood, my town, the place of my birth.

"All right, all right," Mr. Zukerman finally said. "He's going to go to Kurov no matter what we say." He turned to me. "But listen, Nachemia, go only to two people there: Levi Weinbuch—you remember him?"

"Of course." I nodded my head, remembering Levi. "He's alive?"

"Yes, and his wife and son. God knows how. Also, Antek Kordovsky is still in Kurov. With those people you will be safe. Promise me."

"I promise, Mr. Zukerman."

Yes, I thought, I would be safe with both Levi Weinbuch and Anton Kordovsky. I could still hear them in my family's kitchen as I hid behind the alcove wall, arguing about, bemoaning the plight of, the Jews before the war. I recalled the real affection between Daddy and Mr. Kordovsky—that Kordovsky had been instrumental in getting Daddy on the city council. Fleetingly, I remembered Mrs. Kordovsky presenting us with cakes and cookies in our store, admonishing us to save them until after dinner.

Suddenly I turned to Mr. Zukerman. "Mr. Zukerman, what are the *Bhricha?*"

A dead silence fell over the room.

"What's wrong?" I asked.

"*Bhricha* is flight, Nachemia—"

"Yes, I know."

"All right. *Bhrichas* are runners—smugglers, if you will. They have contacts with the Russians to get Jews out of Poland—preferably to Palestine—but in any case to a place were we don't have to hide and sneak around afraid of being attacked. You know they won't give Jews visas. The *Bhricha* will smuggle you out, for a price."

"Are there many around?"

"We don't know for sure. We know how to get in touch with one if we feel we must leave Poland."

"Yosek, put on more tea," Mr. Zukerman said.

A snowfall had begun by the time I set out the next morning. Kllrov was about twenty miles from Lublin, and I was lucky; I hitched a ride practically all the way.

From a distance, the town resembled a set of broken teeth. Some houses clustered in one area, then, sparse groups of houses, then rubble with two or three houses still standing.

As I made my way closer to Lubelska, the soft grays and whites I remembered faded from my mind: what I saw was the black of charred ruins, the harsh, dirty grays of slush underfoot, the dingy white of snowdrifts. Lubelska was a stretch of rubble, broken here and there by what appeared to be recently erected shacks. Clearly, nothing had been done about rebuilding the original houses since the Germans had bombed the town in 1939. I headed toward what had been our house.

Some blackened walls stood encased by a charred heap. I made for the stairway to the cellar. *Could we rebuild in on the foundation of the cellar?* Then I discovered that the heap of rubble was piled up from the floor of the cellar. I couldn't even recognize bits of furniture or other furnishings.

I stood there for a long time, covering every inch of the ruin with my eyes. *Well, what did you expect?* I thought despairingly. *You saw it go up in flames yourself.* It was hopeless. It was gone. They had obliterated my childhood.

I could see the water pump in the middle of the market square. There had been about five houses between our house and the square. Now there were two or three recently erected wooden cottages. How would I know which one was Levi Weinbuch's? I approached the nearest one and knocked on the door.

Mr. Weinbuch had aged. He didn't recognize me. We all stood there silently for a moment.

David Weinbuch pushed past his father and threw his arms around me. "My God, my God," he moaned, "you're back from the dead."

He turned to the older man, who was just beginning to realize who the stranger was. "Papa! It's Nachemia Wurman! Don't you know him?"

Mr. Weinbuch's face lit up. "Nachemia! Henoch's son." He put his arms around me.

"Come in, come in." He put his arm around my shoulder. "It's not the house we had when we were all here together, of course not, but—I stayed in Kurov, as I told your Daddy I would—and we survived. Here, give me your coat. A Russian uniform. Nachemia, what is this?"

I could hardly get a word in edgewise.

"Chasia," he called to his wife, "come see who has come. And make us some lunch."

Mrs. Weinbuch came in from the other room. She flew to me and threw her arms around me. "Nachemia, Nachemia, oh God, Nachemia," she crooned. "I never thought I'd see you again." Tears began to run down her face.

"Sit, Nachemia, sit." David pulled a couple of chairs close together.

"Tell us what happened to your family," Mr. Weinbuch said. "Henoch, is he—" He hesitated as if not wanting to finish the question.

I shook my head slowly.

He bowed his head. "Ah, Henoch, Henoch," he moaned. "A giant among men. A true son of God. What happened, son?"

His face, when he looked at me, was tear-stained. I felt the tears begin in my own eyes. I sat there looking at him for a long time before I could speak.

"It was in Lager—the concentration camp outside Ostroviec. Those of us in the camp worked in the nearby factories. They had Daddy maintaining the barracks—he thought it was because he was older. Anyway, in October 'forty-three, the Jewish police came into the hut with a list of names. Daddy's was one of them. He—and the others—were taken outside and made to line up."

I sighed deeply. "When I finally managed to get information, I learned they were taking them to Radom Firley."

"A death camp," Mr. Weinbuch said soberly.

"Yes. Mr. Weinbuch, Chania and I—I can't bear the thought even now—ran to *everyone* in Lager trying to get five thousand *zloty* for Daddy's ransom."

"Five thousand!"

I nodded. "It seems they really only wanted forty men— but they'd rounded up sixty. Twenty could be ransomed by their families."

"Did you—"

I shook my head slowly. "No. Anyone who had money had already given it for ransom or had had it taken from them. No. We weren't able—" I stopped. It was some time before I could go on.

"Two trucks pulled into the camp in the afternoon. Thirty-eight were shoved into the trucks. Daddy—"

"—was among them," he finished for me.

"He blessed us as they shoved him into the wagon, Mr. Weinbuch." Tears ran unashamedly down our faces. "And—" my voice was beginning to crack. Would I ever be able to relive that scene without choking on my own pain and rage? "—and Chania and I blessed him, also."

"What more could you have done, Nachemia? Nothing, nothing." He stared out the small window. "Henoch," he mumbled to himself. "Ah, those nights in your father's house, the tea, the cake, your mother was—your mother! Is she—?"

"I don't know." My face tightened angrily. "I registered my name and Chania's at the registry in Lublin."

"Is Chania alive?" David interjected.

"Yes." I nodded positively. "And let me tell you how I found out."

"Tell us what happened after you left Korev with your family, Nachemia," Mr. Weinbuch asked.

Lunch was ready by the time I finished telling the Weinbuchs of my experiences. We sat down at the small well-shined table, and I turned to them.

"Now," I said, "What happened to you?"

"Well, you know, Papa was determined to remain in Korev," David began as his mother ladled out the soup.

"I remember. I heard the conversation in our house," I said, passing my plate.

"While you were supposed to be asleep, right?" Mr. Weinbuch grinned, one bushy eyebrow raised.

The image of Heinz flashed through my mind with that gesture. I gulped and refocused on those at the table.

"Well . . . yes," I grinned back.

David raised his wine glass. "Well, somehow we managed to escape—many times it was a narrow escape, believe me." David turned to his father. "Remember the time we were all in the cellar and they came down with flashlights? We thought it was the end. That they would shoot us right there."

"None of us dared even breathe," Mrs. Weinbuch chimed in.

"Well, in April of 1943, they got us. Rounded us up

with the rest of the Jews left in Kurov. Marched us towards the train station."

"We knew what *that* meant," Mr. Weinbuch interjected gloomily.

"We escaped—" David exclaimed vehemently.

"How?" I asked, looking intently from one to the other of them.

Mr. Weinbuch raised his voice, seemingly determined to speak.

"Somehow, the guard was slack at our section of the line—they were talking to one another or something. You know the forest right on the edge of town—well, we weren't twenty-five feet away from the trees. We looked at each other. Papa scrutinized the guards. They weren't paying any attention. We made a dash for the trees—about six of us. They didn't even know what happened."

I shook my head. "What did you do then?"

"We travelled through the forests towards Lublin until we finally met up with a partisan group that accepted us as members. Seems most partisans are afraid Jews won't fight, or something."

"And that they won't separate from their wives and children," I added.

"Yeh. Well, anyway, this group did. We lived in bunkers for about a year. We were able to get quite a few Nazis. The Soviets supported us."

"They dropped supplies and weapons?" I asked, although I knew the answer.

"Yes. We also got weapons—as you did—from the Nazis we killed. We hid in the trees and shot before they could turn around."

"I know." I looked around the table.

"Nachemia," said Mr. Weinbuch soberly, "it is the Soviets who are setting up the new Polish government. They are putting the leaders of the partisans into the positions of militia, security and administration. The Soviets were active in the underground."

I nodded. "So that's how they knew how to drop the supplies to the partisan groups," I exclaimed.

There was the slightest of pauses.

"Of course," he smiled.

"Is Poland going to be a Soviet state?" I asked.

Mr. Weinbuch frowned. "Who knows? Who could have foretold what has happened in the past five years? Whatever, they must be better than Hitler."

"Papa," David put in, "you know most Poles are just as anti-Semitic as the Nazis."

"True, true," Mr. Weinbuch shook his head sadly. For a moment I watched him as if from a distance.

He's aged. God, how he's aged, I thought. I remembered him as young and vital from the gatherings in my family's house on Lubelska. *But—haven't we all aged?* I asked myself.

"Mr. Weinbuch," I ventured. "If I may make a suggestion. I know you love Korev—your family has been here for generations . . . But wouldn't you be better off in Lublin, where there are strong Jewish organizations to help the survivors? Or even Ostroviec? My friend Abek Fridenthal and his father—"

He cut me off abruptly. "No, Nachemia. Here we were born; here we will die. Look—I told your father we'd survive and stay in Kurov, didn't I? And here we are."

There was no changing his mind.

"Will you stay with us, Nachemia?" Mrs. Weinbuch offered kindly.

I shook my head negatively. "Thank you, Mrs. Weinbuch. But no, I must find Antek Kordovsky. Perhaps he can give me information about my family . . . what's left of them."

"Ah, Kordovsky. Yes, he is still here, also," Mr. Weinbuch said quietly. "You remember his house on the edge of town? It is still there."

I felt tears rise to my eyes and pushed them back.

"Yes. And thank you for lunch. And—for being alive." I stood up. The family stood. Each embraced me in turn. "Go with God, Nachemia," Mr. Weinbuch said. "We will meet again."

"We will," I assured him.

Kordovsky's house was undamaged, as far as I could see. Two-story, cream-painted brick—just as I remembered it. I knocked on the door.

I didn't recognize the woman who opened the door. She looked aging; her hair was almost completely gray.

"Yes?" she asked without expression.

"I'd like to see Mr. Kordovsky, please."

"Who are you?" The old woman stared at me.

"Nachemia Wurman."

She began to tremble. "Who?"

I grew alarmed. Who was this? "Nachemia Wurman," I repeated.

Suddenly my mind spun back to my days in Kurov and I recognized her.

"Mrs. Kordovsky?"

"Nachemia," she said in a broken voice. "Oh dear God, come in. Come in. I didn't think there were any Wurmans left alive." She turned into the house. "Anton!" she called.

I recognized her husband immediately—although he had also aged. Tall, broad shoulders, well built—he had always resembled my father. He was about fifty by now—my father's age. "Yes?" he said tonelessly. He didn't recognize me.

"Mr. Kordovsky—Nachemia Wurman."

"Oh my God! A miracle." He grabbed my hand and shook it. He grasped my shoulder in the other hand and led me towards a sofa.

"Vanda, make us some tea."

A warm feeling came over me. As we settled ourselves in the living room awaiting tea, my mind wandered back to before the war, when I would come to Kordovsky's shoe shop to be measured for a pair of boots. He was one of the best shoemakers in Kurov, and his specialty was leather boots. He made boots for all my family, and I suspect he didn't charge my father what he'd charged everyone else. The boots were dark, sleek and very beautiful. I remembered how proud I'd been when, asked by my friends who made those boots, saying "Kordovsky."

As we sat there another picture came into my mind; Mrs. Kordovsky and my mother deep in conversation in our shop in Lubelska, where Mrs. Kordovsky came often to shop. They were almost like family.

We were no sooner seated on the sofa than he asked about Daddy. "My friend—my dear friend—Henoch, Nachemia, where is he?"

Yes. He *was* a dear friend—to all of us. "Mr. Kordovsky—" I choked on the words "—I'll tell you everything, if you want to know—"

"Of course I do," he interjected.

"But my father . . ." I gulped.

"No, Nachemia." He looked away for a few moments and then met my eyes again.

I sighed and continued, "—was sent to the death camp while we were imprisoned outside Ostroviec."

Wordlessly, he bowed his head and tears began to pour down his face. We sat there silently. My thoughts turned back to childhood when Kordovsky would bring little games or toys for Chania, Chaike, Moshe and me. Sometimes he'd bring a cake his wife had made to the gatherings in our house. There was real affection between him and Daddy. The mutual admiration.

He broke the silence. "Your mother, Sarah? Your sisters and brothers—Eliezer?"

"Eliezer died a hero's death, Mr. Kordovsky. With weapons in his hand. Three hours before liberation."

He shook his head again. Again, he wiped away more tears. I could hear Mrs. Kordovsky preparing tea in the kitchen.

He leaned forward in his chair, his finger stroking his chin thoughtfully. "Tell me everything, Nachemia. What happened after you left Kurov?"

"Nachemia, you must spend the night here," Kordovsky said after I'd completed my story. "You cannot go out into the streets. Some Poles are worse than the Nazis."

I shrugged. "Thank you, Mr. Kordovsky. But I think I will return to Lublin tomorrow."

"Then we'll get you there," he said firmly.

Mrs. Kordovsky prepared a large breakfast for us early the following morning.

"You need it for the journey," she smiled. I was still having difficulty associating this aged gray-haired woman with the vivacious, brown-haired one that was the Mrs. Kordovsky of my childhood.

Kordovsky drove me to Lublin himself in his horse-drawn carriage. He drove right up to Lubartovsky, where the Zukermans now lived. He hitched the horse's reins to the carriage, reached in his pocket and took out a roll of bills. He pressed them into my hand.

"Mr. Kordovsky, what—"

"Shh, Nachemia. Not a word. I owe your father this—" here his voice broke "—and much more—"

Tears filled both our eyes as we looked at one another.

"—but this is all I have now. Please—please take it." He took the money from my hands and pushed it down into the pocket of my jacket.

We stood there wordlessly looking at one another. Our eyes spoke.

Finally, he put his arm around my shoulder. "Go with God, Nachemia."

"Go with God, Mr. Kordovsky."

I stayed two more days at the Zukermans. On the second day a tall, olive-skinned man—whom I did not recognize—arrived from Kurov. Yosek, of course, made lunch and we sat in the fading afternoon light of the kitchen.

"You know Levi Weinbuch?" the man asked me.

"Of course." I nodded. "I was just at his house. He refused to ever leave Korev. Said he was born there and would die there."

"He did," the visitor said barely in a whisper.

"What?" I asked confused.

"Two nights ago. Goddam Poles broke into the cabin he

and his family were living in. Killed him right there. Mrs. Weinbuch and David escaped."

No one said anything for a long time. I watched the shadows lengthen across the kitchen floor.

I took the train back to Krashnik. From Krashnik I hitchhiked back to Ostroviec.

I vowed never to return to Korev again.

March 1945

When I returned to Ostroviec, Aharon Fridenthal had intervened with the Polish authorities on Chania's and my account. We'd been granted a dry goods store that had once belonged to a cousin, Shlomo Wortzman.

"The store is ours, Nachemia. It was once in the family, anyway. We'll have to get some merchandise . . ." Chania could barely contain her excitement.

The Germans had appropriated the store in 1941 and had turned it—and the stock in it—over to Polish collaborators. With the liberation of Ostroviec, Polish authorities took over the store—and many others that had been stolen from the Jews—and held it in trust. Mr. Fridenthal had seen to it that it came to Chania and me.

"How are we going to obtain stock?" I asked, as excited as she.

"We'll get a loan from the Committee—Mr. Fridenthal will help us."

And he did.

We spent a lot of time with Abek Fridenthal and his father. Mr. Fridenthal was a lawyer and accountant. He had spearheaded the centers and committee to aid the survivors of the camps, the forests, and the fields. He'd been able to obtain several apartments that had once belonged to Jews, so most of those survivors that streamed into Ostroviec were able to find living quarters. Sometimes crowded—but living quarters nonetheless. His committee virtually took survivors by the hand and helped them with their first steps back into freedom: clothing, medical aid, food.

Misha Rosov was a frequent guest in our apartment. He seemed to go into ecstasy over Chania's meals and never failed to compliment her enthusiastically. Chania did quite well with the sparse cooking equipment we were able to obtain.

I wondered from time to time whether Misha and Chania would be attracted to one another.

Misha often sang Russian songs at our gatherings. He had a deep, resonant voice. I would think of Heinz then. Tears welled in my eyes and I would dash them away before anyone saw them. Occasionally Misha brought his violin with him and kept us enraptured with the sweet, sad sounds he got out of it.

One night we made a deal. Misha knew a little Yiddish, but did not know how to read or write it.

"Nachemia," he said one evening after dinner, "an exchange: you teach me to write and read Yiddish and I will teach you Russian."

"Good! Yes." I was pleased.

"Then you can wear that uniform of yours legitimately," he twinkled.

We all laughed.

Most of the Jews coming into Ostroviec arrived with no food, little clothing, and less hope. Through the committee the Fridenthals set up—and on which I helped when I wasn't in the store—the shell-shocked Jews regained all three. Apartments were found for them. Funds arrived from the United States, supplied from Palestine through the Jewish Agency of Palestine. Promise: you could feel it in the air.

"Nachemia, do you intend to wear that Russian uniform forever, or can we get you some clothes?" Abek asked one evening.

Aharon and Abek Fridenthal had escaped from camp during the summer of 1944—Mrs. Fridenthal was sent to Firley during the *aktsia* of October 1943—at about the time my father was sent to his death.

"We left my other son, Samuel, and two daughters in 'Kazet.' " Mr. Fridenthal shook his head. "We haven't heard from them since."

It was then that the tragedy struck. The "A.K." (Land Army) organized an attack on one of the houses newly occupied by survivors. They murdered five people. Two of them, Faiga Krongold and Haya Spiegel, had managed to survive the entire war on faked Aryan documents. Leibl Lustig, who had just returned from the Glewitz concentration camp, we later learned, begged his killers for mercy, while he pointed to the number tattooed to his arm. They shot him through the head.

It went through the Jewish community like wildfire. I spent a lot of time in the committee's offices, attempting to dissuade Jews from leaving town.

They ran into the office. "Please, please. I must leave. I don't want to be next! Please."

I was not quite as successful as Aharon Fridenthal in calming them. I heard him say, "Lightning does not strike twice. Ostroviec is an important assembly point for surviving Jews. Here we can provide them with shelter, clothing, food, perhaps work—for pay—a new beginning to life. Believe me, the new government will find those murderers and that will be the end of them—and such tragedies as happened the other day."

People went away comforted. I soon learned to deal with the panic-stricken in the same manner.

But the A.K. was not the only tragedy. The Russian soldiers stationed in Ostroviec had apparently taken to entering houses where they knew girls resided and raping the girls. They would do this in the course of patrolling the streets.

In fact, it happened to us—almost.

I remember distinctly that Misha was entertaining a group of us at our apartment with stories about "Mother Russia," "Comrade Stalin," and other Russian heroes who were fighting a bloody war against the German invaders.

Suddenly a loud knock reverberated through the rooms.

I got up and opened the door. Two Russian soldiers, completely drunk, forced their way past me into the apartment, shouting *"Dzievushke, Dzievushke, Dzievuske!* (The girls, the girls!)" As they lunged for Chania and her girlfriend, they took out their automatic rifles. Chania and Dorka ran to the nearest cupboard.

Misha stood up and drew out his automatic from his belt. The soldiers, seeing the officer's uniform, froze in their tracks.

"Give me your weapons," Misha said quietly. The two handed them over meekly.

"Put your hands up," he continued. They obeyed.

Misha removed their documents from the closed pockets of their uniforms. He was as cool and calm as if he were conducting a routine inspection. The soldiers, both fairly tall men, hung their heads.

"Now," Misha said when he had the weapons and the documents. "Won't you join us in some tobacco?"

The soldiers looked up at him, astounded.

"Come," he said. "I've some tobacco here." He gestured towards the sofa. The soldiers stumbled towards it. Chania and Dorka had emerged from the cupboard and stared from Misha to the soldiers.

Misha, calm and collected, sat down on the chair in which he had been sitting when the soldiers broke in and took out a pouch filled with tobacco. The soldiers removed pieces of newspaper from their boots in which to wrap the tobacco.

"Be my guest," Misha said, and offered them the thin paper designed especially to wrap tobacco which he carried with him all the time.

Sheepishly, the soldiers accepted it, murmuring thanks.

After about an hour, during which Misha continued the conversation as though nothing had happened, he returned their documents and automatics to them—but kept the bullets. He had written down the information about their status and service in the Russian Army.

"Now, comrades," he said as he stood up, which was the signal for them to stand also. "Please report to the Commander at 8:00 tomorrow. Don't be late."

"We—we're sorry," they turned to each of us as they practically fell over each other moving toward the door. They saluted Misha and left.

When they had left, Misha turned to Chania and Dorka. "Ladies, I heartily apologize for this disturbance. I am ashamed that they are Russian soldiers."

"What will happen to them at the Commander's office?" Chania asked.

"They will be punished according to Russian military rules, don't worry," Misha said with a dismissive gesture. "I assure you all, the Russian heroes of whom I've been speaking would never, never do such a thing . . . Now, where were we?"

One day as Abek and I made our way toward the public kitchen for lunch, we saw two Polish men about our age. Suddenly my head spun; where had I seen them? I knew them! Where? Then it struck—like a thunderbolt.

"Abek," I grasped his arm. "Remember the two 'Heivies' I told you about who informed on me in the German Army?"

Abek nodded his head.

"There they are!"

We didn't lose a moment. We spun around as one and seized them from behind, raining blows on their heads and chests. They began to scream. A crowd formed immediately.

"Jews are beating Poles! Jews are beating Poles!"

"Save Christians from Jewish bullies!"

We might as well have been beaten ourselves. The "Heivies" struggled mightily, but Abek and I held them with the tenacity of fury. It wasn't long before the police appeared. I couldn't believe my eyes; one of the police was a man who'd served with me in the partisans.

"Mr. Shvidersky," I shouted, "these two are traitors to Poland. They willingly served the Nazis."

The police arrested them on the spot. Abek and I followed them to the police station.

"Abek," I breathed as we followed them close behind, "I can still see the way they looked at me that morning; I can still hear the way that one—" I pointed to the man on the left "—told that one—" I pointed to the man on the right "that I'm a Jew."

Abek patted my arm.

"I can still see Emil roaring into the kitchen to tell Heinz."

"It's okay, Nachemia." He patted my back. "Now you will be avenged.

The crowd grew larger as we neared the police station. There, the officer behind the desk ordered a search of the men's apartment.

They found German uniforms, with the well-known emblem, "Heivie," sewn on.

The two were immediately ordered to put the German uniforms on. Back at the military headquarters, cardboard signs with the words I WAS A TRAITOR AND INFORMER FOR THE NAZIS were made up and hung around their necks. The military police ordered them to parade up and down on the square in front of the headquarters for the week preceding their trial.

Chania, Abek and I managed to stop in the square at least once a day to see them.

"Now if we could only get the men who took Daddy away," she confided one day, her face pale, her voice shaking.

"We will, Chania." I put my arms about her and held her.

At the trial, I testified:

"They were known as 'Heivies,'" I told the judges. "They voluntarily served the Nazis—for pay. And food. It was the Seventy-Second Fusiliers Battalion."

"What were you doing there?" one of the judges asked me.

I sighed. Again I had to prove myself. For a moment I felt despairing. Then my resolve hardened. This was for a good cause. Finally, those who had betrayed us were being brought to justice.

"I was a spy for the partisans—the First Battalion of the First Brigade of the 'Langevich' group under Lieutenant Czeslov Borecky. We called him 'Bzioza.' "

"And?" one of the judges inquired.

"I was able to give them the password. They got into the encampment without any trouble and stole a truck full of munitions."

The Heivies scowled.

The judges looked at them.

Suddenly the younger Heivie spoke up. "We had no choice. We were afraid we would be taken for forced labor into Germany."

"They could have joined the partisans," I observed.

The trial lasted no more than half an hour. The two were found guilty of collaboration with the German Army; of voluntarily enrolling in the German Army; of informing on a partisan to German authorities; of betraying a Jew to German authorities.

"We did not know he was a member of a partisan group," the younger Heivie shouted.

They were sentenced to death.

So should Emil have gone, I thought.

June 1945

The dry goods store was doing well. Chania was managing it beautifully. I spent more and more time on the committee.

Kielce was the primary source of supply for clothing. We were running low on clothing in Ostroviec as more and more Jews arrived virtually naked. I was one of the five delegates chosen to go to Kielce to bring back supplies of clothing.

It was still dangerous for Jews to travel. Nationalistic Polish groups, renowned as anti-Semitic, ambushed Jews and usually killed them. They wanted to finish off the work Hitler had begun, they claimed.

The Polish security service sent an officer with us, and, moreover, supplied documents, signed by the military commander of Ostroviec, requesting assistance from the governmental office for our safe passage.

"Shall I wear my Russian uniform?" I asked Abek.

There was no hesitation. His voice was jovial. "Oh come on, Nachemia. Do you want to roast to death? You've got protection. My father's seen to that."

Silence. I drew a breath. "All right, all right, Abek."

The four other men also wore civilian clothes. The security officer was in uniform.

He showed our documents to the authorities at the train station in Ostroviec. I looked around the station. I would never forget it. It was only yesterday that we were forced to run from the ghetto in Ostroviec to what we were sure was the train station, the Ukrainians goading us to sing, and had run past it to the camp.

Come to think of it, I'd never seen the inside of the station. It was all dark, glistening wood—typical of nineteenth-century architecture.

Well, you're here now on a mission of freedom. And you're free, I told myself confidently.

We were assigned a special cabin on the train.

"We'll have to change in Skarzisko," the blond-haired boy-faced security officer said.

"So? All right." I glanced at my wrist watch. "As long as we get to Kielce."

The security officer was Jewish, we learned. A partisan, he had been appointed by the new government as part of security.

It was about a two-hour ride to Skarzisko, maybe more. "It's a three-hour wait," the officer said.

We groaned. All of us.

"But look," he placated us, "we're in the first-class waiting room."

Although it was well into the evening, the station at

Skarzisko was thronged with people—people trying to get back to their home cities; people returning from the forced labor camps.

We sat and watched through the glass-windowed doors.

"Rather be in here than out there," Shlamek remarked.

"Yeh. Looks kind of crowded," I mused, leaning forward.

"Is it really going to be three hours?" Shlamek ran his fingers through his thick hair.

"Why should he lie to us?" I muttered.

"Anyone got cigarettes?" Shlamek inquired.

"No," the officer shook his head.

"I haven't," I said disinterestedly. I cared only for getting to our destination. For me the time would drag by with or without distractions.

"Can we get some?" Shlamek wasn't easily put off track.

"There's probably a shop in the main lobby," I observed.

"Who wants to go out *there*?" the officer said irritably.

"I'll go," I said.

There was a snack bar in the main waiting room that sold refreshments and cigarettes. It was slow going over there. I had to walk around milling people. Skarzisko must be a main transfer point, I thought. Idly, I wondered how many of these people were headed for Ostroviec.

I bought five packs of cigarettes, thinking that would hold us until we caught our train to Kielce. Suddenly a scream pierced the study buzz of voices:

"A German! A German!" an elderly, hoarse-voiced man shouted.

I looked around. Who were they screaming at? Then I saw the Pole who had screamed pointing his gnarled finger at me. People turned to look.

I broke into a run for the first-class waiting room. Some began to run after me. I slammed the door shut and locked it.

"What's going on?" my group asked almost in chorus. By then there was loud pounding on the door.

"They think I'm a German," I told our officer breathlessly. "Someone has remembered me wearing the German uniform."

"All right, we'll take care of it," he said.

But now the pounding on the door was accompanied by loud voices: "Polish militia! Open the door."

Our officer drew his pistol and opened the door.

Two militia entered, rifles aimed at us.

"What do you want?" our officer demanded.

"We want to see your documents."

Our officer kept level-headed. "May I see your identifications?" he asked, his pistol still in his hand.

The militia took out their cards; our officer showed them our documents. Apparently satisfied, they left.

"Now—who wants cigarettes?" I said mischievously.

"Why did they think you were a German, Nachemia?" Mundek, one of the committee asked.

"I served the partisans by 'joining' the German Army," I replied. "I guess whoever it was that began screaming out there had seen me while I was in the German Army."

"Oh."

Ten minutes hadn't passed when the militia returned—with the Pole who had pointed me out.

"We want him to go to the police station with us." They pointed at me.

"Absolutely not," our officer replied. "We are on our way to Kielce."

"The commander orders it," one of the militia snapped.

"I don't give a damn *who* orders it," our officer snapped back. "It is dark. You think we don't know what can happen on the way to the police station on the pretext that someone attempted to run? We've shown you the documents. They're in good order. Now get out of here."

The militia drew their guns; just as quickly, our officer drew his.

Shaje stood up and went over to where the three were staring each other down.

"There is no need for this," he said in Polish. "There is

no need for murder right here in the station. He is not a German," he pointed at me. "You've seen the documents," he addressed the militia. "Let us have a compromise—but Nachemia cannot go to the police station."

The four of us sat on the edge of our seats, listening intently to Shaje. We felt the tension begin to die down.

Finally, one of the militia growled, "All right. But I will stay here to watch you. You," he turned to his companion, "go call the commander."

During the next ten minutes there was a tense silence in the little waiting room. The five of us exchanged glances but said nothing. Finally, I addressed the militiaman:

"Would you like a cigarette? After all, that's what started this whole thing."

He looked at me in astonishment, then broke into a broad grin.

"Yes, thank you," he said.

He took a couple of puffs; the three of us also took the opportunity to light up. Then I asked him, "Who were those men out there and why did they accuse me of being a German?"

"They were the two who came in before," the officer said, relaxing visibly. "They say that you were one of the Nazis that rounded them up to ship them off to Germany for forced labor."

"Where did they say all this took place?"

The Pole looked thoughtful. "As a matter of fact—they didn't."

"I never rounded anyone up for forced labor or deportation, I swear it." I looked him right in the eyes.

He looked at me. "Were you ever in the German Army?"

I took a deep breath. "Yes," I said. The Pole's eyes opened wide. "I was in the German Army—as a spy for the First Battalion of the First Brigade of the 'Langevich' group."

"Who was the leader of that group?" the militia asked, visibly excited.

"Lieutenant Czeslov Borecky. Known as 'Bzioza.' "

"Oh my God . . ." the Pole said.

Just then the door opened. We all stood up, not knowing what to expect. We could see that a rather large crowd had gathered outside, obviously curious.

"Must be the commander," Shaje muttered.

I stood rooted to the spot. That build, those broad shoulders were recognizable anywhere in the world. The commander began to stride into the room—then froze in his tracks.

"TADEK!"

"BOLEK!"

We rushed across the room, fell into each other's arms, laughing, slapping each other on the back. Tears ran unheeded down our cheeks. The others stood gaping. We stood there a long time.

The militia who had accompanied Bolek into the room stared uncomprehendingly. The militia who had been "guarding" us while the commander was on his way understood perfectly. He knew Bolek had been a leader in my partisan group. He smiled broadly.

"All right," Bolek turned to the other militia. "Everyone out."

He put his arm around my shoulder and led me to one of the benches. The rest of the group faded to the other side of the room.

"Tadek—"

"Bolek. Commander Bolek. I mean—it was the password I gave that helped you into the battalion to steal the truck, wasn't it?"

"Absolutely. You know, we even got a couple of those stupid German guards in the munitions storeroom to help us load the truck."

We both laughed uproariously. Out of the corner of my eye I noticed the others in my group laughing and shaking their heads.

"How did you get to be commander of this militia, Bolek?"

"Well, they made practically *all* commanders of partisan groups commanders in security, militia and in administration. The Russians, that is. They knew who the partisans were."

"Of course. They helped us through the underground."

"Tadek, where are you headed?"

"We've got to get the train for Kielce. I'm on the survivors' committee in Ostroviec and we're going to get some clothing for the new arrivals. They are pouring into Ostroviec daily."

"So you returned to Ostroviec—"

"And met my sister."

"A miracle, Tadek, a miracle." He shook his head.

"Life is a miracle, Bolek," I half whispered.

He didn't answer. But he heard.

"Tadek, let me accompany your group on the train to Kielce—I guess you have enough room in your cabin?—and we'll tell each other how we got out of the war."

"That would be wonderful."

"Tadek, you know you saved my life that day in Volka Voynowska."

"So—you saved mine when you allowed me into the partisan group."

It was the happiest train ride of my life. When we got to Kielce, Bolek made arrangements to catch the train back to Skarzisko. Just before he turned to go, he said, "Tadek, tell me one thing."

"What?"

"What is your *real* name?"

"Nachemia."

He embraced me once more. "A good name. I will never forget it—or you."

There were tears in my eyes as I watched him walk away.

It took us half the day to secure all the clothing we thought we'd need for the new arrivals in Ostroviec. We went to the Jewish Committee offices and Soviet-run centers.

By two o'clock we had the clothing boxed and piled

outside one of the committee offices, ready to be taken to the train station.

"When is the train back to Ostroviec?" I asked.

"Four o'clock," our Polish security officer said. "Why?"

"I have something to do before we return."

"What is it?"

"It's—personal."

The officer's face slowly spread into a grin. What could he want, I wondered.

"All right," he finally said. "Do you have your papers with you?"

I felt in my inside jacket pocket. "Yes," I answered.

"Four o'clock. Sharp. Don't be late."

I set off in the direction of the municipal buildings, where I'd observed the Russians had set up offices. I hoped and prayed, as I trudged along, that someone there would speak Polish.

Finally, I arrived at the municipal building. It seemed that all municipal buildings were old, stone-faced and weathered. This one was no exception. People milled about. I walked up the cracking front steps and pushed against the dark wood front door. Inside was a long dark corridor. Walking down it, I slipped quietly into what appeared to be the busiest office. Russian soldiers and some civilians stood and sat around. I stood near the wall and listened. Finally, I observed one Russian soldier speaking Polish. I approached him.

"You speak Polish?" I asked.

"Yes," he replied shortly.

"Are you an officer?"

"No. Why do you need an officer?"

"I—have something to ask."

He looked me up and down. The worst he could do, I thought was to order me out.

"You want an officer that speaks Polish?" he finally asked.

"Yes—thank you."

He stared at me again. Then he jerked his thumb

towards a uniformed Russian sitting at one of the tables. "Try him."

"Thank you very much."

I approached the table. The officer looked up and I immediately noticed the contrast between his light green eyes and his black hair and moustache.

"You speak Polish?" I asked.

"Yes. Why?" he said in a standoffish voice.

"Can you tell me—what happened to the German battalions that retreated toward Kielce last January?"

His eyes sharpened to pinpoints. "Why do you want to know?"

My mind raced. "A woman—a fellow partisan—I was in a partisan group—worked for the Germans in the kitchen of the Seventy-Second Fusiliers Battalion. I—want to know what happened to her. Whether she might still be alive . . ."

His glare seemed to soften. He absentmindedly began to tap his knee with his left hand. "As far as I know, those who were not killed outright during their retreat were taken to labor camps in the Soviet Union. I don't know exactly any facts about the particular battalion you're talking of, but I can tell you that's what usually happened."

"Thank you for the information," I barely whispered. "You are kind to tell me."

As I began to walk away, he called out to me. I turned.

"She must have meant a lot to you," he smiled.

I could only nod.

Tears blurred my eyes as I walked toward the railroad station. I must have sent Heinz to his death or to a labor camp. The Soviets would not have known about the retreat had I not informed on the *Wehrmacht* in Konsk.

I hardly spoke on the train back to Ostroviec.

August 1945

Chania and I asked every Jew who arrived in Ostroviec if they'd heard anything about Mother, Chaike, or Moshe. We thought perhaps someone had been in a camp with one of them.

We'd come to the conclusion that Mother was gone. But no one could give us concrete information about Chaike. We heard that Moshe had been sent to Pleshov, near Krakov, then transferred to Flossenberg, a camp in Germany. There the information stopped.

Meanwhile, Chania travelled fairly routinely to Krashnik, Lublin, and Lodz to obtain fabric and other merchandise for our flourishing shop in Ostroviec. I'd given her directions to Leon Brenner's place in Krashnik; if she had to stay overnight, he would probably be able to give her lodgings, I told her.

"Your friend Leon—he's very nice," she said the first time she returned from Krashnik.

I looked at her more closely. Was that a smile on her face?

"Yes." I nodded, trying to restrain my own smile. "He was very hospitable to me while I was in Krashnik," I answered.

She said nothing.

One day, she reported that as she was returning to Ostroviec from Lodz, a man of about twenty-five approached her on the train.

"He came up to me, sat down, and said 'How are you?' as though we'd known each other for years," she told me. "I just looked at him and nodded. And he persisted. He said that he'd just seen me two weeks ago in Zellsheim, of all places, in some survivors' camp. I was sure he was just looking for company."

"So what did you do?" I grinned. Chania was so proper. I could tell she must not have appreciated what she thought were the man's advances, yet could find no gracious way to change seats.

"I pretended to watch the scenery out the window," she smiled. "Then he took a pack of pictures out of his back pocket, picked one out and handed it to me. It was a picture of a group of youngsters—and there was Chaike!"

"Chaike!?"

I took a deep breath and walked over to where she stood. "Chaike," I repeated.

She nodded her head vehemently. "Yes. And that's why he thought he knew me. He thought I was Chaike! In fact, after I had nearly fainted with surprise, he said, 'See, I wasn't being fresh'—I guess he knew what I was thinking—'You look so alike.' Well, at this point I was crying for joy, and could hardly speak to him."

I interrupted her excitedly. "Where is Chaike, then?"

She brushed back the hair which had fallen over her eyes.

"Zellsheim. Outside Frankfurt. It was built for the Nazis who worked or were somehow connected to the chemical industry there. He says it's a beautiful little suburb—trees, flowers. It was left intact. The American generals—Eisenhower and Clay—ordered the Germans to vacate it so displaced Jews could stay there. Wait. I have the picture."

She jumped up and ran to get it, pulling out her wallet. "Here," she said excitedly. I stared down. Chaike looked content in the picture. She, too, looked older. Which of us didn't?

"He couldn't tell me much about Chaike," Chania continued, "except that she seems happy in Zellsheim, she helps out in the kitchen area."

"I don't suppose he knew anything about Mother or Moshe?"

"No." She shrugged sadly.

We both spoke at once: "Let's go find her."

"What about the store?" Nachemia asked.

"It can wait." Chania's eyes glistened with tears.

In the meantime, another "miracle" occurred. Two of the Russian-backed Polish security came to the committee headquarters.

"We are detaining a field gendarme who worked for the Germans. He claims he is a Pole and a Jew," the officer said. "Can someone from the Jewish community here come with us to Opatov to determine if the man is telling the truth?"

Opatov! Where I'd been captured by the Luftwaffe and where the young military policeman had told the Germans that I was not a Jew but a Pole. Whatever had happened to that young officer? Could it be . . .?

"I will go with you," I said.

They broke into smiles. The senior officer waved his arm in a polite gesture. "Thank you. We have a jeep outside."

"Let me see if Abek Fridenthal will go with us," I said. "Two are better than one."

They chuckled.

It was a one hour ride to Opatov. I explained the strange feeling I had to Mr. Fridental.

"You think it might be the same man who saved your life with the Luftwaffe?" he asked.

"I don't know," I mused. "Yes. It strikes me that if he *is* a Jew—and he is that man—it certainly explains why he took my part—"

"—and treated you with such kindness," Mr. Fridental finished.

I was gratified to see that the Polish security occupied the German military police quarters where I'd been interrogated when the Luftwaffe had captured me.

"He's in there," one of the security men at the desk pointed to an adjacent room.

The man of whom they spoke sat slumped against the wall. For a moment I was unsure. I drew closer. He had a full beard, and there were reddish as well as black and blue marks on his face. But it was the same young officer. I could still hear him as he'd turned to leave before locking the door to my cell: "Don't be frightened. Be strong."

He looked at me in utter astonishment. Then a smile broke across his face.

I smiled at him. "Don't be frightened," I said. "Be strong."

Both he and Mr. Fridental understood immediately.

I walked back into the other room. "Who is the officer in charge?" I asked.

A dark, stocky middle-aged Pole stood up. "I am."

I turned and faced him. "That man in there is no German. He is a Pole. He helped me very much when I'd been captured by the Luftwaffe last year. He was never on the German side."

He mulled that over for a moment.

"He worked for the Germans," the commanding officer said.

"So did I," I replied. "I 'joined' the German Army as a spy for Commander Bzioza's partisan group."

"Bring him out here," the officer ordered one of the men.

The "gendarme" stumbled as he entered the room.

"So?" the commanding officer said.

The man blinked in the strong light and swallowed nervously. "I've told you, I got into the service of the Germans with faked papers. I had to survive."

"I believe him," I interjected. "Otherwise, he never would have told the German police that I was a pure Pole when I am a Jew. They ordered him to lock me up, so he had no choice but to do so. But before he left he brought me food." I turned to the man. "Amchu?" I asked.

He nodded, smiling.

"He is Jewish," I said to the commanding officer.

"All right, let him go," the short, stocky man said.

The three of us walked out of the building together. He put his hands on my shoulders. "How can I thank you?" His grave eyes met mine.

"How can *I* thank *you* for what you did for me?" I asked, my voice breaking.

"You just have."

September 1945

It had been five days since Chania had left for Lublin and Krashnik to purchase goods for the store and I was beside myself. She was supposed to have returned in three days.

I had heard about anti-Semitic Poles who threw Jews out of train windows for no reason.

I closed the store early. I couldn't keep my mind on business. I headed for the Fridenthals' apartment, and as I walked I wept. Suddenly, I was a little boy without a mother, and the world trembled under my feet.

The Fridenthals' apartment was locked. I stumbled back down the stairs into the street. Dusk was approaching, and the light was a soft gold. The end of the day—the end of Chania's life?

I headed toward the committee office. Panic rose like a bile in my throat. I couldn't see for the tears—I made my way toward the office instinctively.

Chania, Chania, I thought, *have we gone through Hitler's hell, to obtain freedom for this? Why? Why does God continue to punish us—hasn't there been punishment enough? Isn't it enough that they've taken our parents, Eliezer, and Moshe?* I tried to push these thoughts away, but they taunted me.

I felt that the world was falling in. I had not felt this way in the five previous horrible years.

"Nachemia, where are you going?" Abek stood in front of me. I had been totally unaware of him.

"I don't know," I sobbed.

"Hey—what is it? You're as white as that building. Tell me, Nachemia—are you going to pass out?"

"I—"

"You look so awful," he interrupted. "Did Chania come back from Lublin?"

"No," I choked. "Abek, I have a bad feeling. I closed the store and went to see your father—but he's not in the apartment. I need his advice. He can help me out, tell me what to do. Five days since Chania went to Lublin, and she promised me she'd be back within three days—"

Abek put his arm around my shoulder. "Come, Nachemia," he said.

"You know very well what's going on on the roads and on the trains—how the Poles attack the Jews and sometimes throw them out the windows while the train is going—" I was practically babbling.

"My father is in the office; come." He led me away.

Several Jews newly arrived from the concentration camps were in the office when Abek and I reached it. Mr. Fridenthal stood up the minute I staggered in with Abek. "Nachemia, what happened?"

Abek answered for me. "Chania has not come back yet from Lublin; she was supposed to be here the day before yesterday. Nachemia doesn't know what to do."

Mr. Fridenthal came to me and put his hand on my shoulder. "Nachemia, everything will be fine, don't worry. Listen, perhaps there is no transportation back here right now. Maybe the trains have been delayed."

He guided me to a chair and sat me down. A couple of new arrivals stepped back. "Nachemia," he patted my shoulder, "look, calm down. You are not fainthearted: you escaped a concentration camp, joined the partisans, blew up trains, gave the partisans the password from the *Wehrmacht*. You are no coward. Come, now."

His words made me feel better.

"Everything is going to be fine," he went on. "Chania knows how to get around, don't worry. If she knew how to get out of the *gendarmie* and the Gestapo, we can rely on her. She's all right, I know it." He got up, went to his desk, and motioned me over.

"Have you any address or name where she is supposed to be staying in Lublin?" he asked.

"No," I replied, calming down, "the only people I know in Lublin are the Zukermans, but when I was there nine months ago, I didn't see any telephones."

"Wait," Abek spoke up suddenly. "Didn't Chania say she might stop in Krashnik?"

"Oh—yes." I suddenly remembered.

"Well, whom would she be staying with there?"

"Probably at my friend Leon Brenner's apartment."

"Okay," Mr. Fridenthal smiled. "In a small town it should be easy to find a telephone number by name. Come," he said, rising from his seat.

"Where?" I asked.

"The post office," he replied. "They close at 5:00; it's 4:30 now. Maybe we can do something."

The post office was not far from the Jewish Committee offices. We were there in minutes. Mr. Fridenthal went straight to the man in charge of the telephone.

"I would like to make a phone call to Krashnik and to speak to a man named Leon Brenner." His tone was polite but urgent.

The clerk, short and painfully thin, squinted at us. "Do you have a phone number?" he asked in a monotone.

"No," Abek replied impatiently.

"Does he have a telephone, this Brenner?"

"No," I said dejectedly.

"Do you know his address?" Abek prodded.

"I can't remember."

"How can I call anyone without a phone number or address?" the clerk asked, nearly exasperated.

"You are absolutely right," Mr. Fridenthal reassured him. "But this call is very, very important. A matter of life and death. Could you please do me this big favor and try to put this phone call through? I don't care how much it costs."

The clerk relaxed. "I'll do my best," he said.

"Thank you," the three of us said in unison.

He called the Krashnik post office and asked them to locate Leon Brenner in the local register. We all waited in silence for what seemed like years. "Okay," the clerk finally said into the phone, "will you go to his address and ask him to come to the post office tomorrow morning at 9:00 and wait for a telephone call from Ostroviec?"

We were disappointed.

"That is all I can do right now," the clerk sighed. "Come back tomorrow just before nine and we'll make the call."

"Nachemia, stay with us tonight," Abek urged as we walked back toward the committee offices.

"Thanks, Abek. But—no. Suppose Chania comes back tonight."

"I can understand your wanting to be there," Mr.

Fridenthal nodded. "But at least let us go to the Jewish kitchen and have some dinner."

We ran into Misha at dinner. He scanned my downcast face. "My God, Nachemia, what's the matter?" he exclaimed.

"Chania was supposed to have returned from Lublin— or Krashnik—two days ago," Abek explained.

"Chania—?" Misha's brow rose.

"Yes, Misha," I sighed. "You know how dangerous it is to travel these days. Oh God—" I shook my head.

"But we've put in a phone call to Krashnik," Mr. Fridenthal said determinedly. "She might be delayed there. Try not to worry. We'll see tomorrow morning."

"Please God that's all it is," Misha sighed.

I didn't sleep a wink. Every little noise or eerie whisper on the stairway caused me to jump and run to the door. I thought the morning would never arrive.

When the sun began to rise, I went over to the window to watch it. It was just before 6:00. Below the window, workers made their ways to their various jobs, watched by guards.

I recalled how, three years previous, I also had gone to work—marched, really—on that same road, with the Ukrainian guards watching for the tiniest misstep, rifles ready to shoot. I heard again their shouts, the sound of rifle butts against heads, the orders to "Sing, you bloody Jews!"

I remembered afresh the march to "Kazet." I could see the cobblestones running red with blood, the bodies on the sides of the roads. I had survived it all. Chania had survived it all. For what?

The fierce knocking on my door made me jump. I ran over to the door. "Nachemia, Nachemia," Abek called from the other side. "Open up. Come on—we have to get to the post office."

Once inside, he looked at the steel bar across the door. "When did you get that?" he asked.

"Right after the night the Russian soldiers broke in— remember?"

"Oh, yes," he murmured soberly. He patted my shoulder. "Listen, we just have time for breakfast. At our place. Come on."

"No, listen," I protested. "I have bread and butter and eggs and coffee right here. Let me make you an omelet. You can start the fire in the stove, okay?"

Abek grinned wickedly. "Yeh, I almost forgot, Nachemia. You were the chef of the *Wehrmacht.*"

"Let's hope I haven't forgotten how," I shot back.

I made two fairly decent omelets. Abek gobbled his. I toyed with mine.

"Eat, Nachemia; look, I've already finished," he said.

"Abek, please." I pushed my plate over to him. "Do me a favor and finish this, too. I can't."

He looked at me and nodded understandingly.

"Coffee is all I want," I explained lamely. He nodded.

At 8:30 we locked the apartment and sprinted over to the post office. People in the streets stared at us, wondering, no doubt, what the big hurry was.

The clerk recognized us immediately. "Where is the other gentleman?" he asked.

"My father is very busy on the committee today," Abek explained.

"Well, who's going to pay for this call?" he asked suspiciously.

"Don't worry—I am," I answered. I took out a roll of bills from my back pocket and displayed it. He was convinced.

"All right—it's not quite nine yet." He glanced at his watch.

Abek and I busied ourselves with the notices on the bulletin board. After about five minutes the clerk called me: "Go to that telephone booth over there and pick up the receiver." I rushed over.

There was a disturbance on the line. I shouted into the receiver. "Leon—Leon—are you there?"

The clerk signalled me not to shout. "If you speak quietly and slowly they'll hear you better," he called.

"Nachemia?" It was Chania's voice.

"CHANIA! Thank God. Are you all right?"

"Yes, Nachemia. I'm all right. What's the matter?" she asked.

"What do you mean, what's the matter? What are you doing there? You were supposed to be here two days ago—you promised. I'm going out of my mind and you ask what's the matter."

"All right, Nachemia. You're right. When you come here I'll explain."

"Where am I coming to?"

"To Krashnik," she answered.

"For what?"

"I have good news."

"Well—tell me," I demanded.

"We're engaged."

"Who's we?"

"Leon and I," she said.

I burst into joyous laughter. "MAZEL TOV!" I yelled. Everyone in the post office looked around. "I'm on my way to Krashnik," I added. "See you."

Abek was right next to the phone booth. "Why 'Mazel Tov'?" he asked. "Is Chania engaged?"

"Yes—to Leon, the guy I told you about, the one I met the first time when I was in Krashnik nine months ago."

"Oh, yeah. You like him." He smiled in amusement. It was more a statement than a question.

"Yah. I'm glad." I heaved a sigh of relief. "God, I'm glad!"

"Abek," I clapped his shoulder as we made our way to the committee offices. "Come with me to Krashnik for the engagement party. You're family."

He shook his head sadly. "No, Nachemia. I cannot leave my father for even one day by himself. But, tell you what—I'll watch the store. You'll be a few days."

For a moment, we were both silent.

"Thank you, friend," I said, patting his shoulder.

Mr. Fridenthal was waiting impatiently. As soon as he saw the smiles on our faces he said, "As I thought. She's all right, isn't she?"

"More than that," Abek said before I could. "She's engaged. To Leon Brenner."

Mr. Fridenthal clasped my shoulder. "See, Nachemia, what did I tell you. Don't ever lose hope. Now—let's sit down and drink *L'chaim.*" He bent down and brought a bottle of vodka and three glasses from the desk drawer.

He set the glasses on his desk and poured the transparent liquor into them. They caught the morning light streaming through the windows. We each picked up a glass, stood up, and clinked the glasses together. *"L'chaim,"* we said in unison.

I felt lightheaded almost immediately.

Mr. Fridenthal went back into the drawer and brought out two sandwiches. "Here," he said, "you probably did not have any breakfast. So I took these with me."

"Thank you, Mr. Fridenthal," I said. Suddenly I was starved. "Abek had a double share of breakfast at my place. And I'm real hungry now." I ate both sandwiches. The Fridenthals laughed.

I spent only a few hours in the store that day. I wonder what the customers thought; I was almost completely distracted and totally happy. I closed at about 3:00 and headed to the apartment to pack for the trip. I planned to catch the 7:00 p.m. train to Krashnik, but I kept changing my mind about which clothes to bring, and when I finally got to the station, I had missed the 7:00 p.m. The next train was due to leave at 10:00. With three hours on my hands, I decided to return to the apartment and change into my Russian uniform. It would be safer.

Unfortunately the 10:00 train went to Rozvadov. It was not a through train. The train to Krashnik would not pull in until 7:00 in the morning.

"Ah well, I missed the 7:00 through my own stupidity," I mumbled as I searched the station in Rozvadov for a place to sleep. The benches were all occupied.

I leaned back against the wall to think. Young girls walked around the station approaching men. They seemed particularly attracted to soldiers.

It wasn't long before one of them got around to me. Short, dark-haired, overly made up, she wore high heels and a red satin dress underneath her jacket.

"Would you like to come over to my place and spend the night?" She spoke half-Russian, half-Polish.

I answered in Polish. "I *am* looking for a place to sleep—but not with you."

"Crazy bastard," she called. She turned and walked over to a stout middle-aged woman who appeared to be taking everything in. She whispered a few words to the woman who looked at me with watery eyes.

Before I knew it the woman had waddled over to me. "Are you looking for a place to sleep?" she asked in harsh Polish.

"Yes, I am."

"You can stay at my place until morning. But you must pay me in advance. Fifty zlotys."

I paid her and followed her out of the station, praying the place was not rat- or roach-infested.

She led me to a decent-sized apartment not far from the station. As we entered I noticed people already sleeping on mattresses on the floor. She beckoned me to the large kitchen. I looked around. It seemed clean enough. The woman heaved a bench from under the table, went to a cupboard, and pulled out two woolen blankets and a pillow.

I didn't realize until right then how tired I was. The woman stared at me as I began to unbutton my overcoat. "Are you waiting for another train?"

"Yes," I replied, stifling a yawn. "The seven o'clock to Krashnik."

"The seven. Very well. I'll wake you shortly after six, so you can make it."

"Thank you."

She continued to gaze at me. "So," she said slowly, "your little 'friend's' loss is my gain."

I looked at her sharply.

Her coarse features seemed to soften. "Don't judge those girls harshly. They see no choice but to be what they are. Most have lost all family, all money. They have nothing else."

I folded my coat and placed it over the back of a chair. "Perhaps you're right," I mumbled.

"I know I am," she said softly. "Well, good night."And she was gone from the kitchen.

I put out the lamp and found my way to the bench, where she had already laid the blankets and pillow.

As she'd promised, she woke me a little after 6:00. I hurriedly splashed water over my face, combed my hair, and dressed. I grabbed my rucksack from under the bench.

"Thank you for the bed . . ." I smiled at her.

"Thank *you,*" she smiled. "I hope you have a good journey. And remember what I said. We are all human beings."

Her words ran through my head as I sprinted towards the station. That was what Heinz had said to me the night he told me he would protect me.

The train was already in the station. Quickly, I boarded it. I wasn't going to miss *this* one. I got a seat next to the window. I wanted to watch the scenery, and I was fairly certain that, with my Russian uniform, no one would attempt to throw me out.

The countryside was beginning to turn toward autumn. Yellow glaze appeared in the fields, even in some of the trees. The train engine created billows of smoke, matched by those inside the car from cigarette smoke. Somehow this softened the scene. The two men and woman who had moved into the seats nearest me were asleep within the hour. I was left to my thoughts.

Should I be angry with Chania, because she didn't come home when she said she would? For the hell she put me through? For not trying to even contact me?

The train pulled into Krashnik at 9:00. The town was bustling with the day's activities. Vendors stood about the station, plying fruits, vegetables, sweets, drinks. Horse-drawn buggies waited at the curb. I hailed one of them and gave him Leon's address.

Outside Leon's apartment building, I paid the driver and began to run up the stairs. Chania stood at the top of the stairwell. She glowed. I could not spoil her happiness with reproaches.

"Nachemia—"

"Mazel Tov, Chania, Mazel Tov." We hugged each other. "Your happiness is my happiness."

But she sensed my previous thoughts. "Nachemia, I hope you're not angry with me—but maybe you are, a little? She looked searchingly at me. "I really tried to let you know I would be delayed in returning to Ostroviec, but there were no ways, believe me. A letter would have taken a week. I feel badly about it. I really do."

"It's over, Chania. Yes—I was out of my mind with worry, as I told you. But let us not spoil the happiness of this day."

"Such wonderful smells!" I inhaled as we entered the apartment.

"For the party tonight," Chania smiled.

"So, Chania." I put my rucksack down and began to unbutton my coat. "No wonder you've made so many business trips to Lublin and Krashnik."

Chania blushed. "Have you had breakfast?" she asked.

I hadn't, I remembered. And suddenly I was very hungry. "No. Will you make me some?"

"Of course. Coffee first?"

"That's great. Chania, I am delighted. Delighted to have Leon for a brother-in-law."

Chania smiled gently. "That's good, Nachemia. He is a good man."

Chania's influence had already made itself felt in the apartment. There were flowered cushions on the one rickety chair that I'd remembered, and another, more comfortable chair stood opposite it. There was a lace covering on the table.

"Chania," I sighed as I sank into the comfortable chair, "tell me one thing. How come it was you who answered the telephone in the post office yesterday morning when I called Leon?"

She turned from the table towards me and grinned. "Oh," she chuckled, "I had a feeling it would be you calling. So I went down with Leon."

We went out about noon. Chania felt she needed more food for the party. We walked around Krashnik. The sun was still warm, but the air was becoming brisk. People smiled at us. From Chania's expression they probably thought it was the two of us who were engaged. Once I put my arm around her shoulder impulsively. "You deserve this happiness, Chania. Every bit of it. And I know you'll have a good life with Leon."

She looked up at me and smiled.

Leon got to the apartment around 4:00. We hugged each other.

"Now, are you still angry with her for not returning when she said?" He held me at arms' length.

"Not anymore."

"Good." He grinned. "Now what do we need to do for the party?"

"I think we've done it all," I grinned back. "Let's relax." Chania and I sat in the two guest chairs. Leon pulled a chair from the table near.

"Here is the plan, Nachemia," he said. "What do you think? You and Chania will return to Ostroviec tomorrow morning. I have to wind up some affairs here in Krashnik, and will come to Ostroviec within the week. Do you think they could find me a room near you?"

"I'll put Abek right on it," I said reassuringly. "This is wonderful, Leon. I am so glad Chania and you found each other."

No one said a word. We all smiled.

It was a wonderful party. The apartment was packed with people. Hersh introduced me to a few other men who'd fought with the partisans, and Chania and Leon had to pry

me away from my conversations with them to introduce me
to other friends.

"Chania, this is the most joyous occasion since . . .
since . . . before the war."

She sighed. "If only—" We looked into each other's
eyes. We each knew what the other was thinking: if only
Mother and Daddy and Eliezer could be with us.

Meanwhile, the wine and vodka flowed like water.

The next morning, Chania and I left for Ostroviec on
the eight o'clock train.

October 1945

The news came through the committee. There had
been a pogrom in Kielce. Forty Jews had been slaughtered—
by Poles.

Which town was going to be next?

"We've already had our pogrom here," Abek said between gulps of coffee.

"Not necesarily, Abek." His father shook his head.
"That was only one house—five people. Oh God—saved from
Hitler's beasts, only to be murdered in cold blood by Poles—
who have no reason to hold anything against us."

Suddenly Chania spoke with a determination I had not
heard from her since we'd been in our parents' home in
Kurov. "Nachemia, we will leave here. We will leave Poland.
The earth here is soaked with Jewish blood. We will go to
Chaike."

We all stared at her wordlessly.

She was right.

ELEVEN

October 1945

It wasn't going to be easy. The borders were patrolled by both the Russian and the Polish armies. It was impossible to obtain passports.

We talked of nothing else, with each other, with Abek and his father.

Mr. Fridenthal advised us that we had a better chance of making contact with the *Bhricha* in Lodz.

"There is a denser Jewish population there," he said. Consequently more *Bhricha* go there to help Jews reach Israel—or at least safety."

Chania's face lit up. "Nachemia, we have a cousin in Lodz—Lazar Weinberg. He went to Lodz several months ago. He has his wife and daughter with him. Let me see—Devorah is his wife's name. You remember him, Nachemia. His mother was our mother's sister. They used to live in Gneivoshov."

Then I remembered. When I was about ten Mother had taken me to visit her sister in Gnievoshov—my Aunt Tova. Gneivoshov was about twenty miles from Kurov, and much smaller. Even at ten, I had been struck by the sharp division of the place into Old Gnievoshov and New Gnievoshov. My aunt and uncle, who were very wealthy, lived in New Gnievoshov, where there were paved roads and sidewalks, elegant homes, and shrubbery and flowers on everyone's property. Uncle Pinchas owned a brick factory about six miles from Gneivoshov. Every morning a carriage hitched to two horses pulled up in front of the house. Uncle Pinchas would get into the carriage, which drove him to his factory. Lazar was in charge of Uncle Pinchas's flour mill, which was also outside of the town. Lazar was already married at that time and living in his own home.

"Anyway," Chania broke into my thoughts, "Lazar and Devorah and their daughter—Rivka—were bounced around from one concentration camp to another. God only knows how they survived and stayed together."

"Just like you two did," Abek put in, "with fortune and luck."

Chania and I smiled.

"But," she continued, "they were afraid to go back to Gnievoshov because of the anti-Semitic Poles. So they went to Lodz. Now Lazar has a leather business—he sells leather to shoemakers—"

"Chania, how do you know all this?"

Her eyes had a momentary glint of amusement. Then they became serious. "Well, last time I was in Lodz I visited him. He lives on Kilinska Street. In two small rooms."

"You never told me you visited him."

"No, I didn't . . . I guess I forgot."

"That's because she detoured through Krashnik after she left Lodz," Abek grinned. We all laughed—Leon loudest of all.

"Well, anyway," Chania's cheeks were pink. "Lazar isn't in the best of health—and he's kind of depressed. Except for Devorah, he's lost all his family—Aunt Tova, Uncle Pinchas, all his brothers and sisters."

The lamp on the table guttered. It rasped loudly in the deep silence of the room. No one spoke for a long time. Finally, Mr. Fridenthal heavily sighed," . . . ah, who hasn't?" he said in barely a whisper.

We each looked at one another. Then I grasped Chania's hand—at the same time Abek clasped his father's shoulder as if to give each other courage.

"But," Chania resumed in a low voice, "I think Lazar knows *Bhricha*. I overheard two youngish men come to Lazar's rooms one afternoon and speak with him in Hebrew. I was in the other room with Devorah, but I understood a few Hebrew sentences from Beh Jacob School. They spoke of Israel—and of flight. Well, after they left, I asked Lazar who they were. All he said was 'Jews.' So I asked him why they spoke Hebrew. He said he was doing business with them, and they spoke Hebrew because they saw a strange girl and didn't want strangers to know what they were buying, for how much and with what coins.

"Well, I got a little vexed with him. 'Don't sell air with air,' I told him. 'You know very well that I understand some Hebrew and that those two told you that some group is about to leave tomorrow and that they have some problems.' Well, Lazar actually smiled—for the first time. He said to me, 'Chania, I can't lie to you. You are too clever; you are Henoch Wurman's daughter.' "

We all broke into laughter, remembering my father's pithy wisdom. Mine, as was Chania's, was tinged with mourning.

"By then Devorah was also annoyed with Lazar. 'She's your cousin,' she yelled at him. 'You can trust her; you always spoke of your Uncle Henoch with respect and admiration.'

"Poor Lazar—beset on two sides. 'Okay, okay,' he finally said."

Chania sat back and furrowed her brow. "I am trying to remember Lazar's exact words, because I think they are valuable to us.

" 'This is very secretive,' he said. 'If the authorities find out we are in very big trouble. There is a Zionist movement, called *Bhricha*.' "

Mr. Fridenthal was nodding enthusiastically.

" 'Their mission is to save Jews and free them from Poland to reach D.P. camps in West Germany, Austria, and Italy and go from those camps to Eretz Israel. They do not take money for their work unless they have to pay off an official to obtain documents—or a Russian officer that can help or bribe border police.'

"I asked Lazar if he belonged to the *Bhricha*. He answered, 'I don't belong directly. I'm too old—I'm forty. I don't have the strength anymore. Escorting people across borders is arduous. These are the new generation of young men and women sacrificing their lives to save the Jews that survived the Holocaust—and to help them reach Israel.' "

"So should we all," Mr. Fridenthal intoned.

"Yes," Abek added.

"Lazar's role was to assemble candidates that were willing to leave Poland—and to check if these people can be trusted. I asked him how he determines who wants to leave Poland. He said, 'We walk among Jews—especially near the Jewish committee offices in the city. We listen; we write notes; we check them out. Then we ask the promising candidates to come for an interview. Those of whom we approve we give a meeting point from which the *Bhricha* take them to the other side of the border.' "

"Yes, that is the way it's done," Mr. Fridenthal observed. We all stared at him. How deep was his involvement with the *Bhricha*?

"Who are these 'Fliers,' Mr. Fridenthal?" I ventured.

He leaned back and folded his arms across his chest. "Most come from Eretz Israel—two groups, mainly: the *Haganah* and the *Etzel*. They are underground movements fighting for the liberation of Israel from British rule. And they have an iron-bound determination to free as many Jews as possible."

"Yes, that's what Lazar said," Chania said slowly. "He said he has the highest respect for them—they are strong, intelligent. They speak English, Russian, French, Polish, German . . ."

"Chania, do you think Lazar would help us make contact with the *Bhricha*?" I asked.

The room suddenly became completely quiet. Not even street sounds penetrated the silence.

"I know he will, Nachemia," Chania said so softly we had to strain to hear her.

"Why?" Mr. Fridenthal scratched his head absentmindedly.

"Because I asked him." A spark of the old animation lit her eyes.

Then everyone spoke at once. Plans were suggested and discarded. Mr. Fridenthal's was the coolest head—as usual.

"It is best that Nachemia go to Lodz, make contact with the *Bhricha* through Lazar; get to Zellsheim, then send word to Chania. Meanwhile Chania and Leon can proceed to close the shop here."

"Well, we have to let Lazar know I'm coming." I observed.

"Of course," Chania agreed.

We sent Lazar a letter. Within two weeks we had the reply: "We are waiting for you."

I put some underwear, a couple of shirts and another pair of slacks in my rucksack. As I did, I heard, as if she were in the room, Mother's voice when she had packed rucksacks for us as the war broke out:

"My children, there is a war going on. We don't know what will happen tomorrow. If, God forbid, we have to separate or if we lose each other, you must have money at least to buy food."

I began to cry. I would give anything to have had her here as I packed by rucksack to go to freedom.

Chania sewed a pouch inside the waistband of my slacks into which she put money—including gold coins.

I was ready.

Chania and I hugged each other close a long, long time.

"It's freedom, Chania. And you'll be coming, too."

She managed a smile and reached for the tissues behind her. "I know, Nachemia. It's not as though you're preparing to escape. 'Kazet.'"

"If only—" I drew a breath and stopped.

Chania interrupted. "I know, Nachemia, I know. Mother and Daddy are no longer with us. But—" the tears began to pour down her cheeks. "They are aware. And they're glad for us. And we've still got Chaike. And—who knows—perhaps Moshe is still alive."

I met her eyes and held them. "I will try to find out—"

She whispered, "I know."

"I will send word when I arrive in Zellsheim. With Chaike." I looked intently at her. Chania had always been beautiful to me, but now she glowed. Leon's love became her. "Chania," I whispered, "I am so happy for you." I held her tightly. "I know you will be taken care of. I know that with Leon you will make it to freedom also. Just remember. The two of you must be careful. There is still danger here in Ostroviec."

I stared at her anxiously a moment more. She stayed with her head down pressed against me, but gave a faint nod. "We are constantly on guard, Nachemia, you know that."

"Still—"

"Leon has a weapon, you know. And we are always together."

"Yes, that's right," I assured myself.

"Come, Nachemia, the train leaves in an hour." Suddenly Leon came into the room. "And you want to say goodbye to the Fridenthals."

Leon and I strode briskly to the Jewish committee offices. The fall air was crisp, clean. I looked around the town as we walked. How miserable I'd been here shut up in the ghetto—then the ghetto had been made even smaller. I shuddered. How well I remembered how the streets had run with Jewish blood. I also remembered the good times we'd had at Uncle Matityahu's house—even though we were in the shadow of constant danger; how happy we'd been when Daddy and Chania had arrived in Ostroviec, when they had escaped from the stable to the small ghetto. Then I remembered "Kazet." In all the time we'd been back in Ostroviec I hadn't once gone to see the camp; I had no idea whether it was still there. I'd had absolutely no desire to see it—even if it had been in ruins.

"Here we are," Leon broke into my thoughts.

As usual, the committee office was busy and crowded.

Mr. Fridenthal got up from his desk immediately, came around and put his arms around me.

"How can I thank you for all you've done for us, Mr. Fridenthal?"

"Shhh, Nachemia. No thanks are required. We are here to help one another."

We stood silently, our arms about each other's shoulders. People in the office stared. Finally, Mr. Fridenthal said, "Don't worry. We will watch over Chania and Leon until you send for them."

"Thank you," I said. I felt the tears well up in my eyes.

Suddenly Abek was at my side. "I'm going with you to the station," he said.

Mr. Fridenthal put his hand on my shoulder. Words sprang to my lips and they seemed as natural as breathing. "See you in Israel," I said.

"In Israel," he echoed.

The train for Lodz puffed into the station.

"This is it," Leon said.

"Yep," Abek confirmed. He turned to me. "Nachemia—" We put our arms around each other. "My good friend—" Again the tears sprang to my eyes.

"This is not goodbye, Nachemia. We will see each other again." Abek clasped my shoulder.

"Yes," I rasped, "when we are all truly free men."

"Please, God, bring that day soon."

"He will; He will."

I turned to Leon. "My brother," was all I said. We embraced silently.

"Take care of Chania, Leon."

"You know I will. And we'll see you in Zellsheim."

The train whistled. We all jumped.

"Quick—before it starts for Lodz without you," Abek urged.

I ran for one of the doors. I waved at them until they were out of sight.

Cattle grazed in the meadows. Wagons piled with hay and straw jogged along the roads that criss-crossed and paralleled the train tracks. The grass was beginning to dry up. The leaves were yellow and beginning to fall. There was a poignant loveliness about the countryside.

Somehow the ride to Lodz seemed much shorter than to Krashnik—but then, there was a direct connection, since Lodz was a fairly large city. We pulled into the station in the late afternoon. The noise and smoke assailed me as soon as I stepped off the train. The tiles in the station amplified the noise from vendors, from stationmasters announcing departures and arrivals, from children crying, parents calling after them.

Lodz was primarily an industrial city, dominated by textile manufacturers, and the factories had resumed operation almost immediately after the war. There was a bustle, a busyness about it which I hadn't seen in Lublin.

I asked a vendor just ouside the station where Kilinska Street was.

"Oh, I think if you go down that big street there," he pointed with a greasy finger, "Kilinska runs off it."

As I walked down the street he indicated I noticed that most of the shops reflected the city's major product. No wonder Chania had been most successful in obtaining goods for our shop in Lodz. Textiles of every description filled the windows. I wondered how Lazar's leather business fit in.

I couldn't locate Kilinska. Finally I stopped a man in a suit. "Please—where is Kilinska Street?"

"Well, that's in the older part of town," he said. "It's several blocks from here. Go down here—" he pointed "—then turn left . . ."

It took about half an hour. It was, indeed, the older part of town. The row houses seemed to cling to each other when they weren't separated by tiny alleys. As I searched for Lazar's place I noticed postage-stamp-sized backyards attached to most of the buildings. I guessed that each two- or three-story building was cut up into as many apartments.

It was quiet here. This must be a strictly residential section, I thought; everyone's in the other part of town working.

Finally I found his building. His apartment was on the street level. The entrance was through the yard.

As I walked around the house towards the entrance I noticed that it was old but solid. And probably nothing like what Lazar had occupied in Gneivoshov.

Devorah answered my knock. She was slight, and had obviously been beautiful once. The previous six years had taken its toll on her, as it had on everyone. Her eyes were a deep blue.

"Devorah?"

"Nachemia?" I was astonished. How did she know me?

We embraced. Rivka stood up and came towards me. "Rivka, this is your cousin, Nachemia Wurman." Devorah put a hand on each of our shoulders. Rivka and I smiled at each other.

"Come in, Nachemia."

"How did you know it was me, Devorah?" I asked as I entered.

"Oh—we knew you'd come here sooner or later. When Chania asked Lazar if he would help you make contact with the *Bhricha*, we knew we could expect you any time."

The apartment was small and neat. We stood in the kitchen-living room. There were two small bedrooms off it; each had a dresser and a bed. A feeling of warmth permeated the small rooms.

"Where is your luggage, Nachemia?" Devorah broke into my thoughts.

I pointed to my rucksack.

"That's all you have?" her eyes widened.

"Yes, this is it. I left Korev with a backpack, and I'll leave Poland with a backpack—to find my future."

She gazed at me, and a smile played around her lips. Finally she said, "There is a saying, Nachemia. 'Where the water was, the water will be.' You are young, yet. The whole world is waiting for you." She turned toward a counter, where Rivka had been chopping vegetables. I looked at Rivka. She was slender, about eleven, with a straight, proud carriage. I thought of Aunt Tova.

Feeling my eyes on her, she turned toward me. "You remind me of Aunt Tova—your grandmother, my mother's mother," I said.

"That's what Papa says," she smiled.

"Go get some more vegetables from the bin, Rivka," Deborah said gently. "We'll need them."

"Where is Lazar?" I asked.

"He'll be here shortly. Would you like to wash up?"

"You have running water here?" I asked, surprised.

"Yes," she grinned. "This is Lodz. A big city. Not Gnievoshov or Korev."

It felt like an absolute luxury.

Lazar walked in the door about twenty minutes later. He stopped in the middle of the kitchen. "Nachemia?"

"Yes, Lazar."

He embraced me. "I almost didn't recognize you. I remember you as a small child. Ten years ago. Now you are a man. In spirit as well as in body. Chania told us everything. But," he held me at arms' length, "you must tell us again. I want to hear it from you."

"But first, dinner." Devorah said.

It was delicious. There was barley soup with dill, which gave off a wonderful aroma, vegetables, potatoes, and meat. "What is this meat?" I asked, not wanting to sound disapproving.

"Veal cutlets."

"Veal cutlets?"

"You were a chef in the German Army and you never had veal cutlets?" Lazar asked in mock astonishment.

"Oh, we had cutlets." I replied, "but not veal—horses."

"Well, how was it?"

"Wonderful," I replied sarcastically.

We all laughed.

"We were never short of food in the German Army, that is for sure," I mused. "Heinz and I ate the best of what was in the kitchen."

"Heinz—" Lazar looked at me intently. "Who was Heinz?"

"Didn't Chania tell you?"

"Not everything, I guess."

"Heinz Klockmann is responsible for my being alive today."

"A German Army soldier?"

"A sergeant."

"A German saved your life?" Lazar's jaw dropped.

"Yes—" I gazed out the windows. The day had slipped into dusk. Devorah suddenly got up from the table to make tea.

"Let us sit over here with our tea," Lazar gestured toward a group of three chairs. He and I got up and walked toward them. Rivka and Devorah began to clear the table.

"Yes, Heinz was a sergeant in Hitler's army," I said slowly as we settled into the chairs.

"Wait, Nachemia," Devorah called out. "I want to hear, also."

I told them everything.

"Do you mean Heinz said nothing to you after the other sergeant told him you are a Jew?" Devorah asked, wide-eyed.

"Well—after a while he told me he knew I was Jewish and said, "As long as I'm alive, you are okay.' He said he would take me back with him to his family when the war ended."

"Where is that?"

"In Hamburg."

The lights in the room had grown bright as it got dark outside. I thought of the many nights Heinz and I—and Michel—had shared rum or cognac in our quarters. Here I was with my family. But somehow, despite my constant fear, Heinz and I were also closely tied to each other. Lazar read my mind. "Where is Heinz now?" he asked.

"I'm not sure. He may not be alive. Maybe he was taken to a Russian camp—the Russians had surrounded us on our retreat. Chania told you I got to the Soviets, didn't she?"

"And that you walked around in Russian uniform all over Ostroviec," Lazar grinned.

"Well, the uniform is warm. I'll probably wish for it from now on."

"This Heinz—do you think he got back to Hamburg by any chance?"

"I don't know. I hope so. When I get to Germany I'm going to try to track him down."

"You want to go to Germany?" Lazar asked, raising his eyebrows.

"To find Chaike—and, yes, to find Heinz."

"Chaike is alive?" Lazar asked, just as Devorah came to me and began kissing me.

"Oh, thank God, thank God," she said. "Are you sure, Nachemia?"

"Yes, she is. Truly. She is in a D.P. camp—'Zellsheim,' near Frankfurt."

"Why didn't Chania tell us?" Lazar wondered.

"I think at that time she didn't know," I mused. "Yes— it was on the train from Lodz, in fact, that she found out. Let me tell you how it happened."

We were all laughing by the time I finished telling them of the man's approaching Chania on the train.

"I remember Chania," Devorah chuckled. "So proper. Of course she thought he was flirting with her."

"So how do you expect to get to Germany?" Lazar asked. I knew he knew my answer.

"I'm hoping you can help me."

Lazar and Devorah smiled at one another.

"I suppose Chania told you I'm connected with the *Bhricha*?"

"Yes, she did."

"All right. Rest assured I will see to it that you see Chaike soon. And have the chance to look for Heinz." We talked late into the night. Rivka went to bed about midnight.

"Nachemia," Lazar finally said about two in the morning. "You know you are a true hero—what you've survived; what you've been able to do."

"I'm not alone, Lazar. There are thousands like me—

only we'll never hear about most of them. Look at Eliezer, for example."

"Yes," Lazar nodded slowly, his face furrowed in pain. "I hear about Eliezer from men who were in his partisan unit." Lazar stared into the lamp for a few seconds. "You know, I remember Eliezer when he was Betar Commander in Korev. Why, I remember he visited us once in his Betar Army uniform. He was so proud of it. *We* are proud of him, Nachemia." Lazar stared at me intently. I could only nod. I felt the tears welling up in my eyes. "We are proud to be Eliezer's—and Henoch's—family. And I'm proud of *you*. You are walking right in Eliezer's footsteps.

I turned my head to cry wordlessly. Devorah clasped my hand.

No one said anything for a long while. Two of the lamps began to sputter. Devorah got up and turned them down a little..

Lazar finally broke the silence. "You know, Nachemia, I lost my whole family."

"But you've got Devorah and Rivka," I interrupted.

"Yes, thank God," he intoned. "That's why I told myself, immediately after the war, that I must help our Jewish brothers. It was due to a few good people that Rivka was saved from the Nazi angel of death."

I looked at him questioningly.

"Rivka was in all sorts of work camps," he continued. "And whenever there was an *aktsia*, other Jews hid her— sometimes under mattresses, sometimes underneath the barracks floors. I have a moral obligation to save and help people who are running from death."

"We all have, Lazar."

For the next couple of days I walked around Lodz. At times I dropped into Lazar's shop, helping him if I could. Lodz consisted mainly of factories, which belched smoke continually. Yet there was the bustle to it. People were running. Lazar told me that before the war there had been two hundred fifty thousand Jews in Lodz, and there were now eight thousand.

One evening Lazar walked into the apartment with a man abut twenty-five years old, tall, blond, slim. He stood for a few moments, his intense blue eyes taking in everything in the room, without saying a word.

Lazar locked the door. "Nachemia, this is Gideon."

Gideon held out his hand. "Shalom," he said.

I realized instantly that Gideon was from the *Bhricha*.

"Nachemia is my cousin," Lazar said. "He wants to cross the border to West Germany, to Frankfurt. His sister Chaike is there. You can trust him. He was a partisan in the Sadlovisna Forest."

Gideon had not taken his eyes off me. Finally he asked in Yiddish, "Are you alone, or do you have family who would like to join you?"

"I have an older sister—Chania—and her fiancé, but they are still in Ostroviec. They will join me when I reach Frankfurt."

"How?"

"I will send word that all is well."

"Why don't they join you now?" Gideon asked.

"It has been my experience that during war it is better for families to separate. We escaped from 'Kazet'—the concentration camp—separately, although she didn't know I escaped, and I didn't know she escaped, and we were with different partisan units. We were both captured; we both survived. It was good that we were apart during those times because, God forbid, had something happened at least one of us would have survived."

Gideon looked at me.

"Gideon, I think he's right," Lazar finally said.

"Fine," Gideon stated. "Let us sit down."

We headed for the group of chairs.

"Nachemia, I'll need a picture of you—for a certificate. Chances are you'll need it. Can you be prepared to leave in two days?"

I nodded, overjoyed.

The following day Lazar walked me to a tiny photographer's shop on a side street. He took my photograph for a few zlotys. It wasn't a good picture, but would do for a forged document, I thought.

That evening, Lazar again locked the door of the apartment as he entered. "We must be at the train station at seven tomorrow morning," was all he said.

Devorah, Rivka, and I smiled. Finally Lazar did, also.

"Let us have "La Chaim" with dinner to celebrate Nachemia's freedom," he said.

Devorah wakened me at 6:00. She'd already set out coffee, bread, butter and jam for us.

"You should wash up," she said. "Who knows when you'll have another chance?"

She was right.

Over breakfast Lazar informed me, "Your first stop will be Poznan. And there are five of you. Everything's taken care of." He looked at me intently.

"Lazar, why don't you and Devorah and Rivka get out of Poland?"

"I feel our place is here, as I told you the other night," he said, "helping Jews who want to escape. Someday, maybe . . ." His voice trailed off. Devorah smiled at him.

The streets were busy at 6:30 as we made our way to the station. "It's a lot faster route than when I first got here," I observed.

Gideon stood just inside the station with two men about twenty-five years old and two girls of about twenty. Even at that hour the smoke seemed to fill the station.

"How do you stand the smoke, Lazar?"

"You get used to it." He shrugged. "It's the least of our worries."

Lazar and I embraced.

"Lazar, will you please let Chania know I'm on my way?"

"Of course I will, Nachemia. Go with God."

"Go with God, Lazar."

He turned abruptly and disappeared into the morning bustle.

Gideon distributed a ticket to each of us. "Come," he said, "the platform is over here."

It took about four hours to Poznan. We had a private cabin so that Gideon could tell us the plans without being overheard.

"We have a rented apartment in Poznan. It is our meeting place. I have to get your documents sorted out; you can visit the city, but be back at the apartment by six. It is on a side street and not that easy to find. I will give you the exact directions—but do not write them down." He looked at us. "In fact," he continued, "we'll go there first so you can put your bags there and better mingle with the crowd. Then you'll have no trouble returning to it."

Poznan was the first capital of Poland. It is about one hundred and seventy-five miles west of Warsaw and about one hundred and fifty miles east of Berlin. I remembered that it is situated on a wide plain on the Warta River and was founded in the tenth century. It boasted a medical academy, an agricultural college, a college of engineering, an observatory, five museums, an opera house, and the first Roman Catholic Cathedral in Poland. It was also the first big city in Poland annexed to the Third Reich: the German Army had invaded Poznan on the very first day of the war in 1939 and had evacuated all Jews.

"Wonder what the place looks like now," my companion on my right broke into my thoughts.

"What do you mean?" The two girls sitting opposite us looked at him.

Mote Mietek was blond and narrow-faced; he reminded me of Yosek Zukerman. "Well, you know," he said, "Poznan was a battlefield between the Soviets and the retreating Nazis last February."

"There's not that much damage," Gideon interjected. "Yes, buildings are scarred—but nothing like Warsaw."

We were all silent for a few minutes. Warsaw—Poland's pride—in ruins.

We arrived in Poznan around 11:00. Mote, for that was his name, and I sort of naturally gravitated toward each other.

"I think all train stations are noisy," I observed.

"They probably are. So much going on."

It was about half an hour's walk to the apartment. There was an old, settled, mellow quality about the city. History, rather than industry, permeated the air. The buildings seemed as though they'd been there forever—ancient, knowing seers. The trees that lined many of the streets were full-grown and seemed almost part of the houses they shaded.

The route to the apartment was, as Gideon promised, complex. Perhaps he was deliberately taking a complicated way. Our heads spun as we frantically made mental note of the street signs and important-looking structures at the turning points.

"How are we ever going to find this again?" one of the girls breathed.

"You will," Gideon said cryptically. He was right. When something means enough to one, one does what is necessary.

"Here we are," he finally said. It was a tiny, old, four-story building on a side street that ended in a cul-de-sac. "We're on the third floor. Try to climb the stairs quietly so that it does not sound like an invading army."

There seemed to be no one about as we climbed the stairs. For some reason I saw, clear as a photograph, Michel and me climbing the stairs to Heinz's living quarters on the evening I'd first come upon the Headquarters Battalion of the Seventy-Second Fusiliers.

Heinz, where are you? I thought.

Gideon wasted no time once we reached the apartment and dropped our bags on the floor.

"Let me have your pictures, so I can get the documents drawn up," he instructed.

We all fumbled in our bags for the photographs, each handing a photograph to Gideon as we found it.

"Okay, you are free in the city for the afternoon," he finally said. "But remember—be here at six. We will eat here; I will give you your documents, then we will prepare to leave.

"Another thing," he said as he folded a paper around the photos and put them in his pocket, "call each other by Polish names in the street. Don't arouse any suspicion whatever. Needless to say, do *not* chatter about what we're going to do."

Mote and I set out for the center of town. "Okay," he said, as we turned into the first main street, "call me Mietek."

"Call me Tadek," I said automatically.

"Tadek?"

"That was my name while I was in the partisans."

"You too? Where?"

"In the Sadlovisna Forest. The First Battalion, under Commander Bzioza."

"Tadek, there's a small luncheonette. Let's get something to eat." He pointed to a little clean-appearing restaurant.

A waiter seated us immediately. As soon as the waiter moved away from the table, Motel continued.

"I was a partisan, too. Stationed in the forests of Volhiyn in the Ukraine. General Kovpack. He was Russian. Tens of thousands of partisans fought under him—many Jews."

"Not all partisan units accepted Jews," I observed. Motel nodded. "I had difficulty convincing Bzioza's unit to accept me. But—I helped blow up a munitions train."

He suddenly took a box from his pocket and opened it. Inside were two medallions from the Russian Army; one was a red star. "This," he pointed to the red star, "I received from General Nikita Kruschciov. The other I received for bravery."

I was impressed. "What are you doing to do with these medals?"

"I will give them to my children and tell them how the Jews fought against the Nazis. And that not all Jews went to slaughter without any resistance." He closed the box and sat back.

The waiter reappeared, interrupting him.

"What do you have today?" I asked.

"Cabbage with goulash and potatoes. That's all."

We looked at each other and shrugged. "All right," Mote said. The waiter turned.

"Wait a minute," I stopped him. "What kind of meat in the goulash?"

"Pork," he replied, "what else?"

"Then give me only the potatoes and milk, please."

"Me, too," Mote said.

The waiter shrugged and walked away.

"Anyway," Mote continued, "I have fought enough for countries and armies that don't need or want me. After all this, I have to smuggle myself across borders to reach the promised land. The time has come—I want to fight for myself, and for my own independent state that needs and wants me. I don't want to know of pogroms and persecutions. I want to reach Israel."

"Israel is not an independent state yet," I put in.

"It will be—be assured of that." He was emphatic.

The waiter came to the table with two bowls of potatoes and two glasses of milk.

He looked from one to the other as he put them down on the table.

"It's one thing to eat whatever you can to keep the body alive," I commented, "but now we can choose to observe Kosher laws." Mote nodded vigorously. The waiter had returned to the kitchen and appeared not to hear.

"Mote," I asked, "can you speak Russian?"

"Of course. I learned while I was with the partisans." He looked at me. "How is *your* Russian?"

"Probably not as good as yours. I learned from a Russian major, a Jew. Misha Rosov. It was in Ostroviec. I taught him Yiddish; he taught me Russian. I don't know if he wasn't attracted to my sister, Chania. She is beautiful. And a beautiful person."

"So—was he? What happened?"

I told him the story of Leon and Chania.

"Tadek," he said slowly, "with all you had been through up until then, why did you feel as though Chania's disappearance was the end of the world?"

I had thought about that many times. "I think it was just because of that. Chania and I had found each other again—neither of us knew who of our family was alive—as if by a miracle. A gift. We were all we had, except for Chaike, who is in Zellsheim—my other sister. We, of our whole family, considered that we were the only survivors. I suppose I just could not reconcile our both having come through the hell of the war and then losing her to some Polish bandit, or whatever—at least that's what I thought had happened."

Mote nodded slowly. "An irony beyond all ironies. Yes, I see. It would have been a tragedy."

We lingered at the table for some time. We ordered two or three more glasses of milk so the waiter would not tell us to leave.

"Motel, your family—" I began once.

"Gone. All of them. Even the girl I was going to marry." He looked off into the distance. His ascetic features seemed to draw into themselves, to become pinched. His black eyes seemed unfathomable. As I looked at him, I detected a few white hairs in his dark brown cap of hair. I wondered if I had any white hairs. I would have to look closely in a mirror, I reminded myself.

After a long silence, I said softly, "Why don't we explore what we can of the city? It's only two o'clock."

"All right," he said, digging into his pocket for some money.

We returned to the apartment at dusk. We had difficulty finding our way and were initially afraid to ask people in the street for directions.

"Oh look," Mote finally said. "Let us ask for the street that the side street runs off. How can that arouse suspicion? I'll bet the others are asking directions."

It was dark when we arrived. The others were already inside.

"We were worried," one of the girls said. "It is already six-thirty."

"So were we," Mote quipped.

We all found we were tired, and decided to lie down on the beds to relax.

Suddenly Gideon arrived. He had our documents—and good news. "There is a train leaving for Berlin at two in the morning. Are you all ready to leave?"

"Now?"

"Not right now. There are instructions and uniforms to pass out. But—other than that—have you all your things together?"

We nodded.

He passed out our documents. Each of us had a new name. I was "Vladimir Voronov." And I was a doctor in the Russian Army.

"All you men are doctors; the girls are nurses. You're going to the Russian military hospital in Berlin. Do not talk to anyone except yourselves, and keep that to a minimum. Someone at the border will do the talking for you. Now—" he turned to the bag he had brought with him, "here are your uniforms. Notice the armbands with the Red Cross insignia. Any questions?"

"Who is the man that will accompany us to Berlin?" I asked.

"A Russian major, Major Popov. He himself *is* a doctor, and he's in charge of personnel at the Berlin military hospital."

"Is Popov Jewish?"

"No," Gideon replied. "This is his second occupation."

"Can we trust him?"

"Absolutely. It is by no means the first time he's doing this. And by the way," Gideon added, smiling, "he gets two gold coins from each of you. In fact, give the gold coins to me now, so I can give them to him before you get on the train."

"When must we leave?" one of the girls asked.

"By midnight," Gideon answered. "There is some time to rest. An army truck will be waiting for you downstairs. Remember—do not talk to anyone other than yourselves— and among yourselves, keep your voices low so no one can detect you're not talking in Russian. You'll have a first-class cabin on the train to Berlin, but even so, it is better to keep your voices low."

He stayed with us while we donned our new uniforms. The coat and pants assigned to me were a bit big, but I pulled the belt in. I thought longingly of my Russian uniform in Ostroviec. A gift from my friend Lonka. I'd never see it again.

I took out two gold coins sewn in my pants. They were five rubles, and dated back to the time of the Czar. I sighed as I handed them to Gideon.

Gideon left at about ten o'clock. I think each of us wanted to become acquainted with the others, but we were all suddenly exhausted.

"Girls in one room; men in the other," the other men quipped.

We did not need a second suggestion.

It did not seem like more than three minutes before Gideon was back. I was suddenly wide awake, although I thought I'd been worn out. This was my escape to freedom.

"Go downstairs one at a time, and *do not make a sound*," he ordered. "Watch those boots on the steps. Just get into the truck. Make sure you have all your belongings."

I winced at every creak on the old steps, sure it would wake someone in the adjoining apartment. The truck had no lights on, but I could make out the Russian army insignia on the side. The driver was dressed in Russian uniform.

When we had all gotten into the back of the truck the driver pulled it out on the small street. He did not put the lights on until we were on a main street. It took about half an hour to get to the station. He must have gone all over Poznan to throw off anyone following us.

I knew who Popov was the minute I jumped down from the truck at the station. Tall, about forty-five, a serious face atop an immaculate Russian uniform bearing many medals. He looked at us without a word.

Gideon took him aside and handed him the small bag of coins, then returned to us.

"Do not talk among yourselves. When he asks for your documents, just hand them to him. Above all, do not say a word when you reach the border—to the police or anyone. Major Popov will handle everything. Go with God."

"Do Suidania, Good-Bye," we reponded in Russian.

We watched him walk back to the truck and stood there until it disappeared down the street.

Popov cleared his throat, and we turned to him. "Let me have your documents," he said.

We handed them to him, and he placed them in a leather briefcase. "I'll have to show these to the police at the border. You will remain in the cabin while I do this."

The train was late. Silently, we looked at one another. No one dared voice what was on each of our minds—had we come this far to be stopped by a train that wouldn't materialize?

"Don't worry, it will be here." Popov was calm.

It arrived at three o'clock, or shortly thereafter. "I will secure a cabin," he said as he lay us toward the train.

We waited on the platform. After what seemed like hours, he appeared at the door of one of the cars and gestured to us to come with him. Our cabin was about halfway down the car. Popov had hung a sign on the door which bore a red cross and wording in Russian which, according to Motel, read that we were doctors in the Soviet Army and not to be disturbed.

The cabin seemed roomy enough. We weren't crowded in the seats. Popov sat with the two girls; Motel and I and the other man sat on the other seat. We put our baggage in racks above our heads and stretched out our legs.

The other man went to sleep almost immediately.

It was pitch black. We couldn't discern what sped by outside the train window, try as we might.

"How long do you think it will take to the border?" I whispered to Mote.

"I dunno. Shall I ask Popov?"

"See if he answers."

Mote addressed Popov in Russian. Popov looked surprised at this, then simply said, "About two hours."

Two hours to freedom, I thought. Then I began to muse on freedom. Hadn't I made it to freedom when I escaped from the iron factory—from Lager?" Hadn't I been free when I'd been fighting with the partisans? Hadn't I been free these last months in Ostroviec, with Chania? Or had I? Why was I so exultant now? Hadn't the shadow of death always hung over my head—and still hung there, at least for the next two hours? Even in Ostroviec, hadn't we put a steel bar across our apartment door in fear of Polish bandits or drunken Russian soldiers? What was freedom? Perhaps it depended on where you had been just before you'd arrived at where you are now.

Everyone but Popov dozed off—even Mote. Perhaps I did, also, because the next thing I remember was the train's coming to a stop.

It was light out. Then I heard the voices in German and in Polish calling for all passengers to leave the train and stand on the platform. Through the window I saw that people were already descending the steps of the train and forming in groups outside the cars.

Popov rose. "Stay inside and don't talk," he said. He unlocked the cabin door and locked it again behind him. The voices approached. He spoke to them in Russian. Mote and I caught some of the words he exchanged with the Polish border police. "Can't you read the sign? These are doctors— they cannot be disturbed."

I whispered those phrases I understood to my companions. We giggled silently.

People milled about on the platform as the militia went through the train. A few caught sight of us through the cabin window. Their reactions were obvious: how come we were so privileged as to remain in our cabin while they had to inconvenience themselves?

Finally they were allowed to reboard the train. Then the Soviet border police made their inspection, scrutinizing all documents. Again Popov stood outside our cabin. He silently handed the Russians the documents.

The inspectors saluted him.

At last, the train started on the last leg of the journey to Berlin.

We arrived at the Alexander Place Station in the Soviet-occupied zone.

"Okay, I will escort you to the center for survivors," Popov said. "From there you will find a way to get into the free zone."

Remnants of Jews from Poland, Russia, Hungary, Rumania, Czechoslovakia, and even Greece were at the center on Oranienburg Street. They all had one goal in mind: they wanted to get out.

By now Berlin had been divided into zones: Soviet, American, British, and French. The center was in the Soviet zone. But the entire city was surrounded by Soviet troops, which controlled large areas of now-defeated Germany. While it was relatively easy to travel from one zone to another, it was virtually impossible to leave Berlin itself. We reached the conclusion rather rapidly: the only way to get out was to be smuggled across the border.

The first thing we did at the center was to eat. Then we began to make careful inquiries about smugglers to help us.

It didn't take long.

There were seven of us: five men and two women travelling together. The false documents were printed in Russian, English, French, and German. Mine said that I was a German, a refugee from West Germany, returning to my native Frankfurt. The documents gave us free passage to the border of the American zone.

The leaves had turned. The air was beginning to chill. The train sped by forests, burned-out villages, next to roads decorated with the charred remains of jeeps, trucks, cars, and tanks. Occasionally I glimpsed a few cattle grazing in a field. Freedom—I was riding to freedom. *Please, God, let us make it*, I prayed.

I studied my fellow escapees. I looked into their faces to see if each reminded me of someone—from Kurov, from Ostroviec, from "Kazet?" Was there a certain look about survivors of hell? Was it in their eyes? I remembered the shell-shocked Jews who come back to Ostroviec while Chania and I were attempting to start over there—how their faces had slowly begun to register hope and had reverted to despair after the A.K. had murdered the five Jews in the apartment building. I looked around at my companions on the trip, wondering why had those who had survived done so, while countless others had not.

As we sat in the cabin, we exchanged our histories. Mania and Krisia had managed to survive the entire war on faked documents as Aryans. I looked at them more closely. Krisia had long blonde hair and blue eyes; Mania had light brown hair and hazel eyes; both spoke excellent Polish. Surviving must not have been too difficult. Abraham had also escaped a concentration camp and managed to find a partisan group that accepted Jews. Heavy-set, dark-haired Meir was sent to a labor camp near the German border practically from the outbreak of the war; he never thought he'd ever live to see liberation. Alex and Schmuel, who sat a little apart from us, were reticent.

By the time we reached Leipzig, where we had to change trains, I was wishing for my Russian overcoat which I had left in Berlin. We brought only what we could carry in knapsacks. I hoped my heavy sweater would keep me warm.

As we stood on the platform waiting for the train to the border, we all agreed on one thing: the absolute irony of Germans escorting Jews out of the reach of the Nazis.

The train to the southwestern border of Germany was not as comfortable as the one we'd left in Leipzig.

That was the least of our worries.

"I don't believe it," Abraham said a few times, "we're riding to freedom."

"Listen, we're not there yet," Meir muttered.

"Oh, stop it, Meir. Of course we're going to make it," Krisia snapped.

"What do you think, Nachemia?" Alex turned toward me.

"I haven't a doubt in the world," I said.

But I could not help thinking it interesting. What was

the source of Meir's pessimism, of Krisia's optimism? I shrugged. It was hard to tell. Mania just smiled.

Our destination was a small village about four miles from the border. Two Germans led us to a cluster of wooden, thatched-roofed huts among copses of trees. "These are used as 'way stations,'" one of them explained. "The huts are not occupied, but food is always left in them for those crossing over."

"A popular route, eh?" Abraham grinned.

The younger German smiled. Who knew better than they, I thought.

"Do we spend the night here?" Mania asked, running her fingers through her hair like a comb.

"We wait for a rainy night, when we will be least detected getting into the American zone," the other German explained.

"How long is that going to be?"

"Oh—it's the end of November. Any day now."

The two days we waited for the proper weather for crossing passed slowly. Mania and Krisia shared a hut; Abraham, Meir, Alex, Schmuel and I another.

"Do you think those other two were 'Judenrat'?" Abraham asked on the second day.

The rain began about 6:00 p.m. And it had begun to get dark.

"Now we'll find out if the roof leaks," Abraham joked.

"We aren't going to be around that long," I exclaimed. "Thank God."

"Thank God," the other two echoed.

The Germans, who shared another hut, Kurt and Fritz—"Probably the best-stocked one," Abraham quipped—called us outside at about 9:00 p.m. We could hardly see one another.

Lightning suddenly rent the sky.

"My God," Mania exclaimed.

"Don't be afraid," our smugglers offered. Here they removed a long rope from one of the knapsacks they carried. "Now the border is this way—" we could hardly make out which way he pointed in the blackness, "—and it's rough: mountains, woods. Fritz will lead; I will bring up the rear. Whatever happens, don't let go of the rope. If you do, you will lose the way and never make it. Place the girls in the middle, separated by one man."

"What's your name?" Krisia said.

"Kurt."

"All right."

Kurt and Fritz spaced us about three feet apart. Then they tied each end of the rope around their own waists. Abraham was between Krisia and Mania; I was behind Mania. "You must hang on, no matter what," Fritz said. "And follow us—you will be able to just see us even in the darkness. When lightning comes, throw yourselves onto the ground— we don't know who will be around, and we might be shot."

The rope was rough; it afforded a good grip. We needed it: by now the ground was an endless swamp. The mud was so deep it was a struggle merely to put one foot in front of the other. I could barely make out Mania's outline in front of me.

We walked through thick, vegetated fields, through murky woods.

"Ouch! I'm into a tree," I heard Meir yell.

"Do not deviate from the line!" Fritz shouted about the rain.

Meir said nothing—that we could hear, anyway.

Lightning lit up the landscape when we were in the middle of a field.

"Hang onto the rope as you hit the ground," Kurt screamed.

We were covered with mud. But it wasn't long before the waterfall that poured out of the sky had washed it off us.

"Who is so damn mad at us?" Meir complained behind me.

"Wait, wait, I've fallen," Mania suddenly cried. We all stopped. I was nearest her and helped her back to her feet.

The first hill we went up was so slippery that the seven of us slid backwards. Fritz and Kurt held fast to the rope as we laboriously regained our balance.

"God in heaven, is it worth it?" someone mumbled—I think it was Alex.

"Yes," I replied automatically.

I think it was the pitch blackness that was so frightening. The lightning bacame almost a relief.

Each of us fell a number of times. It was impossible not to.

"Are we all still here?" Abraham called out once.

"*I* am," I heard Krisia cry. "You think I'm going to lose myself *now*?"

We travelled slowly. I thought of the days I hid out in the ditch under the iron factory, waiting to make the break out of slavery. This could not be as bad, I told myself.

"Oh God, let's go back to the huts," I heard Schmuel cry after the fourth or fifth slip backwards down a hill. "We'll never make it."

"*You* go back," Mania cried. "*We're* not going back."

"We can't even see; we'll never get there," Meir moaned.

"Listen," I cried. "Why have we come this far? Only to turn around? Of course we'll make it. Come on. The storm is our cover—miserable as it is—a small price for freedom."

"He's right," Abraham shouted above the rain.

"Come on, Meir, Schmuel—you can last," I entreated. "We all will. Would you rather be in the labor camp?"

"Would you rather be on the way to Auschwitz or Treblinka?" Krisia rejoined.

Alex and Schmuel said nothing. It made me wonder again. What *had* they been doing during the war?

I was bone tired.

The tremendous claps of thunder caused us to jump.

The mud mixed with rain often caused one of us to fall.

I suspect it meant nothing to Krisia, Mania, Abraham and me.

It took us eight hours to travel the four miles. We crossed into the American zone as dawn broke. Our smugglers headed for a small house.

We fell on the floor of the house. "Ach, poor youngsters," said a voice in German. The peasant, obviously the owner of the house, had a broad, kindly face. "It's all right," he continued. "When you get up, there's hot tea."

We drank the tea as though it were manna from heaven. "More, more," the peasant's wife pressed bread and jam on us.

Then we found the strength to take off our shoes and boots. "There is hot water to wash," the peasant smiled.

Now we knew why the people at the center in Berlin had advised us to take a change of clothes and underwear in our knapsacks. Each of us threw the clothes we had been wearing into the garbage heap outside the house.

After each of us washed and dressed, the peasant's wife led us to a room where mattresses were scattered across the floor. Gratefully, we laid down upon them. I for one, and I believe the others also, fell into a deep sleep immediately.

It was past midday when we awoke. The peasant and his wife were out in the field. But Fritz and Kurt waited for us in the main room of the house.

"Now we will help you to the outskirts of Munich," Kurt said.

Our knapsacks were considerably lighter when we strapped them on. Fritz and Kurt knew just how to flag down wagons large enough to hold us all. It took about three hours.

"The countryside is beautiful. Look at the leaves," Krisia exclaimed, smiling. The breeze lifted her hair slightly from her shoulders.

"Are you saying that just because we're in the free zone?" Meir asked.

She nodded happily.

"Ah, it *is* beautiful," Mania added.

"If slightly wet," Alex put in.

"What do you expect?" Abraham turned to him. "Be thankful the rain has stopped."

"I wouldn't care if there was a blizzard right now," I joined in.

"If one comes up we'll know who to blame," Meir said.

"Listen," Kurt said in hushed tones. We all leaned

toward him. "Go right to the Central Committee for Jews in the Prinz Regent," he grinned. "It is in the nicest section of Munich. They will help you with lodgings, with food. You will probably be able to learn about your relatives there."

"Can I get a connection to Frankfurt—to Zellsheim?" I asked.

"Yes, sure. I know you will be able to get there."

About a quarter of a mile from Munich, the Germans stopped the wagon. We all got out.

One by one, we reached into our knapsacks for the German currency we had obtained to pay our guides—our smugglers.

As I handed half to Fritz and half to Kurt, I shook their hands. Without them I would not have made the last miles to freedom.

Perhaps it was because of me, perhaps not, but one by one, Krisia, Abraham, Mania, Meir, and even Alex and Schmuel also shook their hands. The two Germans seemed surprised—and taken aback. And pleased.

"A *strassebahn* (streetcar) is coming now." Fritz pointed in the direction where an old trolley was lumbering down the road toward us. "It will get you right into the center of the city."

The seven of us jumped up and down, hailing the streetcar, which ground to a halt about twenty-five feet ahead of us. We ran for it.

I turned once as we were boarding the car. Fritz and Kurt waved.

TWELVE

Munich had become an important center for Jews after the war. Thousands of survivors of Dachau, Treblinka, and other death and labor camps poured in, as did tens of thousands of refugees from the Soviet Union, Poland, Rumania, Hungary, Czechoslovakia, Greece, and other Baltic countries. Most were lodged in the military camps the Germans had vacated just outside the city itself. Most of the material help came from the American J.D.C. (Jewish Distribution Committee) and from the American occupation authorities, enabling thousands to settle in and around Munich and begin to hope again.

The Central Committee ministered to about five hundred displaced Jews a day. It provided food, work, social welfare, medical aid, and assistance in emigration.

A primitive newspaper, the *Undzer Weg* and *Undzer-world* in yiddish was published to keep everyone current on what was happening. Zionists also had found their way here, and were well organized by the time we reached Munich. They, along with the survivors of Hitler's hell, planned for the Jewish state, "Eretz-Israel." With the prodding of the Zionists, demonstrations against the British Mandate were held almost regularly. They dispersed information to all camps of the American, British, and French zones as well as to refugee camps in Austria.

Munich had suffered very little damage from the war; only the very center of the city had been bombarded.

As our smugglers had told us, the Prinz Regent area

was the most beautiful part of town, and Jewish activities there centered around the Mehlstrasse. Here the Central Committee had its headquarters, and virtually every building bore placards with lists of missing relatives. Ten- and twelve-room houses and villas, which the Germans had fled, panicked, as the Allied forces had moved into Munich, were now occupied by the Committee, as well as by *Malben*, the Jewish Institution for Sick and Elderly Invalids; by the United Nations Relief and Rehabilitation Administration; by *Hias*, a national agency for Jewish immigration and immigrant welfare; by the leaders of the Zionists; and by the editorial offices of the weekly and daily newspapers.

I knew, as we made our way along Munich's streets to the Mehlstrasse, that I would probably have even happier days than this in the future. But at the moment, I couldn't imagine how.

And at last, I thought, *I will find out about Moshe for sure.*

I noticed that we were all smiling—even Alex and Schmuel. Abraham looked at them, looked at me, and winked. Krisia and Mania clasped each other's hands in sheer happy excitement. The sunlight was golden on the sides of the buildings. It somehow didn't seem as cold as it had before.

In the Prinz Regent section, evergreens and pine trees overhung the streets. The palatial houses were framed by well-groomed shrubbery. The Central Committee headquarters was located in the middle of the town.

On our way up the steps of the building, we all stopped at once.

"If we get lost in the crowd—if we never see each other again—" Abraham said. "Let us bid our farewells here, so we have no regrets."

"Yes," Krisia said, her eyes beginning to fill, "after all we helped each other to freedom."

"Shouldn't we try to stick together?" Meir asked.

"If we do, we do," I said. "But I for one have a mission to find out about my brother and then head for Frankfurt where my sister is. Krisia is right: let us wish each other well, so if we get separated we have no regrets."

It was a highly emotional few minutes.

I didn't see my companions again. I've thought about them a lot since then—especially Krisia, with her spirit, and Abraham, with his wry humor. Almost as soon as we got inside the building, I began to make inquiries about Moshe. A place to stay and food seemed secondary, somehow; my entire family, after all, was accounted for—except Moshe.

Every dialect in Europe seemed to be going on at once in the committee's headquarters. There were blue-eyed blondes milling about with short, swarthy, wiry Jews from the Balkan countries, red heads among the brown, black and blonde. Some were in tatters—I guessed they hadn't received new clothing from the committee yet; some were fairly decently dressed. Some wore a hodgepodge collection of clothes. I wondered fleetingly what the reaction to my Russian or German uniform would have been. Then I remembered the scene in the Skarzisko railroad station.

Those at the desks appeared sympathetic, efficient, cheerful. No matter what language was spoken, someone on the staff could grasp it.

At first no one could tell me anything about Moshe.

"Look," one tall, muscular German Jews said, "why don't you go on over to the food center and get something inside your stomach? You'll need it to pursue your brother."

It made sense. He told me exactly where on the Mehlstrasse the food center was. "If you can pay, pay," he said. "If not, they'll give it to you."

I still had some money left. Why shouldn't I pay.

Coffee, tinned meats and vegetables, sugar, sweets, and clothing were in abundance here—as were those anxious to get them. I was astounded when I realized that Germans were also purchasing goods in here. I asked one of the people distributing the food about it.

"They've got a severe food shortage," he told me. "Remember—" he smiled broadly—"they've been defeated."

"Doesn't anyone mind that they are Germans?"

"When they pay—and they do—that is money in our coffers."

I bought some tinned sardines and sweets, then wandered around until I found a place I could eat quietly.

As I consumed the sardines and cakes, and lit a cigarette I'd purchased, I listened to the sound of the city. Yes. It was a happy sound. A sound of hope. It overlay the bewilderment and confusion of those refugees just arriving from the seven circles of hell, because they, too, would soon begin to hope again, to even be happy again.

After eating, I walked by the placards hanging on the walls of the buildings of the Mehlstrasse: if I saw my name— or Chania's, Chaike's, Mother's, Daddy's, or Eliezer's—I think I could assume it would be Moshe that had put it there and that would mean he was still alive, looking for us.

I did not.

I went back to the headquarters building, then to the *Hias*, then to the offices of the *Undzer Weg*, then back to the committee headquarters. By then I began to think of finding lodgings for the night and beginning inquiries again in the morning. Someone at a desk would help me, I was sure.

I suddenly stopped dead in my tracks. Someone had said "Plashov." I whirled around.

"Who said 'Plashov'?" I asked.

"I did," a short, freckle-faced boy of about fifteen volunteered.

"Were you in Plashov?"

"Yes."

"Did you know Moshe Wurman?"

"Yes." He looked at me hard. "Are you Eliezer?"

"No." I felt myself, even then, begin to choke up. "I am Nachemia."

"Nachemia. Yes. Moshe talked about you also."

"What can you tell me about Moshe?" I took his arm. "Can we sit down somewhere?"

"Yah. There are benches outside."

The light was beginning to fade as he began his story.

He hunched forward, head bowed. I watched him intently. In the faint light he appeared an old man.

"Moshe and I were both transferred from Plashov to Flossenberg in Germany. We were slaves. We cut stones for walls. We hauled iron. We . . . dug mass graves."

"Oh God . . ." I whispered.

"Well, early this year the Soviets began to invade Germany, you know, and Flossenberg was fairly near the border, so they were approaching fast."

"What happened?" I bent toward him, my voice quivering.

"Well, the Nazis wanted us out of the camp—fast. Did they put us on wagons or trains? No. They made us walk—in January, in the snow—God knows where we were heading. Maybe they didn't know themselves. We walked for days without food or water. Once in a while we were able to bend down and scoop up snow to drink, but only if the guard wasn't looking. There were hundreds of us, Nachemia. Every hour someone would fall down dead. Those who couldn't keep up— they were sick, or *got* sick—the guards shot right there. And left the bodies."

I sighed heavily. "Go on."

"Moshe and I were nowhere near each other . . . I tried to look for him towards the end when the Nazis were getting really scared of the Russians and weren't watching us as carefully . . ."

He broke off and looked out across the Mehlstrasse.

". . . I think's he's . . . gone, Nachemia."

I sat for a long time in silence. *If Moshe were alive, he would certainly have tried to get in touch with one of us . . .*

"Nachemia, I'm sorry," he whispered. "I'm sorry . . ."

I turned to look at him. Despair in the eyes of a fifteen-year-old. I felt anger rise in me again. Anger at those who make wars, who make old men of children. "What is your name?" I asked.

"Chaim," he replied.

"Thank you. Yes, I think you're right—he's . . . gone. You know, you bear the name of a great man: his name was

Chaim Eliezer, but we called him Eliezer. He was my older brother. Chaim in Hebrew means life."

There was nothing now in Munich for me. I secured lodgings I remember nothing about and left for Frankfurt first thing in the morning.

The railroad stations in Germany had been destroyed. There was a shortage of wagons, and those that were available moved very slowly. Passenger trains were out of the question.

A few freight trains still ran between cities. It didn't take me too long to find one headed in the direction of Frankfurt.

"You can sit in the lumber car until the next stop," the workman told me.

At the stop he pointed me in the direction of another freight train going toward Frankfurt. "You may have to change a lot," he shook his head. "The Allied Air Forces have just about destroyed our transportation. But just keep catching those that are headed in the direction of Frankfurt."

He was right. At virtually every stop, I had to change trains. On most I snuck into the freight car—usually coal or lumber—and hid; once in a while a workman took pity on me and pretended not to notice me. The freight cars were not heated. The tracks were filled with potholes. My stomach knotted with pain. I was afraid to attempt to get food at the stops for fear the next train would leave without me.

Ordinarily, it takes between six and seven hours to get from Munich to Frankfurt. It took me two days and two nights.

Zellsheim is about fifteen miles from Frankfurt. I didn't even think about a train running between the two places. I made my way to the main road. I was half frozen by then, but all I could think about was finding Chaike.

Between walking and hitchhiking I got to Zellsheim in about two hours. It was 6:00 a.m. and still dark. There was a lighted sign:

ZELLSHEIM D.P. CAMP
ASSEMBLY CENTER 557
AREA TEAM 1022

I could make out small villas, trees, shrubbery. *A resort*, I thought. The Nazis had built it for themselves.

To the right of the entrance there was a sign with an arrow that read "Administration Offices," and just below it, another that read "Kitchen." I made for the kitchen.

Even as I approached the building, the aroma of pungent spices wafted towards me. It smelled good.

Inside, several men stood by large steaming cauldrons, preparing food and coffee. I walked toward a short, chubby man.

Remember the last time you approached someone for coffee, I told myself and moved more cautiously.

"May I have some coffee?" I asked him. "I'm frozen."

"Sure," he smiled. He seemed amiable. "Here," he gave me a slice of brown bread and a small dish of currant jam.

"Thank you," I murmured gratefully.

He poured himself a cup of coffee and sat down beside me at a nearby table.

"Where are you coming from?" he asked.

"Right now—Frankfurt," I said wearily. "On what seemed an endless number of freight trains. A terrible trip. Originally, I come from Poland."

He grimaced. "Why have you come to Zellsheim?"

"I heard that my sister is here."

"What is her name?" he asked. Then he grinned. "I know everyone here in Zellsheim."

"Chaike Wurman."

His eyes opened wide. He rose from the table and pulled off his white apron. "Come with me," he said.

I was instantly alert; what was he up to?

"Where?" I asked warily.

He realized he'd alarmed me. He patted by shoulder. "Don't worry," he said. "Come on." He took my hand.

I looked into his kindly face. Somehow I sensed that it was all right. I got up and followed him.

"My name is Noach Chodoles," he offered. He looked at me more intently. "And you are Nachemia."

Now I was stunned. "How do you know that?"

"Chaya speaks of you all the time," he smiled. "And you fit her description. I should have recognized you the minute you walked in."

"You were busy with the coffee," I said politely.

"You *did* need some, you looked frozen," he laughed.

Light streaked the sky as we walked quickly to Chaike's house. The pastel-colored houses looked tidy and well cared for. The house Chaike lived in was two stories and framed by flowering bushes. "I live here, too," Noach said. "In the other apartment," he added.

Chaike's apartment was on the first floor. As we approached, I glimpsed a garden out back, and apple trees were ladened with fruit. I felt relieved. It was a place in which one could be comfortable.

"Nachemia, stay here a moment," Noach asked. "Let me tell Chaya."

He knocked on the door and entered. "Chaya!" he called. "I have good news for you: your brother Nachemia is alive." He motioned to me.

I entered the room. Chaike stood there as if glued to the floor. For long moments neither of us uttered a sound. Then we flew to each other and embraced. Our tears mingled. Finally, she whispered, "I knew it."

"Knew what?" I said.

"That you would be alive."

"How?" I asked in a hoarse voice.

"I'll tell you in a while, Nachemia," she said with that mischievous smile. Suddenly she was my older sister again. "First, you must get comfortable. What would you like—"

"Chaike, is there a way for me to take a warm bath?"

All three of us laughed. I had almost forgotten that Noach was there.

"Of course. And while you're doing that—" Chaike brushed tears from her eyes—"I will go to the kitchen and get us some more hot coffee."

I hadn't had a bath in five years—only showers. As I luxuriated in the hot water, I heard Chaike call, "Nachemia, there are pajamas right outside the door. They're from Noach."

I stayed in the bath about an hour, feeling deliciously pampered. Then I toweled off and dressed in Noach's pajamas. They were long in the arms and legs. But they felt wonderful.

I sauntered out of the bathroom and looked around. Chaike's apartment was comfortable: it consisted of two bedrooms, a bathroom, and a large kitchen-dining room.

She smiled at me. "See, here's the coffee, Nachemia. Here, sit at the table."

She sat opposite me. "Now I'll tell you how I knew you were alive."

She looked out the window for a moment before she began. She wasn't as plump as I remembered, and her eyes, like Chania's, had grown enormous. And the perpetual twinkle was missing.

"They took us to Budzyn," she began.

"I know." I nodded sadly.

"It was July of forty-four," she continued. "The Russians entered through the suburbs of Lublin. The Germans began to evacuate Budzyn as fast as they could. They separated the men from the women. They dragged Moshe away, I saw it with my own eyes. He never took his eyes off Mother or me as they took him. He was crying—he seemed so helpless." She stopped and wiped her eyes.

"He waved to us at the last second," she whispered. "They shoved him into an S.S. truck. Well, then we had to get onto the military trucks. They took us to the train station. They loaded us into freight cars—like cattle—about seventy of us to a car. They locked every car from the outside. The tiny windows of the car had steel bars across them. It was like a steam oven in those cars. We didn't move until midnight—and even then it had not gotten much cooler inside the cars. And—they had given us a half a loaf of bread for each of us.

"We stopped many times to let other trains pass by. By the third day there was no food. The heat intensified, and many of us fainted. Some died. They left the bodies in there. The S.S. were sitting on the roofs of the cars. They could hear us begging for water; they laughed.

"Mother fainted. Fortunately, I had a piece of sugar, which I put inside her mouth, and she woke up.

"From time to time we heard shooting. The guards shot people who tried to break away. Some tried to tear the wood from the floor of the cars, or from the sides . . . Finally the train stopped at a big station. There was a sign that said 'Auschwitz.' We all knew what it was.

"They left us in the cars for a whole day in the station. I was close to a window, and could see the big camp with barbed wire surrounding it. German soldiers swarmed all over the place.

"Suddenly the doors of the car flew open. S.S. soldiers stood there with whips in their hands. They screamed at us: 'Get off the train fast, and start running.' We began to run. But some were too slow, so they whipped them. We had to run a long way—and we were all hanging onto our possessions. I just ran; I couldn't see—or think what I was doing. We ran up to a big wall, where more S.S. stood. There was a gate, where they had written *Arbeit macht Frei* (Work gives freedom).

Then the S.S. shouted 'Men to the right, women and children to the left.' It was all done very quickly; we had no chance to think what was going on. We had no time to cry; we hugged each other and got into the designated line. The men were directed through the gate—they waved at the women—"See you in camp,' they said. We moved to the other side. They had us run again until we reached an empty field. Many fell flat on the ground, we were so weak and exhausted by then. They let us rest a couple of minutes. Then they ordered us up and over to the other side of the wall. There were rows of narrow barracks surrounded with a barbed fence—and it was electrified. Then they shouted to us to line up—fast. They kept shouting to go faster and faster.

"As we were lining up, some high commanders walked in front of us. One of them was Joseph Mengele." She took a deep breath. "Mother and I were standing together. Mengele was there—" she began to choke up, "—to determine who was to live and who was to die . . ." She lowered her head. I sat motionless.

"Anyway, Mother and I were holding each other's hands, Nachemia. And she whispered to me: 'Chaike, I know I'm going to die. I leave the world with a prayer . . . that our youngest, Nachemia, remains alive.' " Chaike stopped to wipe the tears away. "Mother said, 'My heart tells me that he will remain alive . . . And if you live and you meet Nachemia . . . see to it that he says *Kaddish* for me . . .'"

We both broke down. We cried for a long time. "Every morning and every evening," I sobbed, "I will say the *Kaddish* for Mother. And Daddy. And Eliezer. And Moshe."

She raised her head and looked at me questioningly. I could only nod.

We must have cried for a long time. By the time I noticed, the kitchen had grown brighter with daylight.

Then I saw it: a tattoo of the number A21391 on her left arm.

"What is that?" I asked.

"I got it when we arrived in Auschwitz," she said. "I became a number—no more Chaike Wurman." She sighed heavily. "After Mother and I were separated they sent me to work. I had to sort out the clothes of the people that they sent to the gas chambers: children's clothing in one pile, women's and men's in another. Woollen clothing separate from silk, the shoes in another large pile.

"Women supervised us—very cruel women, past criminals from Germany and Poland. They called them *Capos*. And there were women wearing the S.S. uniform who had whips. They whipped us hard at the slightest little thing—like talking to one another, or wiping the sweat off our faces.

"And the smell! There was an awful smell in the camp. It almost choked us. It came from the chimney of the crematorium—where they burned the bodies from the gas chambers . . ."

She broke down. I put my arms around her. "Don't, Chaike. Don't. You'll make yourself sick."

I held her close.

". . . anyway," she finally continued, "they didn't want us in Auschwitz when the Russians arrived. They transferred us to different camps. I was sent to Bergen-Belsen. It is in the northern part of Germany. As usual, we were put in huts with wooden beds on top of one another. Of course it was overcrowded. I was on the second layer. Then the typhus broke out. Everyone got it, It felt terrible—I've never been so sick! I thought I was going to die, Nachemia . . ."

"Chaike, do you know *I* got typhoid in Ostroviec—when we were with Uncle Matityahu! Chania nursed me back to health. My God!"

"Well, perhaps God visits all of us in the same way, since we are family, Nachemia."

Noach smiled at both of us. He had a cherubic face.

"I lay on that plank bed for I don't know how long. There was a girl of about fourteen in the bed next to mine. Her name was Anne Frank, she was from Amsterdam, in Holland. We both had very high fevers—and—ugh!—we both had caught lice! We were both so sick we couldn't even move. Women in the hut were dying around us every hour. We just lay there, waiting for the inevitable. Anyway, once, when we could move a bit—the fever had gone down, or something—I asked Anne for her comb—she had a broken comb—so I could try to comb out the lice, because they were driving me crazy. She was just barely able to hand it to me, and, although I was still flat on my back, I had a little success—I got some of them out. When I couldn't sleep all that night, I would go after the lice.

"Next morning, I thought I'd give her back the comb. "Anne, here is your comb,' I said to her. She didn't answer, so I spoke a little louder. Still no answer. I reached over and shook her. 'Anne!' No answer. Now I shouted at her: 'Anne! Anne!' I rose up on my elbow. Anne was—oh God, Nachemia.—she was dead."

Chaike looked out the window as the tears ran down her face. "Such a lovely girl! She was much younger than me."

"What happened then?" I asked

"Well, that morning the block 'leaders' of the hut came around to remove the dead inmates. I guess they just tossed them into large pits, or something. They removed Anne's body—and, they thought I was dead also and began to pull at my legs! I screamed at them. They left me alone. But I saw them dragging Anne's limp body out.

"Nachemia—it is funny, how God works. I don't know how long it was after that that the English liberated the camp. The Nazis knew they were coming: so they poisoned the drinking water! I was too weak to get down from my bed even to drink—but those that could died horribly. Such pain! Worse than the typhus. I only found this out later—but, as I said, the English came through the huts looking for survivors. They had medical assistants with them. They found I was alive—but not much," she grinned. "One day later, and I would have had to get up to get something to drink!"

I clasped her hands. "Thank God, Chaike, thank God!"

"Yes—thank God! The English got me to some hospital—I don't know which—right away. And here I am. And here you are."

We sat in silence for a long time.

Finally, she stood up. "Nachemia, I work in the kitchen—the main kitchen—here. It is my contribution. Listen to me. Go—sleep. When I return you will tell me about Daddy and Eliezer and Mosher and—"

"Chaike! My god. I forgot. Chania! Chania is alive."

"*Chania!?*"

"Yes."

"Where is she?" Her eyes brightened. She smiled.

I took a deep breath. "I left her in Ostroviec. She will be coming to us soon. My God, I forgot to tell you." I stood up.

She rushed over to me and we threw our arms around each other.

"Chaike, look how much shorter you are than me. Remember when you and Chania thought I would always be short and skinny."

That made her laugh a bit. "Go on, now, get some sleep. We will see you later."

I slept for twenty-four hours.

When I awoke, the next morning, Chaike and Noach took me to the registry office, and I registered as a refugee of the D.P. Camp of Zellsheim. They issued me food and clothing coupons.

Noach took me to the clothing supply. I liked him instinctively. I felt I could trust him. "Noach," I said. "I noticed the tattoo on Chaike's arm yesterday."

Noach grimaced and nodded.

"But tell me something," I persisted. "I noticed, beside the number, a tatoo on her wrist that says, 'K.L.' What does it mean?"

Without a word, Noach rolled up his sleeve and showed me his arm: the letters "K.L." were tattoed there.

"Whoever was at Budzyn," he said, "got this tattoo. The letters stand for '*konzentration lager*.' "

I grimaced. "How did you get to Budzyn?"

"When the war broke out, I served in the Polish army fighting the Nazi invaders," he began. "But we couldn't hold on against them. They were much better equipped—and trained. So we surrendered and they took us to a P.O.W. camp. At that camp—I don't know the name of it—they ordered all Jews to step forward. They said that anyone who hid his being Jewish would be killed immediately. There were a lot of Jews in my brigade. Anyway, I figured that they would kill all the Jews anyway: so I didn't step forward. Well, they separated the Jews who'd stepped out from the rest of the group and asked again if there were any Jews left in line. I held my breath. The guy next to me knew I was Jewish; but we had fought together, so I didn't think he'd turned me in. But the sergeant of our brigade was right behind me and all of a sudden he screamed 'Here is another Jew' and pointed his finger at me. A Nazi rushed over and struck me with his whip—it stung so hard—and yelled, 'Get out of line, dirty Jew.'

"I was sure I would be killed. I stepped out of the line and walked over to the rest of the Jews. We were rushed over to trucks that stood waiting. They took us to a P.O.W. camp which held only Jews. After a while they separated us into different camps. I got to Budzyn in 1942."

I shook my head. "Did you know my mother and my brother Moshe, then?" I managed to ask.

"Yes," he smiled gently. "Your mother was a lovely lady—soft-spoken and kind. Whenever she could she would give me an extra piece of bread or some extra potatoes. When you are very hungry every little bit helps. You can lose your mind with no food. She understood this. She was wonderful. And Moshe. He was an electrician. A nice, intelligent boy. He became like a brother to me. I haven't seen my own family since the war broke out."

"Is there anyone left in your family?" I asked.

He slowed down, his head lowered. I could hardly hear him. "No. No one at all. They are all gone." He took a handkerchief out of his pocket and wiped his face. "When the war was over," he continued in a slightly stronger voice, "I met Chaike here in Zellsheim. You know, she was very sick, but they made her well."

He looked at me and smiled. "And you've made her well. By returning to her."

I clasped his shoulders in my hands. Words were useless.

We had reached the clothing supply building. "Come," he said. "Let's get you some clothes."

They gave me two pairs of trousers, three woolen shirts, socks, shoes, and underwear. And pajamas. "I guess those arms and legs will fit you better," Noach quipped.

Everyone referred to it as Caffe Amchu (folk cafeteria). We played group games, we stood around and talked. Chaike and Noach introduced me to practically everyone present.

And everyone seemed to take it for granted that they were a couple.

Once a week a small band arrived and the dancing began. Practically everyone joined in. I found great pleasure in watching young men and young girls grab each other by the waist to dance the folk dances of their respective countries; especially the Hora an Israeli folk dance. There was a very special spirit there—a special joy that comes from hope reborn. I knew the feeling: it had begun for me on that long, muddy haul over mountains and through woods to the American zone in Germany.

No wonder Chaike had looked so content in that photograph the man on the train from Lodz had shown Chania!

"Come on, Nachemia," Noach poked me on the shoulder. "Pick a girl and dance with her!"

I looked around. A dark, sweet-faced girl sat quietly by herself watching the dancing. I walked over. "Would you like to dance?"

Her name was Golda. She smiled shyly. She would.

It took a little more than two weeks from Chania to arrive in Zellsheim.

She arrived with Leon Brenner.

Chaike, Noach, and I threw a huge party to celebrate their arrival. It lasted well into the night.

By then I knew what my "contribution" to Zellsheim would be.

As I'd learned in Munich, a movement to help and to fight for an independent State of Israel was well underway and becoming better organized every week. Part of the movement included the Youth Movement—the *Betar*. It seemed natural that I became the leader of the *Betar* in Zellsheim.

We were able to obtain part of a building that the U.N.R.R.A. had built in Zellsheim. We turned it into a clubhouse and learning center of *Betar*. We actively recruited youngsters between ten and eighteen: it took very little persuasion. We devoted days to "formal" education: Israel, Zionism, Jewish history and culture. Evenings were given over to discussions, Israeli folk songs and dances, re-enactments of momentous events in Jewish history. There were about sixty youngsters active in it.

During the summer I organized a camp in the adjacent forest—with the help of the United States Army, who supplied us with tents and sports equipment, and often the personnel to teach us sports. The youngsters picked up soccer and basketball as though they'd been playing all their lives! The UNRRA provided us with food. Then the enrollment went up to about two hundred—some from another D.P. camp near Stuttgart.

We organized ships of "illegal" emigrants to Eretz-Israel. What joy there was on the faces of those people as they bid farewell to Europe on their way to the ships!

I threw myself into *Betar* with all my energies and memories of the *Betar* in Kurov. The youngsters sensed my commitment and responded. I would have liked to think I was as effective as my brother Eliezer had been. Perhaps I was.

April 1946

It took me nearly a week to get from Frankfurt to Hamburg. The rail service had not improved noticeably since I'd travelled by freight trains from Munich to Frankfurt.

I had nothing to go on—only the knowledge that somewhere in Hamburg was a gasthaus whose owner's name was Klockmann.

The train pulled into a virtual ruin. The Hamburg station had been bombarded. The city itself was not in much better shape. Everywhere skeletons of buildings—many of which had been quite beautiful—stood like sad ghosts.

Certain buildings had signs on them containing the name "Klockmann." I entered the occupied ones and inquirted of everyone in them about Heinz and his family. No one seemed to know.

I could not find a central administration office or registry anywhere.

I stopped people in the street and asked them where

the Klockmann *gasthaus* was located. The responses ranged from a shrug of the shoulders to outright bewilderment.

Was I in the right place?

Then I began looking for different *gasthauses*. They were not easy to locate among the bombarded buildings. It may have been the fifth or sixth establishment where I got a kernel of information.

"Oh yes, Klockmann. The son. Why, I believe he was in the lists of soldiers who were captured by the Soviets."

I began to get excited. "Is he alive?"

"I don't know. I don't think anyone would know. Probably deep in Russia someplace—if he's alive."

"Where is his family?"

"I can't tell you that, either. I never knew any of them. Only heard about the son."

That was all the information I was able to get. It had taken me three days. I left for Zellsheim.

July 1948

It was time. I was ready to go to Israel.

My family—what was left of them—was happy. Chania and Leon and Chaike and Noach had married in Zellsheim—to no one's surprise. And Leon and Noach each had relatives who had made it to the United States before the war had broken out and were established there. They were able to contact them through the Red Cross.

The relatives had sent affidavits stating they would be responsible for the emigrants. The four prepared to emigrate.

I was happy for them. I enjoyed their joy and anticipation.

Israel—for now it was *truly* Israel—was only two months old.

There were about sixty of us in the group headed for the port of Marseilles.

No more were we slaves; no more did we wear armbands. We travelled legally on trains with legal passports—provided by the State of Israel—under our own names.

The ship was waiting in the harbor: its name was *Atzmauth* ("Independence"). The blue and white flag of Israel flew from her masthead.

I began to cry.

THIRTEEN

July 1948

I found myself in the army almost as soon as I found myself in Israel—or, Eretz-Israel. At that time there was a full-scale war going on, The new-born state was struggling and fighting for its existance.

I was sent to the "Negev" region in the south, where we were in conflict with the Egyptians.

Chania and Leon and Chaike and Noach had all settled in Brooklyn. We kept an almost constant stream of correspondence. Three years after arriving in America from Zellsheim, where they had a daughter, Sara, Chania added twins, Rebecca and Henoch, to their family. Chaike became "Clara." She and Noach had two daughters: Sarah (who became "Shirley") and Jackie.

And I also continued to correspond with Golda, who, not long after she reached America, became "Gloria." She had settled with distant relatives near Philadelphia.

I took odd jobs after my army service. I worked in a laundromat for a while. I worked for a printer, Moshe Adler, in Tel Aviv, maintaining the machines and helping out in general. He lived in the old section of Tel Aviv on the second floor of a building that looked as though it were crumbling daily. He invited me to live with his family, an offer I gratefully accepted.

1950

Gloria, who I still found myself calling Golda, was coming to Israel. Mr. Singer, father of the family with whom she was living, had died, and Mrs. Singer—or Aunt Rosalie, as Gloria called her—had booked a trip around the Mediterranean and had asked Gloria to join her. They would stop in Italy and Greece before arriving at Haifa.

I felt strangely exhilarated as I wrote her to tell her that I would meet the ship at Haifa, if she'd like.

The port of Haifa bustled. It was a windy, cool February day, and the breeze from the sea felt good. I wondered, as the ship docked, how much Gloria had changed. Would I recognize her? She'd be eighteen by now.

I had managed to position myself at the front of the crowd so I could see every passenger who disembarked. If nothing else, I thought, I could look for a young girl and older woman together. My eyes roved over the throng of people coming down the gangway.

My attention was caught by a young woman in a soft, light blue sweater and skirt. Her light brown hair caught the light of the sun and shone gold. She smiled slightly; there was an air of self-possession about her. I looked at her face— it was Gloria! Yes—the tall, chunky woman next to her, clearly must be Aunt Rosalie. I moved toward the bottom of the gangway, reaching it as they stepped onto the pier.

Gloria looked up at me. "Nachemia!"

"Hello, Golda."

The next couple of weeks were a blur of excitement and rediscovery—Gloria of me, I of her. We went everywhere together. Aunt Rosalie wanted to see as much of Israel as possible; I was happy to act as guide. And, more and more, she left Gloria and me by ourselves.

Two nights before they were scheduled to leave, we sat in a coffee house on the outskirts of Tel Aviv. The words came out almost of their own accord. "Golda, you don't have to go back to America."

"What?" Her eyes widened as she turned to me.

"Well, what I mean is—let's—will you marry me? And stay here with me?"

She stared at me wordlessly for what seemed like forever. I swallowed hard. Had I mistaken her feelings?

"Oh, Nachemia," she finally said, "of course!"

We stayed in Israel for seventeen years. We moved to Ramatgan, a suburb of Tel Aviv, and had three children: Hanna, Sarah, and Avi. We exchanged photographs with Chania and Chaike and their families as the years passed. After several months, I met some investors who arrived from Europe. One of these investors knew my family before the war. He suggested that I handle his business affairs in Israel. We formed a company that concerned itself mainly with real estate and construction.

In February 1957, the United States Secretary of State, John Foster Dulles, and the United States Ambassador to Israel, Ogden Reid, and I signed a contract to construct a building for the American Embassy in Israel, in the city of Tel Aviv.

In October 1956, a war broke out between Egypt and Israel. It was known as the Sinai Campaign. I was drafted in the I.D.F. (Israel Defense Force) and fought in the Sinai Penninsula. I helped in tactical support for the Israeli Air force.

In June, 1967, again another war broke out with Egypt, Jordan and Syria against Israel; it was called the Six Day War. After serving in the army for three months, I went to the United States to see my sisters Chania and Chaika in Brooklyn, New York. At the same time I visited Canada to meet with the investors, who by now lived in Canada. They asked me to join them in several real estate ventures in Canada.

Always, in the back of my mind, were thoughts of Heinz. But I never returned to Hamburg.

By 1967 a huge portion of my company's business was in Toronto. And that's where I moved my family.

1981

It began at a Bar Mitzvah. Most of the people at our table were Holocaust survivors, including Rita, who spoke English with a heavy German accent.

"Are you German?" I asked her.

"I was born in Germany; I'm Jewish," she smiled. "My mother still lives in Germany; I visit her from time to time."

We survivors began to exchange Holocaust stories. Suddenly, I turned to Rita.

"Rita, do you think you could possibly help me locate a man in Hamburg? I've lost track of him, and he once saved my life." I told her about Heinz. Her eyes widened and she smiled.

"Of course, Nachemia. I will come to your house tomorrow."

The next day, in my study, she typed out a letter to the Municipal Central Population Office in Hamburg. I signed it.

A couple of weeks passed. Every evening excitedly I went through the mail that Gloria had laid out on the table. Then it arrived:

"Dear Mr. Wurman, We have located the man you are looking for . . ."

I was overjoyed. My mind spun back thirty-seven years. I saw Heinz seated at the table in the cramped attic of the schoolmaster's house in Volka Voynowska, urging me to join him in a cognac. I saw his eyes catch mine and fill with compassion at the Christmas party as we sang "Deutschland uber alles." I saw him on the road to Opoczno, asking the other men if they had seen me. Heinz was alive!

The Hamburg municipal office had included Heinz's business cards and telephone number in its letter. *Zollenspieker Faeherhaus*, the gasthaus, is outside of Hamburg; no wonder I had not found it in 1946.

I decided to wait until the following day to call, so as not to disturb his sleep. As for me, I stayed awake the entire night.

The phone rang four times. As I waited my hands were shaking. Then someone picked up the phone. "Who is speaking?" A deep, resonant voice on the other end said.

It sounded like Heinz, but I couldn't be absolutely sure, not after all this time. "Mr. Klockmann?" I said.

"Yes. Who is speaking?"

"Mr. Klockmann, I want to be sure that I'm talking to the right person. Please answer two questions for me."

"Yes?"

"Could you please tell me in which unit of the *Wehrmacht* you served in 1944 and 1945?"

"I served in the Headquarters Company of the Seventy-Second Fusilliers Battalion," he said. My heart skipped a beat. Now I was sure! It *was* Heinz! "Who is speaking?" he asked again.

"Another answer, Mr. Klockmann, and I'll tell you."

I heard him inhale.

"Do you remember a youngster that worked together with you in the kitchen in 1944 and 1945?"

"*Ja*," he said slowly "there was a youngster—Marion . . . Marion? Is that you? *Marion*" his voice broke. He began to cry.

"Yes, Heinz. It is me." I was beginning to cry myself. "It's really me."

Neither of us was able to say anthing for a couple of minutes.

Finally he managed to ask, "Where are you, Marion?"

"Toronto! Canada" I replied finally.

"Toronto?"

"Yes, by way of Ostroviec, a D.P. camp, Zellsheim, and Israel. It is a long story, Heinz."

"Marion, we must see each other," he was regaining his voice. "But—write me; tell me what happened to you since the war. And I will write you."

I received his letter on April 9th.

Dear Mr. Wurman:

How small this world is—here, Germany—there, Canada, and both of us shared the same fate in hard times in 1944.

We were both very young and today, after a long search, we found each other again.

You, my dear "Marion", followcd my advice. I

thank you very much for your phone calls from Canada, as well as your letter with the attached photograph. You cannot imagine my joy of receiving the above material.

We were separated during the Russian air raids.

I survived several obstacles, including 5 years as a Russian prisoner of war (Gorki). In 1950 I came back to Hamburg. My father was shot in the arm in the concentration camp. It had to be amputated.

Today we own a "Gasthaus" and my family (wife, daughter and my sister) are all very well. The work is hard, but we are content.

Following your request, I enclose photographs of myself dated 1944–45.

Thank you very much again for remembering the German non-commissioned officer of earlier days, Heinz Klockmann.

All the best for you and your family.

Best regards
Heinz Klockman

By mid-May I had completed arrangements to fly to Hamburg. I arrived there by way of Amsterdam on June 6th, and registered at the Intercontinental Hotel, not far from the train station, where I checked my luggage.

It was a different Hamburg from 1946. New modern steel and glass buildings had risen over old, ruined, bombed-out ones; traffic was heavy; the city bustled. I smiled without really knowing why.

The taxi I hailed was driven by a middle-aged woman with a kindly, weather-beaten face. When she looked at the name and address of the gasthaus, which I had written out on my notepad, she turned to me. "It is about a half-hour's ride. Is that all right?"

"That's fine," I answered in German.

As we sped through the streets and towards the outskirts of the city, I asked her if she was familiar with the gasthaus.

"Of course," she replied immediately, smiling. "It is a well known place. I often drive people there to dine. The food is excellent and the gasthaus itself, with its gardens, is beautiful."

"Do you know the owner?" I ventured.

"Yes indeed: Mr. Klockmann," she was grinning broadly now. "Mr. Klockmann is an expert—a genius—at preparing fine food. Delicacies," she added.

"Do you know any of the other family members?" I asked her.

"Not really. But—it *is* a family business. And the Klockmanns are very respected around here."

I leaned back in the taxi, content.

The countryside was bright green with early spring. As we rode further out from the city, wildflowers caught the sun and gleamed white, yellow, and blue. Beautifully groomed houses displayed planters and window boxes of bright red geraniums. Oaks, lindens, and willows nestled close to the Elbe River, which we now paralleled.

"It is beautiful here," I exclaimed.

"Oh *ja*," my driver nodded. "Wait till you see the Klockmanns' place."

She slowed the taxi, turning into a gravel drive, which seemed to curve towards the river. Immaculately clipped shrubbery lined the drive, beyond which beds of spring flowers shone like jewels in the middle of velvet green lawns. I kept turning my head from side to side; wherever I looked the view was breathtaking. The gasthaus suddenly appeared ahead, bright white against the backdrop of the trees that lined the river.

Almost involuntarily, my mind spun back to the large room under the eaves of the peasant cottage in Nova, where I had first met Heinz and which he, Michel, and I shared during my first days with the Germany army. I could see him again as he sat at the table with Michel while I headed for the loft where I'd slept. I could again hear him:

"Marion, some cognac. Come join us."

"*Ja*, you'd make a good soldier," Michel had laughed.

Then we stopped in front of the gasthaus. My thoughts spun back to the present. "Here you are," the woman grinned at my apparent disorientation.

"Oh, thank you." Slowly I looked around and absent-mindedly took out my wallet to pay the fare. "Please keep the change," I said.

"Enjoy your meal," she shouted good naturedly as she drove off back down the drive.

Wood-framed glass doors led into an age-mellowed, quietly elegant lobby. Soft old carpets in deep jewel tones were spread on a wood floor burnished to a soft glow with decades of careful polishing. The chairs and sofas looked comfortable and inviting.

An ascetic white-haired man dressed in a black tuxedo approached me. "May I help you?" he asked.

"I'm here to see Mr. Klockmann," I smiled at him.

"Your name?"

"My name is Mr. Wurman. From Canada."

Suddenly he extended his hand and broke into a smile. "Welcome to the Klockmann gasthaus, Mr. Marion."

I was taken aback. "How did you know—?"

"Ah," he smiled more broadly. "We all know you, Mr. Marion. Ever since Mr. Klockmann returned in 1950, we've known you—from when you were in the *Wehrmacht* together, how he met you, how the two of you parted. And we've known you were coming. Mr. Klockmann will be overjoyed."

"As I will be," I returned the smile.

"Ah—you have no luggage? Well—" he looked around. "There, that is a comfortable chair. I will tell him—"

"Wait," I put my hand on his arm. "Don't tell Heinz it's me; tell him someone would like to see him. I want to see if he recognizes me."

"Oh—*ja*. Good. I will get him." He hurried away.

Looking around I felt very comfortable. Two or three groups of people sat within the large, warm room, talking quietly. I heard soft laughter from one of them. The gasthaus staff moved soundlessly through the halls that branched off from the lobby. I remembered Heinz promising me, eons ago, that I would return here with him after the war. At the time I wondered what would I be doing, what would life be like?

Then I saw them approaching from the hallway. Heinz had changed. He'd gotten heavier—even a little taller. And he'd lost a lot of his beautiful black hair. I sat motionless, watching him approach. His eyes met mine.

"MARION!" he called out in a voice filled with emotion. Everyone in the lobby turned.

He rushed towards me as I stood up. We embraced and kissed. Our tears flowed unabashedly.

"Heinz, Heinz." I could hardly speak.

I don't know how long we stood there. The lobby grew very quiet.

"Come," he finally said. "My family wants to meet you."

We started down the hall. "Where is your luggage?" he asked suddenly.

"At the Intercontinental Hotel in Hamburg."

"Well, why did you leave it there? But it's okay. We'll get it. Fritz," he turned toward the host. "Send one of the men to the Intercontinental Hotel in Hamburg to get Mr. Wurman's luggage. What room do you have there, Marion?"

I told him.

"Oh, and Fritz—call the hotel to tell them that someone is coming, please."

Heinz clapped his arm about my shoulder. I noticed that we were about the same height. As if reading my mind, he said suddenly, "*Ja*, you've grown some," and chuckled.

"That's okay," I responded, "But we are probably both going to start to shrink, soon."

"Please! Not yet!" he said in mock horror.

A lovely looking young woman of about twenty-five rounded the corner. She had coal-black hair and blue eyes—and Heinz's humourously curving mouth.

"Heinz, is—" I started to ask.

"Kati—" Heinz broke in, "do you know who—?" Then he turned toward me. "Marion, this is my daughter, Kati."

"Ah!" her face lighted up into a smile. "Marion. At last.

I am so pleased to meet you!" She took my hand in both of hers. "Papa has told me all about you. How you saved his life."

"Saved his life!" I was momentarily puzzled.

"The snowdrift, Marion, remember?" Heinz grinned.

"Oh, *ja*," suddenly I remembered. I looked into Kati's deep blue eyes. "And did he tell you that he saved mine?"

She smiled softly and nodded wordlessly, still holding my hand.

"Where is Mama?" Heinz asked her. "And Käthe?"

"In the garden," she turned to him. "Getting the flowers for the dinner tables."

"We'll go there," he said. The three of us headed out what I took to be the rear of the building. Here the gardens, which I had not seen on the way up the drive, ran down almost to the river. A breeze ruffled the sheer pastel dresses of two women bent over cutting bright pink daisies. "There they are," I said almost to myself.

Heinz turned towards me. His left eyebrow quirked up. "How do you know?" he asked.

"Why Heinz—I've practically met Käthe and Elsa. Even though it was thirty-seven years ago. You know."

Elsa stood up first, and the breeze ran through her blonde hair. She smiled lovingly at Heinz and Kati. She started toward us.

Then Käthe stood up. She was as I'd pictured her: curly dark hair, plumpish, smiling. "Like Chaike," I thought then, as I'd thought when Heinz had first described her.

"Elsa, this is Marion," Heinz said simply.

Her blue eyes widened. She dropped the armful of flowers she was carrying and, like Kati, clasped my hand in both of hers. I smiled at her warmth as I looked into her eyes. They were as open, as artless, as lovely as I remembered from the photograph Heinz had shown me in another world. She'd gained some slight weight; her face was unlined. I saw tears start in her eyes. Finally she spoke.

"It is a miracle. Heinz never stopped hoping he would find you. Thirty-seven years! Even when he was in the army he wrote me about you—the young man from Poland who was his 'right hand.' I am so glad you are here. I cannot tell you—" she swallowed.

I stood speechless. I was just beginning, I thought, to realize that I meant as much to Heinz as he had to me. Birds sang in the trees on the riverbank. The sound of boat motors reached us from the river. I put my other hand over hers, and without taking my eyes off her, said, "She suits you, Heinz."

Then I looked at him. Tears filled his eyes. He remembered, too.

Elsa looked from me to him. "What—?"

"Sweetheart, that is the first thing Marion said to me when he saw your picture in that God-forsaken village in Poland." He looked at me and nodded slightly, trying to blink back the tears.

"Käthe," he finally said, "Marion."

Käthe's smile was dazzling. Her eyes were merry. "*Ja,*" she said, her voice full of music, "we all feel we know you, Marion."

"You are just as I pictured you," I smiled at her.

"Chubby and all," Heinz teased her.

"*Ach*! He is terrible, Marion. How did you stand him all those months?"

"Well, you had a vacation from me for six years," he retorted, his left eyebrow raising.

"Humph! And you've been making up for it ever since," she pretended to grimace.

Kati and Elsa laughed.

"Come, Marion, let me show you *Zollenspieker Faeherhaus.* Then you'll want to rest before dinner. Your luggage will be here by then." He looked at Elsa and she smiled at him. They seemed as in love as I'd imagined they were thirty-seven years before.

The steady knocking on the door woke me. The curtains were drawn and the room was in semi-darkness. I lay still for some moments, taking in the huge frame of the canopied bed, the softly gleaming wood of the bureaus and cabinets, the large stone fireplace on the other side of the room.

"Mr. Marion. Mr. Marion." It was Fritz.

I stumbled out of the bed towards the door. "Yes?"

"It is seven o'clock," he called through the door. "Mr. Klockmann will be here to take you down to dinner in half an hour."

I opened the door and Fritz smiled at me. "Is there anything I can get you?" he asked.

I thought for a moment. There wasn't a thing Heinz hadn't thought of in the room. "No," I shook my head. "I think you all have thought of everything."

"And your luggage is fine?"

"Yes, thank you."

"All right, then. I'll probably see you downstairs."

I opened the curtains. The room looked out over the Elbe. I could see a small ferry making its way towards the opposite side. The day hung between light and darkness, and the flowers in the oblong beds seemed to be irridescent.

Heinz knocked and opened the door at precisely 7:30.

"Well, Marion! Does it remind you of the chateau outside Volka Voynowska?" He was grinning broadly.

"It's better, Heinz. It's yours."

He looked at me for a long moment, then put his hands on my shoulders.

"Anyway," I tried to keep the mood light. "We don't have to haggle with the peasants anymore."

He laughed, "Come on," he clapped my shoulder. "We've got the best table in the house."

We did. It was situated in a corner of the dining room with an unobstructed view of the river. Darkness was beginning to fall rapidly, and lights reflected and shimmered in the water. A ferry was returning to this side of the river, lights strung out along both its sides.

Neither of us said anything while I drank in the view. Then I heard Heinz say "Champagne. Bring us the best."

I turned. A waiter had come to the table so quietly I hadn't sensed him.

"Let me order for us, Marion."

"Of course, Heinz. As long as I don't have to peel the potatoes."

He laughed uproariously.

Suddenly, we both said almost the same words: "I didn't know whether you were alive or dead."

I let him talk first.

"Most of the battalion got past the Russian encirclement and reached Dresden. But the Soviets were waiting for us. Those they didn't kill they took as POWs to Eastern Russia. That included me—but not before shrapnel exploded into my arm. I still have fragments of it floating around in there.

"I wound up in Gorki. There the head of the camp was a Russian Jewish captain who spoke German. It didn't take him long to make me chief cook of the camp. We became friends—and I had it fairly good as a POW."

I smiled at him.

"Yes," he continued, "—I thought of you many times. It was a sort of reversal of our situations. A few months before that you, a Jew, were looking to stay alive and a German sargent whose nation wanted to eliminate all Jews befriended you. Then I, a German, found a friend in a Russian officer who saw me as I saw you—a human being, not a member of the enemy."

We sat silently for a while.

"Doesn't God work in mysterious ways?" he finally murmured.

I nodded.

"Anyway, Marion, remember when I told you that being a cook in the army is better than being even a general?"

I nodded.

"Well, it was true in Gorki also. I was never short of food. The only disadvantage was that in 1950 I was the last one freed from the POW camp; I had to close the kitchen!"

We both laughed.

We both raised our champagne glasses. "Now, Marion, what happened to you after we separated near Kielce?"

I looked into my champagne and then looked at him. "I thought, for sure, for years, that I had sent you to your death, Heinz."

"Why?"

I hesitated. How was I going to tell him that I had told the Russians of the path of the *Wehrmacht*'s retreat?

"Marion?" he asked gently.

"Because—because I told a Russian army unit of your retreat," I blurted out.

"But look—I am alive. Now—tell me what you mean."

I told him of my escape to the Soviets, of the Russian Jewish captain, Lonka, of my telling of the battalion's whereabouts. "Heinz, I—"

"Wait, Marion. They didn't get us in Opoczno. They didn't catch up to us. It wasn't until we got to Dresden. We avoided them until then. You had nothing to do with my capture."

I looked at him. Tears were burning behind my eyelids. He nodded and smiled. Was it possible?

"The thought has haunted me since—" I began.

"I mean it; you had nothing to do with my capture," he repeated.

Again we sat silently. Again he broke the silence.

"Marion, let me tell you something. The member of the Population Office who located me journeyed out here to show me your letter. He asked me if I knew you. I, of course, didn't know your real name at that point; so I said no. Then the man said that he figured, from the name on your letter, that it was a Jew who was trying to locate me, and if I didn't want to become involved he was not obliged to reveal my identity to you. 'I have no reason to be afraid,' I told him. 'In my eyes all men have always been equal. There is no such thing as a Jew, a Russian, a German—we are men,' I said to him. I gave him a couple of business cards. 'Here,' I said, 'this will make it easier for Nachemia Wurman, the man from Canada who is looking for me.'

His left eyebrow went up. "I think I must have shaken him up, Marion. He may not have gotten over it yet."

We both laughed.

"That is why I am alive today, Heinz."

"Even during the war you were willing to stand up for me Heinz. I patted his hand across the table.

I looked out the window again. The lights had gotten brighter as the sky had gotten darker. Now the lights in the gardens had come on, throwing shadows on the trees and shrubbery. People had begun to stroll through the gardens and were silhouetted against the lights on the opposite shore of the Elbe.

I recalled the many times I had counted myself happy since 1939; not one of those times held the feeling of utter peace and contentment of that moment.

Heinz's voice was very soft, very gentle. "Now, Nachemia, tell me your story . . ."